Dow Scott, Ph.D., Executive Editor

incentive pay
creating a competitive advantage

WorldatWork. Press

About WorldatWork®

WorldatWork (www.worldatwork.org) is the association for human resources professionals focused on attracting, motivating and retaining employees. Founded in 1955, WorldatWork provides practitioners with knowledge leadership to effectively implement total rewards—compensation, benefits, work-life, performance and recognition, development and career opportunities—by connecting employee engagement to business performance. WorldatWork supports its 30,000 members and customers in 30 countries with thought leadership, education, publications, research and certification.

The WorldatWork group of registered marks includes: WorldatWork®, workspan®, Certified Compensation Professional or CCP®, Certified Benefits Professional® or CBP, Global Remuneration Professional or GRP®, Work-Life Certified Professional or WLCP™, WorldatWork Society of Certified Professionals®, and Alliance for Work-Life Progress® or AWLP®.

The Total Rewards Association

www.worldatwork.org

Author Acknowledgments

I was honored to work with many compensation professionals who deserve a special "thank you" for their help in making this book a reality. Dan Cafaro, Book Publishing Manager of WorldatWork Press, very patiently cajoled authors to update chapters and coordinated the WorldatWork publishing process to bring the book to a timely finish. The contributing authors wrote and rewrote versions of their chapters well within the constraints of tight deadlines. Many compensation professionals acted as reviewers and provided detailed comments and encouragement as the chapters took shape.

These individuals included:

Bob Eberhardt, *TransUnion* LLC

Kenneth Gatesman, APAC Customer Service

Joshua R. Goderis, CCP, PHR, Underwriters Laboratories

Les Harper, True Value

Jack Kennedy, Cardinal Health

Sharona Leshem, Life Fitness

Eric Mastny, Northern Trust Company

Ronald T. Miller, CCP, Motorola Inc.

Dennis J. Nirtaut, CCP, CBP, Aon Corporation

John B. Nolan, *Exelon* Corporation

Dewellyn Roepenack, University of Illinois at Chicago

Lisa Ryan, Performance Development International Inc.

Ronald C. Sparks, S&C Electric Company

William G. Walton, CCP, CBP, *ConnectiCare* Inc. and Affiliates

Paul Weatherhead, U.S. Postal Service

Donn G. Willey, CCP, Papa Johns International, Inc.

WorldatWork Press would like to acknowledge the contributions of the following technical reviewers, without whose efforts, this book would not have been possible:

Stephanie E. Abualia, CCP, Compensation Manager, *Cox Enterprises*

Meera Alagaraja, Graduate Assistant, *Texas A&M University*

Carol E. Anderson, CCP, SPHR, Senior Vice President, Talent & Learning, *LandAmerica Financial Group*

Chad R. Atwell, CCP, Global Compensation Solutions Leader, *Hewitt Associates*

Gene C. Baker, CCP, CBP, GRP, Vice President, Compensation/Benefits, *Keane Inc.*

Linda J. Ball, CCP, CBP, Vice President, *Epler Co.*

Jacqueline K. Barry, CCP, Senior Design Consultant, *Hewitt Associates*

Steve Bloomfield, CCP, SPHR, Executive Vice President, Human Resources, *Syclo LLC*

Anne L. Chamberlain, CCP, SPHR, Director of Compensation, *City University of New York*

Leah A. Davis, CCP, SPHR, Director, Global Compensation, *Accenture LLP*

Katherine E. Dixon, CCP, Compensation Consultant, *Nike Inc.*

Ron E. Dockery, SPHR, Director of Compensation, *Medtronic Inc.*

David R. Engelman, CCP, Director, Global Compensation Strategy, *Accenture LLP*

James Gandurski, CCP, Senior Associate, Executive Compensation, *Grant Thornton LLP*

Joi Gardner, CCP, PHR, Senior Compensation Analyst, GFI Software

James "Pat" Grube, CCP, GRP, Group Compensation Manager, Swiss Re

Carl D. Jacobs, Senior Vice President, *Aon Consulting*

Kevin M. Kramer, Ph.D., CCP, Senior Manager, *Accenture Institute for High Performance*

Linda McKee, CCP, Human Resource Manager, *Honeywell*

James E. Mittler, CMC, President, *J.E. Mittler & Co.*

David A. Pierson, Ph.D., *The Pierson Group*

Daniel Purushotham, Ph.D., CCP, CBP, Assistant Professor, *Central Connecticut State University*

John A. Rubino, CCP, CBP, GRP, President, *Rubino Consulting Services*

Doug Sayed, CCP, Principal, *Applied HR Strategies Inc.*

Donald J. Suhocki, CCP, Director, Compensation & Benefits, *Covenant Health*

Table of Contents

Introduction

Incentive Pay Programs: Opportunities and Challenges

Dow Scott, Ph.D., Loyola University Chicago

The purpose of this book is to help compensation and HR professionals and managers contribute to company competitiveness by doing the following:

- Determining under what conditions incentive pay programs (IPP) can contribute value to their organization and to the employees who will participate in those programs
- Identifying IPPs that are most likely to support their business strategy and achieve desired performance goals
- Developing effective IPPs that meet the specific needs of the organization
- Implementing IPPs successfully.

The use of incentive pay programs (IPPs) has exploded in the United States during the last 25 years. Prior to 1980, incentive pay (or what is often called variable pay and pay for performance programs) was limited primarily to annual merit increases for most exempt employees, commissions and bonuses for salespersons, and annual bonuses and stock awards for senior executives. Although gainsharing, Scanlon Plans, nondeferred profit sharing and team incentives were discussed in professional journals, few of these programs actually existed in mainstream U.S. companies.

A recent survey of compensation professionals indicates that 88 percent of managers and professionals receive incentive pay in their organizations, and 70 percent of compensation professionals surveyed believe that incentive pay is either "important or very important" to the success of their companies (Scott, McMullen, Wallace and Morajda 2004). As expected, a Hay Group Compensation Survey Report (2005) found senior managers received much more of their total pay in the form of incentives (25 percent to 92 percent) than employees in lower-level support positions (4 percent to 5 percent). Finally, executive pay has more than doubled in recent years, primarily as a result of pay packages that emphasize a variety of incentive programs that include stock options, restricted stock and annual cash bonuses.

So what caused this proliferation of IPPs? Much like the origination of a "perfect storm," a combination of forces conspired to transform traditional pay programs that almost exclusively emphasized employee benefits and base pay into the incentive pay programs widely used today. These forces include the following:

- Increased market competition, both nationally and globally
- Greater emphasis on and capability of measuring performance at individual, team and company levels
- A realization that because pay represents a large expenditure, if not the largest company expenditure, it needs to be used to create a competitive advantage
- A desire to reduce or at least share the risk of operating or starting a business with employees.

Reacting to these diverse forces, IPPs were extensively adopted as mechanisms for compensating people when the competition for scarce high-tech talent intensified in the late 1990s and corporate earnings were high.

Can Incentive Pay Programs Increase Performance?

Even though many businesses are using incentives, one still must ask, "Does it make good business sense in our industry, for our organization and for the specific jobs we have targeted for the IPP?" The primary rationale managers espouse for installing IPPs is the enhancement of performance by focusing employee attention on performance goals, by motivating increased effort, and, in the case of shared rewards, encouraging cooperation, information sharing and integrated work strategies. Less prominent reasons for installing incentive pay programs include risk sharing with employees (e.g., if the company does not do as well as expected, employees are paid less); attracting and retaining employees where competitors offer such incentive pay; and reducing the need for supervision, especially where employee oversight is difficult (e.g., outside sales and senior management positions). Thus, logic and experience suggest incentive pay programs will increase performance and otherwise benefit the company.

But what does research tell us? Numerous empirical studies indicate that the use of incentive pay programs is related to increased performance in a variety of situations. Based on an extensive review of the literature, Locke, Frederick, Buckner and Babko (1980) concluded that incentive pay programs increased performance an average of 30 percent to 40 percent. Jenkins, Gupta, Mitra and Shaw (1998) examined 39 individual incentive plans with meta-analysis and found, on average, performance quantity increased a whopping 34 percent, but quality did not increase significantly. Team-based incentives or shared reward programs also are found to increase performance and to have a positive impact on quality, according to numerous individual studies (e.g., Scott, Floyd, Bishop and Benson 2002; Welbourne, Balkin and Gomez-Meija 1995).

Of course, it may seem obvious that IPPs have a positive impact on performance since, by definition, incentives are paid for performance. Unfortunately, the desired outcome is not always as clear-cut in the "real world" as one might expect. First, the receipt of incentives may be the result of good performance, not the cause of it. For example, many incentive programs that include merit pay and annual bonuses are paid from budgeted labor costs at the end of the year based on company performance. Because company performance is determined by numerous factors, including economic conditions, technological advances, new products and services, and accounting decisions, the connection to individual employee performance may be difficult to discern. Individuals who actually receive the rewards may perform exceptionally well, but their performance may not necessarily contribute to overall business effectiveness or profitability. For example, a salesperson who increases sales of product X to new customers may receive a bonus for meeting his or her sales goal, but if manufacturing difficulties increase costs or if customers cancel orders because of quality problems, increased sales may hurt the company more than help.

Another problem in making the connection between performance and incentive pay may be the difficulty in determining what represents high performance and which employees are high performers. The decisions that knowledge workers make may literally take years to "play out," and in the "fog" of business, where multiple individuals were involved in bringing a new product or service to the marketplace, their individual contribution to the final results may not be clear.

Second, performance measures can be flawed. Individuals or teams who perform may or may not get the rewards they are due. For example, the accuracy of the performance appraisal process is often suspect for a variety of reasons, including budget restrictions. Making meaningful distinctions between high and average performers may be difficult, if not impossible, due to supervisory biases associated with friendships; preconceived notions about age, race and gender; and abrupt changes in work goals.

Third, incentives may be detrimental to performance. Incentive plans designed to motivate individuals may create a work environment where employees refuse to share information, do not help each other, manipulate incentive pay programs for individual gain, focus on playing political games and not getting the job done, and sabotage their rivals' work. Several studies of certain types of work environments indicate that organizations with more egalitarian pay programs outperform organizations that have larger pay differences (e.g., Bloom 1999; Cowherd 1992; Levine 1991; Pfeffer & Langton 1993).

Finally, employees may not perform because they fear management will make performance goals more difficult next year or reduce payouts. This is a common concern among salespeople, who often go to great lengths to avoid surpassing sales goals by too much.

Are Incentive Pay Programs Worth It?

Given the costs associated with incentive pay programs, and research indicating that incentive pay programs may not have the desired impact, why should management use incentive pay programs? First, theory and research show that incentive pay can substantially increase individual and organizational performance, and can represent a powerful tool for establishing a competitive advantage within an industry. Second, our society prides itself on being a meritocracy; employees and managers feel IPPs are the equitable way to determine what employees are paid. Finally, incentive pay programs can increase employee earnings and reduce the risk that management will have layoffs when economic conditions are difficult.

However, IPPs fail or certainly do not meet expectations if they are poorly conceived and implemented. The answer, then, is not to avoid the use of IPPs but to judiciously use properly designed IPP programs.

Overview of the Book

As stated earlier, the purpose of this book is to clarify under what conditions incentive programs will have positive consequences and to articulate how these programs should be designed to achieve the desired result. This book includes 16 chapters written by compensation experts representing the "best practices" of the full spectrum of incentive pay programs in use today. Eight chapters have appeared as articles in recent issues of *WorldatWork Journal* and *workspan*, and the remaining eight chapters were written specifically for this book. The book is divided into five sections. In Section I, Chapter 1 identifies the key elements of an effective IPP and provides a framework for designing new IPPs or for enhancing the value of existing plans.

Nationally known experts offer unique and in-depth treatment of specific IPPs in Sections II, III and IV. The chapters in Section II feature individual IPPs that include merit pay, sales incentives, piecework and recognition programs. Section III features bonus plans that reward teams, departments and operations, and focuses primarily on productivity improvement. Section IV features equity-based IPPs that include use of restricted stock, stock options and employee stock ownership (ESOP).

Section V focuses on how incentive programs are successfully implemented, effectively administered and evaluated. The authors of these chapters have national compensation reputations in academics, or consulting, or as executives within their companies. The chapters are based on considerable research of or extensive experience with IPPs. The authors present the business case for using a specific type of IPP, specify the conditions under which their program should be used, indicate what specific features of the IPP to include and indicate the benefits and challenges of implementing these programs. The biographical sketch for each author reveals the depth of expertise and extensive experience that is the basis of these great chapters.

Reason for Writing an Incentive Pay Book

I have considered writing a book or at least compiling a compendium of the best incentive pay practices for some time. This year I was forced into action by a less than satisfying search for a textbook for my graduate class on incentive pay. The few books devoted exclusively to IPP were old, and recently published compensation textbooks offered only a chapter or two on incentive pay. As a result, I turned to WorldatWork, which was generous enough to allow me to copy its journal papers for class. My students, many of whom are HR professionals, were delighted with the in-depth, applied treatment the *WorldatWork Journal* chapters offered. The compelling IPP "real world" applications provide a unique and interesting way to develop a fundamental understanding of IPPs and how these programs are implemented effectively.

I was impressed by the stature and expertise of the academicians and practitioners who have contributed to *WorldatWork Journal* over the last 20 years. Thus, I was delighted when WorldatWork offered an opportunity to compile its best articles into an incentive pay book. In fact, I took this as a license to not only pick and choose my favorite IPP articles but to also go back to authors and ask them to update the older articles based on their most current experience with incentive pay programs. I am happy to report that these authors indulged my passion, and more then half of the IPP chapters were written specifically for this book. It has been a pleasure to work with the very capable people in our HR and compensation profession, and I hope that this book can provide you with the many new insights into incentive pay that it has provided me.

Section I
Value Proposition and Fundamentals

Chapter 1

Designing Effective Incentive Pay Programs

Dow Scott, Ph.D., Loyola University Chicago

Even in midsize companies, an incentive pay program (IPP) can distribute millions of dollars to employees each year. One might expect an investment of this magnitude to substantially contribute to company performance by attracting and retaining talented employees, aligning their interests with the interests of the company and encouraging them to put forth more effort. Unfortunately, as most managers know, an IPP may or may not have the expected results. In fact, these programs can cause substantial employee dissatisfaction and performance problems. For example, a customer-service representative who is paid a bonus for the number of calls handled may not take the time necessary to resolve customer problems and may create substantial customer dissatisfaction and callbacks. Therefore, careful consideration must be given to the use of incentives and how an IPP is designed. The purpose of this chapter is to help human resource and compensation professionals and line managers do the following:

- Decide which type of incentive pay program, if any, will deliver the desired performance and represent the best value for the organization and for participating employees.
- Design an IPP that will meet management's performance expectations and be perceived as fair by employees.
- Improve the effectiveness of an existing IPP by aligning it with the organization's business strategy and the needs of employees.

Figure 1-1 on page 10 shows the process I use for designing a new IPP or critically examining the functioning of existing programs. This process is a series of steps that begins with an assessment to determine if an IPP is an appropriate tool for increasing performance, to evaluate the readiness of the organization for an IPP and to build commitment for the IPP. Based on the assessment, specific IPP objectives are articulated that provide a starting point for making program-design

Figure 1-1
IPP Design and Evaluation Process

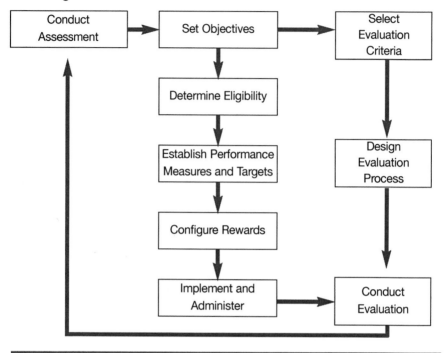

decisions for employee program eligibility, performance measures and targets, and the frequency and amount of rewards. IPP objectives also provide the criteria and suggest an evaluation process for determining the effectiveness of the IPP. Finally, the IPP evaluation provides important information for improving the program design based on employee reaction to the program and the impact of the program on performance.

The remainder of this chapter is a detailed treatment of each step in this IPP design process.

Conduct Organizational or Workplace Assessment

An effective IPP supports the business strategy and thus contributes to the organization's ability to maintain a competitive advantage. To accomplish this, the IPP must have a link between desired outcomes and the efforts and contributions of employees who participate in the IPP. To determine if a linkage can be established, management must clarify and resolve discrepancies among fundamental business strategies, organizational structures, production technologies and human resources policies and programs. For example, some organizations rely heavily on work teams to design and produce products, and they consider cooperative working relationships as a competitive advantage. If the company chooses to implement an IPP that measures and rewards individual performance, employees will receive a conflicting message that can adversely affect performance. Incentives that emphasize cooperation and shared team rewards, on the other hand, will be much more consistent with such a work environment, and the IPP is more likely to engender the support of managers and employees to achieve the desired performance.

An organizational or workplace assessment should provide answers to the following questions:

- What are the business goals to which we specifically require the IPP to contribute? These overall business goals can be to increase market share, develop new products or services, increase revenues or lower costs.
- What competitive strategies do we believe contribute toward obtaining our business goals? How are employees involved in these competitive strategies? If a competitive strategy is to develop innovative products to satisfy customer needs, how are the ideas developed and then brought to market? What employee groups are most involved?
- What employee capabilities and behaviors are required for the company to achieve competitive levels of performance and cost-effectiveness, especially as they relate to potential IPPs? Given the organization and job structure, are employee efforts likely to contribute to desired company performance or outcomes?
- What are the incentive pay traditions within the company, the industry and the occupations of employees who may be eligible for the IPP? For example, mid-level managers often expect that 15 percent to 20 percent of their pay will be based on performance targets and paid as an annual bonus. (This expectation is reflected in pay survey data that tracks average bonuses paid to managers.)

The pay philosophy held by management will influence the choice of incentives and the support the IPP will receive. For example, if management believes that employee rewards should be tied to the performance of the overall firm, it will be difficult to get managers to consider incentives that focus on the accomplishment of specific tasks or objectives that are job related. Likewise, if management believes in individual performance, programs that emphasize team or department performance will probably receive little support.

Even if management can establish a link between business goals, competitive strategies and employee contributions, eligible employees and the managers who supervise them must believe the following:

- Rewards offered fairly compensate them for additional efforts and contributions.
- Performance measures are valid and reliable.
- Management will not unfairly increase performance requirements as a result of performance improvements that are made.
- Their efforts will result in the desired performance or employee behavior.

Particular attention must be given to the effect employees have on performance. In recent years, company-performance formulas based on profits and earnings to fund IPPs have become popular. In fact, employers may offer below-market base pay with the opportunity for employees to receive large bonuses if the company does well. However, if employees have little influence on company performance, then IPPs are simply pay programs where management is sharing the risk of doing business within their industry. Risk sharing can represent a legitimate reason for implementing an IPP, but one cannot expect this type of plan to motivate employees to perform at higher levels. Where employees have limited influence on company performance, they may blame management for making poor decisions or manipulating the books to avoid paying the "promised" bonuses.

A related issue often associated with gainsharing programs that focus on productivity improvement and labor cost reduction is the possibility that the IPP will indeed deliver increased productivity or output. If production becomes more efficient, will employees be laid off, will overtime decrease or are expected increases in customer demand expected to provide work for potentially excess employees? Before committing themselves to increasing productivity, employees will think about how they will be affected.

The "bottom line" is that management and employees who participate in an IPP must trust each other to respect each other's the contribution and needs. Thus, the assessment should examine the relationship between management and employees. If there are issues creating mistrust, the design and implementation of an IPP should proceed with caution. Management can build trust by clarifying the linkages between business strategy and an IPP, demonstrating how the IPP benefits the organization and employees who participate in it, helping employees understand how performance is measured and rewards paid out, and involving employees in the IPP design and implementation process (discussed in Chapter 14).

The organization's management information system (MIS) is a critical element in the effective implementation and administration of an IPP. The assessment should therefore investigate the capabilities of the organization to provide the accurate, timely and understandable performance data that employees need to manage their performance and to understand how performance is rewarded.

Finally, management needs to assess its basic capability in the design and administration of an incentive pay program. Does management have the internal resources to design the plan, make necessary adaptations to the performance management system, provide performance feedback and make the correct incentive payouts? If not, can consultants provide the expertise and the time necessary for designing and implementing the program?

At this point, management needs to carefully consider if the cost of designing and administering an IPP and the cost of the payouts will be worth the expected improvement in performance. For example, sales incentive programs are a fundamental strategy for increasing sales for selected products. However, before implementing a sales incentive program, one should ask the following questions:

- Does the increased cost of selling the product still provide that necessary return on investment (ROI) for the company?
- Does the salesforce have the capability to increase sales of this product (e.g., meet market demand, deal with competition and properly use sales skill)?
- Can the company meet the increased demand for the product?
- What are the negative consequences of redirecting salespersons' efforts to another product?
- Does the company have the ability to accurately measure sales and provide timely feedback and payouts?
- Do the eligible employees believe that they can achieve the performance levels required to obtain the incentive, that the incentive is worth the effort and that management can be trusted to honor the incentive-performance agreement?

Set IPP Objectives

The second step in the design process is to clearly articulate explicit goals or objectives for the IPP. Reaching these goals should support the business strategy and contribute to a competitive advantage for the organization. Useful goals specify performance or employee behavior expectations, the rationale for whom to include or exclude from IPP eligibility and how performance will be measured. Involving management in developing these goals provides a great opportunity to build commitment for the IPP and to reduce the risk that management will be disappointed in the design or in the outcomes of the program.

Again, because they are familiar to most managers, sales incentive programs offer good examples of the types of objectives that will be useful in designing and evaluating an IPP. A goal to simply increase sales for a specific product does not provide much guidance in the design of the sales incentive program. However, a goal to increase sales of specific products to new customers in certain regions provides information that is helpful in determining program eligibility, identifying performance measures, evaluating the program and making other design decisions. For example, goals associated with a sales IPP could include the following:

- To increase sales of product X to new customers (e.g., those who have not purchased a company product in the last 36 months) by 15 percent during the next 12 months
- To increase the number of sales calls to new customers (e.g., those who have not purchased a company product in the last 36 months) by 50 percent during the next 12 months
- To have 90 percent of eligible sales professionals understand the intent and key provisions of the sales IPP
- To have the eligible sales professionals and the managers to whom they report perceive the IPP as fair and the sales goals as achievable.

Although only the first goal and possibly the second goal can be associated with incentive payments, achieving the third and fourth goals are necessary for the IPP to operate effectively. If the sales IPP does not produce the results expected, knowing how employees and their managers felt about the program (goal four), knowing if eligible employees understood the program (goal three) and knowing if employee behavior was consistent with what is required to drive performance (goal two) are important for diagnosing why the program is failing.

A company that utilizes team selling and integrates customer service into the IPP offers a somewhat different set of potential objectives. For example, the goals for the next 12 months may be as follows:

- To increase sales to current customers by 10 percent
- To reduce customer complaints by 20 percent
- To increase cooperation among sales and customer service by timely sharing customer information with each other
- To have 90 percent of eligible sales and customer service professionals understand the intent and key provisions of the sales IPP
- To have the eligible sales and customer service professionals perceive the IPP as fair and the sales goals as achievable.

It is important when setting IPP goals and eventually evaluating program effectiveness to indicate how eligible employees are going to affect performance. If better cooperation is the process goal expected to drive the desired results, then an explicit measure of cooperation tells employees what they must do to earn the rewards and provides management with feedback to determine if cooperation indeed drives performance. The methodology for evaluating pay programs is presented in substantial detail in the *WorldatWork Journal* article "Evaluating Pay Program Effectiveness," which is included in this book as Chapter 16.

Eligibility

Determining eligibility is the next important step in designing an effective IPP. Of course, employees who have the ability to substantially impact IPP goals should be included in the IPP, and those who do not have that ability should not be eligible to participate. This seemingly straightforward rule is often difficult to apply in the real world, where individual influence on performance varies across jobs and levels in the organization. The error managers most often make is that of including employees that have limited or no influence on the desired performance outcomes. First, they fear accusations of favoritism or not appreciating the contribution the "team" makes to performance. Second, managers are rightfully concerned that employees excluded from an IPP may become resentful and unwilling to support— and may even sabotage—the efforts of eligible employees.

Unfortunately, including employees in an IPP who make little or no contribution has negative repercussions. First, if employees are included in a plan where their performance does not affect payout, at best the IPP becomes viewed as sort of a random giveaway, and at worst an entitlement. On the other hand, employees who perceive themselves as "earning" the incentive (e.g., influencing performance) will resent those who do not contribute to performance or receive incentive awards regardless of how they perform. Dropping employees from an incentive is extremely difficult and is thus seldom done.

Careful thought should therefore be given to the eligibility decision. In making this decision, management should consider the following:
- The actual impact that the position has on the achievement of performance targets
- The importance of collaboration among individuals who support employees eligible for the IPP
- Potential role conflicts associated with job responsibilities and attainment of performance goals.

The potential conflict between supervisors and the employees who report to them is an instance in which it may be desirable to exclude supervisors from the IPP. Although supervisors may interact extensively with the work team and have significant impact on the performance of the team, their role of assigning work, monitoring quality, controlling access to production materials and disciplining employees may at times put them at odds with the performance goals of incentive-eligible employees. Therefore, including them in the IPP with their subordinates would not be appropriate, even if considerable discretion was used.

Returning to our example of sales employees, including customer service in an IPP that focuses on increasing sales to new customers may not make sense. But in the case of customer retention, which requires the combined efforts of both the salesperson and the customer service representative, it may be a good choice to include both of them. Who to include or exclude in the IPP, of course, depends on the degree to which these two groups work together to retain customers.

Although impact on performance, cooperation among employees and the position responsibilities may determine who is eligible and who is not, unambiguous communications that explain management's rationale is absolutely essential. Such explanation can reduce perceptions of injustice by framing communications in terms of the employees' "total reward" package, alignment of the pay system with the company's business strategy and a pay structure that uses mechanisms to ensure that pay is fair both internally (e.g., job valuation) and externally (e.g., market price).

Employees should therefore not be included in an IPP just because they perceive everyone else is receiving incentive pay. If it does not make sense to include certain employees in the IPP, but management is committed to incentive pay, it may make sense to create a separate plan for those employees in which the IPP is better aligned with the focus of their work and their impact on performance. Care must be taken not to inadvertently pit two employee groups against each other. A situation to avoid would be one in which sales employees focus on the amount of product sold while customer service focuses on retaining customers. While the sales employees' goals considered alone may make sense, the behavior of sales professionals can negatively affect customer retention and frustrate retention efforts among customer service professionals (e.g., salespersons may make promises that customer service cannot honor).

Performance Measures and Targets

It is important at this point to clearly distinguish between the measures of IPP effectiveness and the measures used to monitor and reward performance. As indicated earlier, an IPP can be judged on a variety of criteria, including employee perception of fairness, understanding of the program, behaviors believed to drive performance and actual performance outcomes. However, measures used as criteria to reward performance are more narrowly focused, and the measures are associated with specific levels of performance or with behaviors required for payouts to eligible employees.

Organizations by their very nature collect many forms of performance data, either because it is required by law or because this information is necessary for managing the organization. The challenge is to select or create one or more IPP measures that are:

- Consistent with IPP goals
- Perceived to be accurate measures of desired performance or employee behavior
- Easy to understand
- Influenced by eligible employees

The organization must be able to provide timely feedback and calculate the payout when promised.

Returning to our sales example, let's examine the first goal:

To increase sales of product X to new customers (e.g., those who have not purchased a company product in the last 36 months) by 15 percent during the next 12 months

Even though this seems to be a relatively straightforward performance criterion, this IPP measure is problematic. First, one needs to know if the sales data are collected and recorded in enough detail to monitor what constitutes a sale to a new customer as specifically defined by the IPP. If a purchase is made from sister divisions or another product line, does this disqualify it as a sale to a new customer, and if so, is this data being recorded correctly? Does a sale count if the customer returns the product or does not pay? It is important to clearly state what is included in the measure and verify if that is indeed what is currently being measured.

A second consideration is the accuracy of data, in terms of its source (who supplies the information) and how the data is processed. Errors can easily be made when data is entered (either intentionally or unintentionally). Having multiple data coders or situations where the coders must use judgment can be particularly challenging. Errors can easily be made in transforming the information by simply misplacing a column of data or using the wrong formula for defining which sales are included or excluded. Carefully verifying the data stream from where it originates to the final spreadsheet that provides individual results for the IPP is always a good investment of time.

Third, managers and employees need to trust the source of the data and to understand how rewards are calculated. Lack of trust or confusion will erode the ability of the IPP to motivate the desired performance. Thus, management needs to scrutinize data sources carefully or even allow employees to verify the data themselves. Keeping calculations simple and making the collection of data as transparent as possible is important.

Finally, the ability to produce this data when needed is essential. As most managers know, employees place great importance on receiving their money when it is due, and immediate payment can strengthen the link between pay and performance. Both quality and availability of individual performance measures vary substantially across jobs. In sales, for example, there is direct customer contact and a measurable output, but in specialized staff jobs there is virtually no measurable output. Measuring performance gets particularly difficult when incentive programs cover a variety of jobs and employee contributions. Many organizations use performance appraisal instruments that allow supervisors to evaluate performance based on goal accomplishment or standardized performance criteria such as integrity, productivity, communication and leadership. Unfortunately, supervisor bias can easily influence how they rate employees, and because of the length of time required to conduct performance appraisals, they are frequently done only once a year. Performance appraisal ratings are thus often the weak link in merit pay increase programs. This issue will be discussed in detail in Chapter 2.

It is not enough, however, to provide accurate (e.g., reliable and valid) measures of performance. IPPs also require establishment of performance targets that challenge employees to perform at higher levels and that are, at the same time, achievable. A target indicates at what level of performance the employee will be entitled to receive a reward. Establishing a target is often a difficult task because future performance is often difficult to predict or is influenced by factors that the organization and employee may not fully control. Targets are most often extrapolated from past performance, either informally (e.g., the manager and employee may negotiate a performance goal) or through specific formulas that calculate a target based on performance achievement during the last year or several years of performance (e.g., rolling averages). Setting performance targets can be a source of conflict for the employee who wants to set a low target (to maximize earnings) and the employer who wants to establish a high target (to minimize the cost of the IPP and maximize performance). If management raises the target each year, with little rationale, that can quickly erode the motivational value of an IPP.

Configuring Rewards: Types, Amounts and Frequencies

Attaching rewards to the performance measures requires management to make several decisions. First, there are a variety of rewards, including immediate cash, deferred cash, noncash (e.g., extra vacation, merchandise or recognition), perks and equity in the company (e.g., restricted stock, phantom stock and stock options). Each of these rewards or payments for performance may have a different value to the employee and different tax consequences. The size the or amount of the reward reflects the value to the employee and the cost to the company. Management must decide what reward type and amount will motivate the desired employee behavior and must effectively determine the performance cost ; it must have a positive return on investment (ROI).

Researchers have made periodic attempts to determine what has been called "just meaningful difference," which is the amount required to get employees to perform at higher levels. A reward of 5 percent to 15 percent of an individual's base pay has been suggested as a minimum. However, common sense indicates that the incentive amount required to produce the desired behavior and obtain the desired results depends on a variety of factors, which include the following:

- The employee's current income or wealth and the value the employee places on the reward (e.g., annual cash payments, stock or deferred income)
- The effort the employee believes must be invested to achieve the reward, taking into account alternative rewards that can be earned by focusing efforts in other venues (e.g., family time at home working late to possibly earn a bonus)
- The employee's perception of the likelihood of actually receiving the reward; in other words, the less likely it is that employee will receive the reward (e.g., the higher the risk that invested effort will produce no reward), the larger the reward amount must be to obtain the desired behavior or results
- The employee's tolerance for risk and pay variability.
- The perceived fairness between the amount of the reward and the value the employee's efforts contribute to the company; if an employee makes a suggestion that saves the company thousands of dollars, he or she may not be happy receiving an engraved plaque and a $25 gift card
- The tradition among employees in that occupation or industry for fixed salary and variable pay (e.g., incentives).

The reward amount or payout also is influenced by the risk the employer expects the employee to assume. For example, some incentive pay programs are based on a philosophy of "pay for excellence." In this case, employees are paid a competitive wage or salary for good performance. Incentive pay is expected to reward excellence or performance substantially better than what one would expect. The pay-at-risk philosophy is where employees are paid less base pay than the labor market indicates they should be paid. Employees expect to make up the difference by good or excellent performance and actually receive higher rewards for the level of performance achieved because they are placing their pay at risk. In the latter situation, incentive payouts must be more consistent and rewards richer, because employees will be tempted to leave for better-paying jobs that are less risky.

The type of reward desired by employees, and employers' preference for using gifts, direct cash and stock equity, are fairly easy to discern. However, determining the amount is more art than science, because few studies have been able to capture the numerous trade-offs that the variety of work situations create. Pay surveys often try to capture the range of incentive pay offered for different jobs and for employees at different levels in the hierarchy.

The frequency of payment is closely related to the decision about the amount of the employee reward. Reinforcement theory and substantial research indicate that more frequent rewards will increase performance. However, simple economics suggests that more frequent rewards must be smaller than infrequently paid rewards. Although the overall annual payout may be the same for frequent and less frequent payments, rewards that are too small may be perceived as inconsequential by the employee. A 5-percent, or even a 10-percent bonus distributed over 26 paychecks may have limited value, while an annual lump sum may be of considerable value.

Other factors that affect the frequency with which rewards might be paid include the availability of performance data (e.g., company earnings may only be calculated annually) and the amount of effort required to generate this information. In any event, a common criticism of most IPPs is that payouts are too infrequent and substantially reduce employee motivation.

As discussed in the previous section, it is important to establish payout targets that are challenging but achievable. Unfortunately, achievement of performance goals can be difficult to predict because work requirements may, and often do, change. Some individuals are more capable than others, and external factors can have considerable impact on the achievement of performance goals. Thus, incentive guarantees and caps are sometimes used to protect the employee and employer, respectively, against circumstances over which they may have no control. Guarantees provide a minimum payment regardless of performance, which protects the employee, and employers are protected if performance exceeds what is normally expected (creating a "windfall") by a cap or maximum payment. Guarantees and caps are often condemned because they may reduce employee performance. If performance goals are difficult, employees may quit trying to reach performance levels where there will be an incentive payout and simply take what is guaranteed, and if employees reach the cap before the end of the performance period, they may stop performing or try to move performance to the next incentive period (e.g., by post-dating sales). However, where employee performance can have substantial variation because of factors outside of the employee's control (e.g., economy, customer preferences or cost of raw materials), or where there is a lack of trust between management and employees, the guarantees and caps may fill an important function.

In an attempt to establish expectations, if not manage payouts, management can establish a desired payout matrix and then adjust the performance targets and payout levels based on experience. For example, management receives no payout during 20 percent of the performance periods for incentive plan driven by corporate performance, at least threshold payments 35 percent of the time, targeted payouts 40 percent and maximum payouts 5 percent of the time. The same kind of matrix can be established for the percent of individuals or team who will reach targeted levels of performance and receive different payout levels. In this situation, management may expect to pay 10 percent of employees the maximum payout, 20 percent an above-average payout, 50 percent an average payout and finally 20 percent of employees a below-average payout or no payout. Requiring a payout distribution may force managers to make distinctions between higher and lower levels of performance.

IPP Funding

Funding the IPP is integral to the design of the program and affects payouts. There are three primary funding mechanisms used today. The first, and the one that offers the most flexibility to management, is discretionary awards. A payout for a discretionary award is determined by senior management at the end of the performance period. The funding or incentive pool is based on what management feels employees contributed to performance, what performance was worth and how much the organization believes it can afford. In other words, incentive pay is distributed at management's pleasure based on whatever criteria and amount it deems appropriate. Discretionary awards avoid commitment until management is sure the performance has occurred and the resources are available to reward employees. The downside, of course, is that employees are not sure what rewards they will receive for what levels of performance. Typically, IPPs funded by discretionary awards have poor "line of sight" and may simply recognize the amount of available resources management has to share but have little connection to either individual job performance or the performance of the organization.

The second method of funding rewards is to budget incentive payouts as simply a cost of doing business. In other words, if the organization budgets $200 million for total labor costs for the upcoming year given sales projections, estimated production costs and expected capital investments, then management decides how much of the total labor costs to allocate to base pay, incentive pay and employee benefits. If 5 percent, or $10 million, is budgeted for annual bonuses, it is then up to management to decide how to distribute the incentive budget based on measures of individual, team or organization performance. Budgeting incentive pay often creates a "zero sum game" because each employee is in competition with every other employee for a fixed amount of budgeted incentive pay. Merit increases that are rolled into base pay are a budgeted incentive payment.

The third method is formula funding. Management identifies appropriate performance criteria associated with profits, earnings, cost saving, quality improvements and so on, and promises to share these earnings or savings with the employees. For example, if the funding mechanism is earnings, and the company is willing to share 50 percent of company earnings that exceed 4 percent return on investment, you have a simple formula that funds the incentive pool. Management typically likes formula-driven funding because there are no payouts unless additional revenues or cost savings are realized, typically above what investors may expect to receive. However, although size of the incentive awards funded by the formula is potentially unlimited, employees may have little individual influence on how much money is generated by the organization. For example, earnings of an orange grower are directly influenced by the economy and the weather. Consumers buy fewer oranges and orange juice during downturns in the economy, and bad weather reduces the supply, which drives up the price. As a result, employees can work hard and exceed individual performance goals but not be rewarded—unless the organization as a whole is generating sufficient earnings. An alternative when outside factors are likely to affect performance is to compare earnings or other measures with those of other companies in the industry.

Even though employees may have limited impact on the money generated by the formula that funds the incentive plan, management can link the incentive pool generated by the formula to performance by specifying how the incentive pool will be distributed. Employees who contribute more, either in terms of the positions they hold or their level of performance, can be allocated larger shares of the incentive pool.

There are, of course, certain positions, such as sales, where individual employees may have a direct and measurable impact on earnings, profits or expenses. In those cases, formula funding can be more easily directed to those who make the largest contribution. However, the problem of external factors affecting payoff still exists.

The effectiveness of incentive pay programs is largely determined by management's ability to determine which employees affect desired performance, to accurately measure performance and establish challenging performance goals, and to provide meaningful rewards for performance. To create an IPP that can meet those design requirements can be very challenging given the complexity of production systems and the effect of external factors on performance. However, employees who are rewarded for performance do in fact perform better, and higher levels of performance can have a dramatic impact on organizational performance.

Implementation and Administration

There is little doubt that it is a challenge to determine if an IPP is a suitable strategy for increasing performance, and to design a program that's appropriate for the unique competitive environment of an organization. And, additional problems often occur in the implementation process and, later, as the programs are administered. It is not enough to have a technically well-designed plan; employees must perceive it as having value for them and must believe that management can be trusted to deliver the rewards promised. Managers and employees want to know how performance is measured and how the bonus is calculated. An implementation process that engages key stakeholders can dramatically increase the likelihood that the IPP will be effective, because such a process will accomplish the following:

- Improve the quality of the program design.
- Build commitment and trust in the program among employees and the managers to whom they report.
- Educate employees about the purpose and key elements of the program.

For the implementation process to be effective, management must recognize that involving key stakeholders must begin when an IPP is first considered. Unfortunately, management often wants to limit employee involvement and even limit knowledge about the company's consideration of developing an IPP because it does not want to build expectations and then later reject the idea or simply not bring the program to fruition. Although limiting involvement in the plan may give managers a sense of control, restricting employee involvement will certainly undercut the value of the implementation process and possibly alienate employees. Thus, management must work to achieve balance between its need to control the outcome of the process and its understanding of the value of involving employees.

A detailed treatment of IPP implementation can be found in Chapter 14.

Once an IPP is implemented, management must collect performance data on an individual, team or organization level, calculate the amount of the reward pool and then allocate the appropriate rewards to individuals as promised. Compensation and HR professionals have traditionally used spreadsheets such as Microsoft Excel to perform these calculations. However, the complexity of many incentive programs and the application of an IPP to large groups of eligible employees has caused this method to be both time-consuming and fraught with errors. Newer and more sophisticated software, however, can directly access human resources or management-information systems. The challenges of designing and using this software are examined in substantial detail in Chapter 15, "The Experience of Changing to an Integrated Compensation-Software Program."

Regular communication about the IPP is important for maintaining interest in the program and reinforcing the link between pay and performance. Providing real-time data on performance and earnings is ideal, but weekly, monthly or quarterly reports can be meaningful as well. Communications need to be easy to access and understand.

IPP Evaluation

IPPs are seldom designed perfectly, and conditions under which they were expected to operate often change. It is the unexpected consequences that create problems for an IPP. One must thus monitor and periodically evaluate the IPP. As noted earlier, IPP goals provide the basis for monitoring and evaluating the program. Those criteria can focus on how eligible employees and their managers react to the program, the level of understanding demonstrated by employees and the supervisor to whom they report, the desired or undesired behavior exhibited by employees and the result or outcomes of the IPP.

Once the criteria are identified, reliable and valid measures of the criteria must be established. The data for each measure must be collected and the findings interpreted. A specific methodology for evaluating a pay program is provided in Chapter 16.

Conclusion

The systematic process for designing and implementing an IPP that has been presented in this chapter is essential for ensuring that the substantial investment made in employee compensation contributes to a competitive advantage for the company. Assessing the organization's strategic purpose, work situation and management expectations offers considerable insight into the potential value of an IPP, builds employee and management commitment to the program and provides a basis for establishing meaningful goals for the program. The explicit goals that result from the assessment provide the criteria and rationales for the following:

- Assessing the value of the program and monitoring its effectiveness
- Determining employee eligibility for the IPP
- Selecting performance measures and targets
- Making reward or payout decisions (e.g., amount and frequency)
- Formulating a process for implementing and administering the program.

It has been my experience that poorly conceived IPPs can do substantial damage to employee trust, performance and morale. An IPP has a pervasive impact on motivation and a critical effect on an organization's ability to attract and retain talent. Given the level of investment involved, it is vital for management to very carefully manage the design process and monitor the effects of the IPP.

Section II
Individual Incentives

Chapter 2
What Have We Learned About Merit Pay Plans?

Jon M. Werner, Ph.D., University of Wisconsin-Whitewater
Robert L. Heneman, The Ohio State University

A challenge facing employers is thinking and acting more strategically with regard to total compensation. Nowhere is this more true than in the area of merit pay. While some have derided merit pay as passé, or even "dead," merit pay remains one of the most widely used forms of incentive pay in the United States. In the research we conducted for our recently revised book on the topic, we found that approximately 90 percent of all private-sector organizations, 88 percent of state governments and 73 percent of local governments have merit pay plans in place.[1] This is an *increase* since 1990, particularly for public-sector usage. The need, then, is to find how to best use merit pay given that employers continue to use it. To demonstrate how to best use merit pay plans, we have reviewed the current research literature and benchmark case studies of best practice. This chapter presents our findings.

Merit Pay Defined

Merit pay is a form of employee incentive where individual pay increases are linked to the rated performance of individual employees in a previous time period. As such, it is a "pay-for-performance" plan. A key distinction in merit pay plans is that there is generally less focus on objective or quantifiable employee outputs such as sales, objects produced or billable hours. Instead, the pay increase is linked to a subjective judgment of employee performance in a recently completed time period. These judgments are most often made by the employee's supervisor, though other raters are increasingly included in the judgment process that forms the basis for a rating and subsequent change in pay.

One assumption many people have about merit pay is that a rating of employee performance that leads to a merit increase will lead to higher levels of performance in the future by that employee. Thus, for merit pay plans to work effectively, there must first be an accurate means of measuring employee performance and translating this into a meaningful pay increase that will motivate future performance. However, a meaningful pay increase does not guarantee that future levels of employee performance will remain at high levels. A recent review of merit pay described the success of merit pay plans as "moderate."[2] Merit pay plans are most likely to be viewed as effective when employees perceive a link between pay and performance, and when they view the system as fair in terms of the process that is used to administer merit pay.[3]

The Importance of Performance Measurement to Merit Pay

For merit pay plans to work as intended, organizations need solid, well-functioning performance appraisal or performance measurement systems. Unfortunately, performance appraisal remains one of those topics that everybody loves to hate. Employees are frequently dissatisfied with both the process and outcomes of the appraisal process, while managers often dislike them because of the administrative hassles and because of frequent negative employee reactions to the feedback and ratings they receive.

For too long, the academic and research communities seemed unduly focused on finding a "best" rating format to rate employees. Whole careers were made arguing the superiority of a particular rating scale. After considerable research, some fairly basic conclusions can be made concerning rating scales:

- It is better to measure more specific behaviors than to focus on broad employee traits.
- It is desirable to measure observable outcomes or results whenever possible.
- There is no "holy grail," no ideal rating format, that works for all employees and organizations.
- A format that looks at both outcomes and behaviors is generally recommended.

An example of an organization that uses multiple measures to rate performance comes from Praxair. Praxair had a management-by-objectives (MBO) system in place that was well regarded. However, in the late 1990s, it added how goals were achieved (e.g., the behaviors involved), as well as the actual goals and results obtained.[4] We recommend that organizations follow Praxair's example and use a strategy for merit pay decisions that evaluates multiple measures of performance. Other best practices in performance appraisal appear in Table 2-1 on page 31.

Table 2-1

Ten Recommendations for Improving the Accuracy of the Appraisal Rating Process

- Link performance standards and ratings to the strategic mission of the organization.
- Base performance standards and ratings on a job analysis for the particular job(s) in question.
- Wherever feasible, use multiple sources or raters to collect performance information.
- Wherever feasible, include raters and employees in the process of developing performance standards.
- Provide adequate training for everyone involved in the appraisal rating process.
- Only use rating formats that are based on sound scale-construction principles.
- Minimize the time between performance observations and ratings.
- Ensure that raters have sufficient opportunity to observe employee performance prior to making their ratings.
- Encourage raters to keep notes or diaries of employee performance as it occurs.
- Hold raters accountable for their ratings.

Source: Adapted from Heneman, R.L., and J.M. Werner. 2005. *Merit pay: Linking pay to performance in a changing world*, 2nd ed. Greenwich, CT: Information Age Publishers.

Merit Pay Policy Issues

Assuming that employee performance can be accurately and fairly measured, the next step for organizations is to translate these performance ratings into actual merit pay increases. To do this, it is imperative that organizations have a sound set of merit pay policies and guidelines in place. Issues regarding budget concerns, guide charts, pay structure, market pricing and plan implementation must all be addressed.

These types of issues are tremendously important, as one of us observed when serving on a merit pay task force at a large public university. One of the more vocal members of the task force was very critical of the university's merit pay system. This supervisor's gripe went something like this: "I have 15 employees. Last year, my merit pay budget was $1,000. The difference between how I can reward my top performers and everyone else comes out to pennies a pay period."[5] His point was that the implementation of merit pay in the organization was faulty—that the differences in how people were rewarded based on this process were so small that employees were not motivated to achieve high levels of performance. This problem seems especially prevalent in public-sector organizations, where merit pay plans are common and are frequently one of the primary means by which individual variations in performance are rewarded.

Just Noticeable Differences. What is the minimum pay increase that employees would perceive as "making a difference" with regard to improving their attitudes and behaviors at work? This amount is sometimes referred to as a "just noticeable difference" (JND). If a merit increase is not large enough to produce a JND, then it is not likely to produce an increase in the quality of future employee performance. A review of 11 studies on this topic concluded the following: "It appears that an estimate of around 7.5 percent is a rough indicator of how large a pay increase needs to be before it becomes just noticeable to employees."[6]

Actual merit increases since the beginning of this decade have generally been in the 3 percent to 4 percent range. For example, average merit pay increases for 2007 were estimated at 3.7 percent in a recent IOMA survey.[7] There is clearly a discrepancy between the average estimate for a JND and the estimated average for actual merit pay increases. This brings into question the ability of most current merit pay plans to actually motivate subsequent employee performance when a majority of employees come nowhere close to receiving a merit increase that is noticeable to them. It seems, then, that budgetary issues can be a serious impediment to successful merit pay plan implementation. The presence of these issues may be why, in the face of tough economic conditions, many organizations revert to low, across-the-board pay increases. However, differences that appear to be little more than a drop in the bucket may do more harm than good.[8] Unfortunately, across-the-board increases do nothing to reward high levels of performance by individual employees.

In a study by the Mercer consulting firm, only 48 percent of the large organizations surveyed reported that their reward programs were effective in differentiating and rewarding top performers.[9] In a study of organizational performance in the trucking and concrete pipe industries, Jason Shaw and colleagues found that increased pay dispersion among employees was related to increased organizational performance, but only when organizations had formalized individual incentive systems in place (such as merit pay, spot bonuses and lump-sum bonuses).[10] This report provides another example of how a proactive and strategic approach to compensation can prevent strong negative employee reactions and subsequent performance issues. Steve Bates has provided creative examples of how organizations can reward their top performers.[11]

Merit Pay Guide Charts. It is recommended that organizations develop guidelines or a merit pay guide chart so that employees can understand the merit pay system and be more likely to perceive a pay increase as fair. A guide chart should thus spell out precisely how the organization intends to link pay to individual employee performance. In its simplest form, a guide chart lists specific percent raises that are linked to each level of rated performance. For example, there will be no increase for ratings of 1 percent or 2 percent, a 3-percent raise for a rating of 3, and so on. More complex guide charts can also take into account an employee's current position in the pay range and may also consider the period of time since the employee's last pay increase. An example of a guide chart used by a public transit organization appears in Figure 2-1.

Moving employees relatively quickly up to the midpoint of their pay range is shown in the guide chart because doing so reduces the temptation for competent

Figure 2-1
A Merit Pay Guide Chart Used in a Public Transit Organization

Performance Level	Quintile (Position in Range)				
	1	2	3	4	5
Outstanding (5)	(a) 9%	(b) 9%	(c) 8%	(d) 7%	(e) 6%
Superior (4)	(f) 7%	(g) 7%	(h) 6%	(i) 5%	(j) 4%
Competent (3)	(k) 5%	(l) 5%	(m) 4%	(n) 3%	(o) 3%
Needs Improvement (2)	(p) 0%	(q) 0%	(r) 0%	(s) 0%	(t) 0%
Unsatisfactory (1)	(u) 0%	(v) 0%	(w) 0%	(x) 0%	(y) 0%

(Letters in parentheses are cell identifiers for reference purposes, and numbers within cells represent percent of pay increase based on position in pay range and performance appraisal).

Source: Scott, K.D., S.E. Markham, and M.J. Vest. 1996. The influence of a merit pay guide chart on employee attitudes toward pay at a transit authority. *Public personnel management* 25:103–117.

employees to leave for higher wages elsewhere. However, the guide chart also presents slower pay increases above the midpoint; only the top-performing employees move toward the upper limit of the range.[12] Cost-containment goals are often given as a major reason for such a pay policy. In the study of public transit authority workers conducted by Dow Scott and colleagues, the use of a guide chart appeared to set expectations about what employees would receive as a pay increase. Interestingly, employees who were rated highest and were at the top of their pay ranges were *not* less satisfied with their raises. Scott and colleagues wrote, "Thus even though merit pay guide charts may successfully slow employee movement through the upper half of the pay range, employee attitudes are not necessarily negatively affected. Overall these results are good news for those companies that use a merit pay system."[13]

Market Pricing and Merit Pay. For decades, the use of job evaluations has been a mainstay of compensation practices, at least for large organizations. The argument for the use of job evaluations is that such evaluations provide an internally consistent structure for the wages paid to different jobs within an organization. Job evaluation efforts should also take into consideration external equity issues; most often this is done by referencing wage and salary survey information. Since the 1990s, however, there has been a concerted effort to reduce or remove job evaluation efforts from the setting of base pay and to rely more on market pricing as the sole or primary source of information concerning base pay.[14]

Job evaluation, as commonly practiced, is often slow, cumbersome and bureaucratic. There is certainly much appeal to moving toward greater use of market pricing in setting compensation, and WorldatWork has an e-learning program set up to guide practitioners in such efforts.[15] However, issues of internal equity do not simply go away when an organization moves toward greater use of market pricing to set compensation levels. A particular question that must be addressed is whether (and how) individual differences in performance will be handled. That is, will some form of pay-for-performance plan (such as merit pay) be used in addition to market pricing? While some initial efforts are being made in linking merit pay to market pricing, it is still too early to say how effective this strategy actually is. If merit pay is to remain as prevalent in the future as it has been since the 1980s, the connection to the current wave of market pricing efforts must certainly be addressed.

Appeals Procedures. To promote perceived fairness in a merit pay policy, employees should have a means to appeal merit pay decisions. A survey from the 1990s found that 32 percent of the reporting organizations had formal appeals mechanisms in place.[16] Anecdotally, it seems that formal appeals mechanisms are much more common in the public sector than in the private sector. An example of an appeal policy for college faculty at Northeastern University appears in Figure 2-2 on page 35.

Pay Secrecy. Many private-sector employers in the United States maintain some form of pay-secrecy policy that provides for disciplinary action or even discharge for employees who discuss pay information with colleagues. Rather disturbingly, in a study by Towers Perrin, less than half of the organizations surveyed communicated details with employees concerning merit pay budgets, salary ranges or average merit increases.[17] In contrast, in a research study sponsored by WorldatWork, more openness and better communication concerning pay issues was associated with increased satisfaction with pay, greater organizational commitment and increased trust in management.[18] It would seem highly desirable, then, for organizations to move toward greater openness about pay in general, including merit pay decisions.

Figure 2-2

A Sample Merit-Appeals Procedure

A. Purpose

The purpose of merit review is to measure and to reward individual faculty members' contributions to the achievement of unit goals, and to provide a process to assess and to facilitate professional development.

E. Appeals Procedure

Each faculty member shall have five working days after receiving the written evaluation to submit documentation for appeal. The faculty member will be provided the opportunity to meet with the persons responsible for the merit review, to discuss any concerns about the results of the review. This meeting shall take place within two weeks after the request is made. The committee shall respond to the faculty member within five working days after the meeting with the faculty member. In the event that the faculty member is not satisfied with the outcome of his/her appeal, he/she may pursue whatever rights are available in the *Faculty Handbook*.

Source: Bouvé College of Health Sciences Merit Policy, Northeastern University (June 14, 2001). Accessed on March 25, 2004, at: http://www.bouve.neu.edu/merit.html.

In the United States, the National Labor Relations Act gives all employees (whether represented by a labor union or not) the right to engage in activity for their "mutual aid and protection." Lawyer Jonathan Segal writes that the National Labor Relations Board has consistently held that this includes the "right to discuss the terms and conditions of their employment among themselves. This includes, for example, the right to talk about what they are paid. Accordingly, employers cannot prohibit employees from discussing their wages. A rule prohibiting discussions about pay is unlawful, even if the employer does not strictly enforce it" (p. 113).[19] We recognize that this is not how most organizations have typically handled discussions of pay within their workplaces, and would thus urge readers to seek legal counsel concerning the implications of this act for all organizational policies relating to pay discussions. We stress the point already made that this issue is not just an issue for unionized employees.

Merit Pay Communications. Within the past decade, a sizable portion of organizational communications about employee compensation and benefits issues has shifted to computerized information systems such as an HRIS or an organizational intranet.[20] For example, Cisco Systems uses a "Managers Dashboard" to facilitate managerial decision-making.[21] According to Brit Wittman, the Dashboard allows managers to "give salary increases, decide annual cash incentive payout amounts, decide on stock option share amounts, pay spot bonuses, assess employees' skills and document corrective action" (p. 49). Wittman argues that the Dashboard has led to large productivity gains and improved communication with employees. While more formal research evidence is needed, clearly this approach appears to be a promising means of increasing and improving organizational communication about compensation issues.

Outcomes of Merit Pay Plans

In our research, we have summarized the results of 34 empirical studies evaluating the outcomes associated with merit pay.[22] Perhaps not surprisingly, there is a great deal of variation in the outcomes achieved by merit pay plans. Overall, merit pay is most consistently related to positive employee attitudes. For example, Jason Shaw and colleagues found that merit increases were significantly related to pay level satisfaction as well as behavioral intentions such as intent to leave the organization.[23] To date, however, merit pay plans have not been found to be consistently related to improved subsequent employee performance. This finding is quite disappointing, given the ongoing prevalence of merit pay plans. Does this finding mean that merit pay plans are ineffective? We simply do not know the answer to that question at this stage. Too many organizations appear to be operating on blind faith that their merit pay plans are effective. When evaluation of merit pay plans are performed, they are too often just a one-shot case study in which results of a single intervention are only collected after the fact. While some valuable things can be learned from such an approach, more rigorous evaluation efforts are definitely needed. Unfortunately, the following summary remains fairly accurate with regard to the evaluation of merit pay plans:

It is an embarrassment to our profession how few well-designed empirical studies have ever been conducted to assess the impact of merit pay, given the overwhelming number of companies that use merit pay and the huge direct and indirect costs involved. At an absolute minimum, companies should routinely collect data on the attitudinal impact of merit pay. Standardized measures of employees' attitudes towards pay, with sound reliability and validity properties, are easily accessible from the research literature (R. Heneman, Eskew and Fox, 1998). Better yet, employers might assess using controlled designs to measure the impact of merit pay on performance and productivity. Unfortunately, the number of studies of this type can literally be counted on one hand (p. 458).[24]

We have seen, however, some positive outcomes from merit pay. As shown in this chapter, merit pay continues to be seen as moderately successful by employers and does improve employee attitudes toward merit pay, which can then influence a decision to remain with an employer.

Conclusions

Incentive plans such as merit pay should work, according to economic and psychological theories. There is strong evidence about the positive impact of contingent rewards on employee performance.[25] While not nearly as strong, there is also evidence that merit pay plans can and do work in practice. Of course, there are many potential problems and pitfalls in designing, implementing and evaluating merit pay plans. Not every organizational setting is conducive to incentive plans such as merit pay. Additionally, there is evidence of considerable individual differences among employees in their preferences concerning merit pay.

What seems most necessary is that merit pay be viewed in the context of total or strategic compensation.[26] It is not enough to view merit pay as a stand-alone or primary means of rewarding employees. For example, in a recent study of a large service organization, Michael Sturman found a greater impact on employee performance for one-time (lump-sum) bonuses than for merit pay increases.[27] At first glance, this may not appear to be good news for merit pay plans. However, there is nothing inherent in merit pay that requires that pay increases be linked to base pay; merit pay increases could theoretically be paid as one-time bonuses, and Sturman's case study provides a provocative argument that such a pay strategy may produce strongly positive outcomes. His arguments are consistent with recent calls for a total rewards management approach.

The call to link compensation policies with organizational or business strategy is not new. The tricky part of such a linkage is in the details. For example, what reward practices will promote a particular business strategy (or mix of strategies)? Some of the business strategies organizations use include the following:

- Reducing costs
- Improving productivity
- Improving financial capital (e.g., using models such as economic value added (EVA)
- Emphasizing the distinctive quality of one's product or service
- Emphasizing innovation and/or time to market
- Emphasizing human capital (e.g., viewing employees as a source of revenue generation, not just as a cost)[28]

The need, then, is to align compensation practices with these business strategies. The available research also suggests that merit pay is most feasible in organizational cultures that are competitive (versus egalitarian), with well-defined job characteristics and high levels of discretion in the work employees perform.[29] Overall, organizations should examine environmental and organizational issues when considering the feasibility of merit pay, and they should consider the characteristics of the supervisors and employees who are or will be involved in the merit pay process.[30] It might be the case that alternate reward strategies are preferable to merit pay in some situations.

In addition to aligning compensation plans to organizational strategy, compensation policies and practices must be aligned with other human resources practices. That is, an organization's staffing, training, appraisal, compensation and employee relations approaches should fit together in a coherent manner. This is sometimes referred to as horizontal fit, in contrast to the vertical fit of HR practices with organizational strategy.[31] It would make no sense, for example, to pursue a staffing strategy of hiring the "best and the brightest" and then pursue a compensation strategy that provides no incentives for creativity or innovation.

We think there is real promise in recent efforts to link compensation plans such as merit pay to an organization's overall performance management efforts.[32] The intent of such an approach is to link together goal setting, appraisal, training and rewards together in an integrated fashion. For example, goals set for individual employees are linked to their evaluations as well as to the training they are provided and the rewards they receive. As straightforward as this seems in the abstract, it can be exceedingly difficult to carry this out in practice.

Thus, as organizations seek strategic and systematic approaches to compensation, merit pay can serve as one such approach. Like any systems approach, it is necessary to assess the situation, design the right approach, implement it well and then evaluate the effectiveness of the intervention. It is often not the idea of merit pay that is faulty, but the manner in which it is implemented. We again stress the need for extreme care and diligence in carrying out any compensation plan, including merit pay. Employees need to understand the compensation system and view it as fair—in the procedures used and the outcomes received. For example, Michael Vest and colleagues demonstrated that the greater the trust that employees had in top management, the more they perceived that their pay was related to performance in an existing merit pay plan.[33]

A final word about the evaluation of merit pay plans: We urge organizations to do more and better evaluation, and to study multiple outcomes of their pay plans. While progress has been made in the past 15 or so years, there is still considerable room for improvement in measuring the impact of merit pay systems on important organizational variables. If we are going to live up to the title of "strategic partners" with top management, we as compensation professionals must be able to demonstrate the effectiveness of our policies and practices.[34] Doing anything less is simply no longer acceptable. Here's hoping for further progress and breakthroughs in the coming years.

Endnotes

1. Heneman, R.L., and J.M. Werner. 2005. *Merit pay: Linking pay to performance in a changing world*, 2nd ed. Greenwich, CT: Information Age Publishers.

2. Heneman, R.L., C.H. Fay, and Z. M. Wang. 2002. Compensation systems in the global context. In N. Anderson, D.S. Ones, H.K. Sinangil, and C. Viswesvaran (eds.), *Handbook of industrial, work & organizational psychology* (Vol. 2, pp. 77–92). London: Sage.

3. Eskew, D., and R.L. Heneman. 1996. A survey of merit pay plan effectiveness. *Human Resource Planning* 19(2):12–19.

4. Harris, B.R., M.A. Huselid, and B.E. Becker. 1999. Strategic human resource management at Praxair. *Human Resource Management* 38:315–320.

5. Heneman and Werner 2005, p. 3.

6. Katkowski, D.A., G.J. Medsker, and K.H. Pritchard. 2002. Literature review of "acceptable" or "just noticeably different" pay increases. Paper presented at the Society for Industrial and Organizational Psychology, Toronto.

7. Setting & Managing 2007 Compensation. 2006. New York: IOMA. Accessed on Jan. 15, 2007 at: http://www.ioma.com/issues/SPCRPT/1610259-1.html.

8. Mitra, A., N. Gupta, and G.D. Jenkins, Jr. 1997. A drop in the bucket: When is a pay raise a pay raise? *Journal of Organizational Behavior* 18:117–137.

9. Fuller, J.J., and R. Tinkham. 2002, September. Making the most of scarce reward dollars: Why differentiation makes a difference. *Employee Benefits Journal* 27(3):3–7.

10. Shaw, J.D., N. Gupta, and J.E. Delery. 2002. Pay dispersion and workforce performance: Moderating effects of incentives and interdependence. *Strategic Management Journal* 23:491–512.

11. Bates, S. 2003, January. Top pay for best performance. *HR Magazine* 48:30–38.

12. Scott, K.D., S.E. Markham, and M.J. Vest. 1996. The influence of a merit pay guide chart on employee attitudes toward pay at a transit authority. *Public Personnel Management* 25:103–117.

13. Scott, Markham, and Vest 1996, p. 114.

14. Barcellos, D. 2005. The reality and promise of market-based pay. *Employment Relations Today* 32:1–10.

15. *Market Pricing in Six Easy Steps*. WorldatWork E-Learning Program. Accessed on January 16, 2007 at: http://www.worldatwork.org/seminars/generic/html/seminars-market-pricing.html .

16. Cited in Nadler, D.A. 1998, March 15. *Ten steps to a happy merger*. New York Times, pp. 3, 14.

17. Towers Perrin. 2000. *Meeting the global rewards challenge*. Accessed on March 23, 2004, at: http://www.towersperrin.com/hrservices/webcache/towers/United_States/publications/Periodicals/worldwide_pay/2000_09/worldpay_2000_09.pdf .

18. Mulvey, P.W., P.V. LeBlanc, R.L. Heneman, and M.McInerney. 2002. *The knowledge of pay study: E-mails from the frontline*. Scottsdale, AZ: WorldatWork.

19. Segal, J.A. 2004, March. Labor pains for union-free employers. *HR Magazine* 49(3): 113–118.

20. Allard, B. 2002. Improving compensation management through technology. *Employee Benefit Plan Review* 57(2):41–42.

21. Wittman, B. 2003. Cisco Systems puts its HR programs and processes on the line and reaps big productivity gains. *Journal of Organizational Excellence* 23(1):43–54.

22. Heneman and Werner 2005, pp. 232–247.

23. Shaw, J.D., M.K. Duffy, A. Mitra, D.E. Lockhart, and M. Bowler. 2003. Reactions to merit pay increases: A longitudinal test of a signal sensitivity perspective. *Journal of Applied Psychology* 88:538–544.

24. Heneman, R.L. 2001. Merit pay. In C. Fay (ed.), *The executive handbook of compensation* (pp. 447–464). New York: Free Press.

25. Stajkovic, A.D., and F. Luthans. 2003. *Behavioral management and task performance in organizations: Conceptual background*, meta-analysis, and test of alternative models. *Personnel Psychology* 56:155–194.

26. Martocchio, J.J. 2006. *Strategic compensation: A human resource management approach*, 4th ed. Upper Saddle River, NJ: Pearson Prentice Hall.

27. Sturman, M.C. 2006. *Using your pay system to improve employees' performance: How you pay makes a difference.* Cornell University, CHR Reports, Vol. 6, No. 13, October.

28. Heneman, R.L. 2001. *Business-driven compensation policies: Integrating compensation systems with corporate strategies.* New York: AMACOM.

29. Heneman and Werner 2005, p. 80.

30. Heneman and Werner 2005, p. 59.

31. Werbel, J.D., and S.M. DeMarie. 2005. Aligning strategic human resource management and person-environment fit. *Human Resource Management Review* 15:247–262.

32. Lawler, E.E. III, and M. McDermott. 2003, Second Quarter. Current performance management practices: Examining the varying impacts. *WorldatWork Journal*, pp. 49–60; O'Neill, C., and L. Holsinger. 2003, Second Quarter. Effective performance management systems: 10 key design principles. *WorldatWork Journal*, pp. 61–67.

33. Vest, M.J., K.D. Scott, J.M. Vest, and S.E. Markham. 2000. *Factors influencing employee beliefs that pay is tied to performance.*

34. Strategic HR. Tips for expanding your corporate role (2003, September). HR Focus, 80(9), 1-15.

Chapter 3
Designing Sales Incentive Pay for Competitive Advantage

Jerome A. Colletti, Colletti-Fiss LLC
Mary S. Fiss, Colletti-Fiss LLC

As companies strive to develop and execute a sustainable advantage over competitors, one source of competitive advantage is the talent a company deploys in its sales organizations. Salespeople can and do make a difference when customers choose to buy from a company instead of from its competitors. This is especially true in highly contentious markets—markets characterized by high product parity—where all the major players offer equally high levels of product quality and customer service. In such situations, one advantage a company can leverage is the quality of the relationship between the customer and the salesperson.

Across a wide variety of industries using quite different sales models, we have observed that in this type of competitive environment companies often "shrink-wrap" the salesperson around the offering so that the company employee becomes a significant source of competitive differentiation. When this is the case, the sales compensation plan—particularly the incentive component—can play a pivotal role in attracting and retaining the sales talent required to make that type of competitive advantage a reality.

The overall objective of this chapter is to discuss how to design a sales incentive plan that contributes to a company's advantage over competitors because of its effectiveness in attracting, hiring and retaining top-notch sales talent. A fundamental premise of this chapter is that high-caliber sales talent contributes to a unique competitive advantage with customers because it outperforms peers in other companies. Thus, incorporating the concept of competitive advantage into the sales-incentive plan design process can ultimately contribute to high performance for a business.

We first look at the positive business outcomes that a sales incentive plan can contribute to when designed with competitive advantage in mind and what you must therefore understand about your company's current business strategy and goals. Next, we identify and suggest how to design the elements or features of a sales incentive plan to support a company's competitive advantage. For the purposes of this chapter, sales incentive compensation—commission, bonus or both—is defined as individual or team incentives, or a combination of both, where the measurement period is short (typically a year), the eligible positions are customer-facing and the reward currency is cash. Finally, we discuss plan practices, typically referred to as either terms and conditions or plan policies, that can sustain a competitive advantage through the plan on an ongoing basis. The benefit we hope you gain from this chapter is an understanding of the concepts, principles and best-practice techniques that you can use to help your company realize an increased competitive advantage through the sales incentive compensation plan.

Positive Business Outcomes

A sales compensation plan's principal objective is to direct a company's salespeople to effectively sell to and interact with customers. Whether a company wants increased volume, a better mix of customers or product sales, or more new accounts, the right sales compensation plan can help accomplish those objectives. A sales compensation plan—particularly the incentive component, because it frequently represents 25 percent to 50 percent of the cash compensation opportunity—can help increase business results. It does so because it is a "signaling system" that communicates to the salesforce what results are important, how to prioritize and allocate their time, and how they will be recognized and rewarded for their performance. This is one reason that top sales executives think first of the sales compensation plan when a change in a company's sales model is planned. Thus, designing and managing the sales incentive plan without considering its competitive advantage could be a significant missed opportunity.

In companies where the sales incentive compensation plan is designed with competitive advantage in mind, top management believes that the plan contributes positively to five business outcomes.

• **Growth.** Creating new markets, winning new customers, selling new products and continually improving processes to retain current customers and sell more products to them is a top priority at most companies. Research into how companies achieve their sales objectives shows that the growth strategy they most often pursue is that of winning a greater share of business with current customers. This suggests that these companies use a basic blocking and tackling approach to growth—selling more to current customers, either by new product sales to current buyers or by more sales to new buyers in the same customer account or the same demographic profile. This may explain why it is not unusual in many companies to find that 75 percent to 85 percent of sales incentive compensation dollars are earned for performance with existing customers.

- **Profits.** In good and bad economic times, top management wants salespeople to focus on profitable business. Many companies have implemented a CRM (customer relationship management) system that is used, in part, to assemble meaningful information about total customer purchases, the mix of products purchased, resources associated with servicing the customer (e.g., cost to service) and, ultimately, the profit contribution of the customer to the business. To succeed in an increasingly competitive business environment, top management must articulate a clear customer strategy—the plan for acquiring, retaining and expanding business in a profitable manner. This means that top management and the sales leaders must understand the sales job's impact on profitability and, in turn, must determine the right measures to use when evaluating and paying for salesforce performance. When those decisions have been made effectively, the measures can be related to the incentive opportunity and thus contribute to achieving the competitive advantage a company seeks when winning and retaining business with customers.

- **Customer loyalty and satisfaction.** The salesforce touches the nerve endings of a company's customers each day. Sales representatives are a company's face to its customers. They interact with buyers and buying influences at multiple levels throughout the customer organization. Frequently, how a customer feels about a supplier is largely influenced by contact with its sales representative. The sales organization is an integral player in sustaining and improving customer loyalty and satisfaction. Its success in doing so can be measured by revenue retention and incremental sales to customers. Thus, the sales incentive compensation plan must strike the right balance between motivating aggressive sales behavior and rewarding performance associated with meeting (and, ideally, exceeding) the customer's expectations of what was purchased and how the offering was sold. When it does so, the probability of increasing the share of business done with customers and, thus, the probability of outflanking competitors, materially rises.

- **Sales talent.** In most companies, top management looks to the sales compensation plan to help attract and retain the caliber of people it needs to successfully sell to and interact with customers. Attracting and retaining top-notch talent is one of the most serious human resources challenges faced by companies. This is because the labor pool for sales talent, most commonly those individuals who fall in the range of 25 to 40 years old, is actually shrinking. In many industries, this means that it has become harder to attract and retain high-caliber salespeople. Sales executives look to the compensation plan as a source of differentiation in the labor markets in which their company competes for talent to enhance its competitive advantage over others in the industry.

Sales productivity. Top management looks to the sales compensation plan to help it increase sales productivity. Increasingly, companies are faced with the challenges of price competition in global markets and shrinking profit margins, particularly for established brands—both products and services. To justify investment in sales incentive compensation in sales situations involving potentially smaller margins, one or both of two things may have to happen: (a) volume will have to be higher, usually 50 percent or more than it was in the past, and/or (b) the mix of business will have to change in what customers buy and/or in which customers are addressed. If the salesperson's average productivity was $1 million a year, it may now have to be $1.5 million with an improved product and customer mix so that a company will get the better margin with volume. The reality of the contemporary business environment is that the sales compensation plan must direct and complement top management's requirements for increased productivity. Doing so clearly contributes to helping a company realize a differential financial advantage over its competitors.

Understanding Business Strategy and Goals

Understanding a company's business strategy is essential to determining how the sales incentive plan should be designed to reflect the competitive advantage desired by a company. Typically, a company's business strategy includes a description of the markets served, products offered and sales model used to interact with customers. Each year, new requirements are placed on a business as it strives to achieve its growth and profit objectives. That means the combinations of these three variables—market, products and sales model—are likely to impact the sales incentive compensation plan. Changes to any one or all three of the variables could impact the plan's effectiveness in an upcoming fiscal year.

Most companies have a formal business plan that describes the strategy and financial goals for a fiscal year. That document often does not provide a narrative description of what is changing and why. The most effective way to quickly gain an understanding of a company's business strategy—what it is, how it is changing—is to talk with the top executives who are responsible for formulating and executing it. The following are members of the top management team in most businesses: CEO/general manager, top marketing officer, top sales officer, CFO/top financial officer for the business and top human resources executives.

To confirm the business strategy for a particular company or operating division, the following questions should be discussed with the top management team relative to the company's next fiscal year:

- What is the business growth objective and how was it determined?
- Where will the growth come from—which markets, products or both are expected to grow—and do growth rates across them vary? What assumptions have been made about the economic climate and the expected growth rate of the market? What assumptions have been made about availability of products to sell, particularly if a significant percentage of the sales are expected to be achieved through new product sales?
- How is the sales organization expected to change to help the company achieve its business strategy in the coming year? Will the sales model remain the same, or are there changes planned for sales channels, direct sales resources or both?

The answers to these questions provide useful and relevant information about how the sales organization must operate in the coming year and the behavior and performance that the sales incentive compensation plan must therefore reinforce. This information essentially provides a foundation for understanding the competitive advantage that a company seeks in doing business with customers.

In recent years, shifts in business strategy to address "slow" or "no growth" economic environments, particularly in the North American marketplace, have motivated top management to change how its companies interact with customers. For example, four relatively common changes in sales coverage have been to do the following:

- Recharter business-to-consumer sales jobs (retail, counter, services) with a focus on customer satisfaction/ease of purchase in order to facilitate additional purchases by the same or new customers.
- Introduce telesales coverage in both business-to-consumer and business-to-business environments in order to focus on customer retention and customer reorder purchases.
- Reduce the number of business-to-business sales generalists (e.g., territory sales representatives) and add sales specialists (e.g., product or solution sales specialists).
- Expand the role of customer service representatives in order to identify

opportunities for "upsell" or "cross-sell" that can be followed up by either field or telesales reps.

One or more of these changes, motivated by altering business strategy, will likely affect sales jobs' duties and responsibilities and thus create the opportunity to rethink how the incentive compensation plan must be altered to support the competitive advantage a company seeks. A clear understanding of business strategy and how it will affect the salesforce's tactics means that changes to a sales compensation plan are given proper consideration rather than changed through trial and error, which is likely to occur without that knowledge.

Sales compensation is the caboose, not the engine. It cannot create a successful business strategy. Before top management can determine how to use compensation to direct, motivate and reward its salesforce in order for the company to realize a competitive advantage, it must be clear about what it is trying to accomplish with the business. Thus, a company's strategy describes how management expects to compete for and win business with customers, and what its expectations will be of the salesforce. When interpreting business strategy and how a company intends to realize a competitive advantage in the marketplace with the help of the sales compensation plan, the following three broad sales-effectiveness objectives should be considered, because they are the most likely ones to impact the types of performance measures used in the plan:

- **Improve sales productivity.** The principal way companies seek to improve their sales productivity is by realizing more volume and profit from their current investment in sales resources. The alternative—reducing sales expenses, principally head count—is a short-term solution; it ultimately penalizes a company through lost market share and growth that is slower than that of competitors. If a company's business strategy includes improvement in sales productivity, one or more of the following measures should be included in sales-incentive compensation plan design in addition to "growth" or undifferentiated volume:
  - New-customer sales volume
  - New-product sales volume
  - Balanced product-line sales
  - Reduced "churn" among current customers.
- **Improve sales coverage of current customers.** Regardless of the industry, customers want flexibility, customization, faster response and personalized service. To meet these requirements, market-leading companies continually improve the coverage of their current customers. This often means invest-

ments in new ways to interact with customers. New sales jobs are implemented to replace or complement traditional jobs in order to improve sales coverage of current customers. When this is the case, the measures used in a sales incentive compensation plan that is aligned with competitive advantage goals include the following:

- Overall account volume
- Greater share of the account's business
- Achievement of customer objectives
- More lines of business sold
- Account profitability.

- **Grow sales overall.** Because the first and, generally, the most important measure of business success is sales, business strategy typically emphasizes achieving top-line growth. When this is the case, it is important to track the percent of sales realized from the following:

- New direct customers
- New distribution channels
- New products.

To ensure direct alignment with the company's strategy for the next plan year, it is critical to understand the tactical requirements of that strategy, including a clear definition of the sales model, job charters and performance expectations of the customer-coverage resources. The process for gaining and using that information should be completed prior to plan design so that decisions can be accurately reflected in the new plans and related systems and documentation can be developed.

Designing a Plan for Competitive Advantage

There are five elements of the sales incentive compensation plan that can be designed to help a company create and sustain its competitive advantage. Those five elements or plan components are as follows:

- Competitiveness of the incentive opportunity
- Leverage associated with the incentive opportunity
- Plan type
- Performance range
- Terms and conditions.

1. Competitiveness of the Incentive Opportunity

A clear definition of the duties and responsibilities of a sales job is the starting point for determining an appropriate incentive opportunity to pay for business results. Typically, reputable compensation surveys are a useful source of data for assessing the total cash compensation level and incentive opportunity offered to comparable jobs. However, determining if the incentive opportunity should be designed as a source of competitive advantage—that is, if it will be materially more attractive than the opportunity provided by other companies—requires going beyond this basic step. The following three factors should be considered in making such a determination:

- Competitive pay position in the labor market
- Role of the sales job in the sales process
- Performance expectations.

Careful consideration should be given to a company's competitive pay position in the labor market in which it competes for talent. We often find that companies have a default competitive position, which is to price its sales jobs at the same market level (e.g., 50th percentile) as all other exempt jobs are priced. In many cases, this is appropriate because the salesforce represents a talent pool from which other functions—marketing, store or branch management, product management and customer service—may select employees for promotion, rotational assignments or both. Thus, a common labor-market positioning for job pricing makes it less challenging to move employees out of the salesforce to other assignments within the company.

While maintaining that positioning for base pay may be the most practical solution in companies that offer that type of developmental movement, the default competitive position could create a competitive disadvantage if applied to either total cash compensation (TCC) or the available incentive opportunity. This is because in many industries companies have concluded that they can compete more effectively with fewer, but more highly paid, salespeople. These salespeople are deployed in jobs that focus on doing business with a company's top-tier customers. Those jobs—global account manager or strategic account manager, to name a few—often must be priced in the labor market at a higher level than median or 50th percentile because people with the necessary talent and skills are in short supply. Particularly for these kinds of jobs, more aggressive pricing will determine the appropriate TCC and the "mix" (proportion of TCC related to base and to incentives) to be applied to each job to establish the incentive opportunity.

Knowing the recruiting and hiring practices of direct business competitors and the talent pool available in the relevant labor markets from which to choose qualified salespeople helps a company determine the extent to which its labor market pay position should be customized to the requirements of the sales organization.

In situations where a company does decide to selectively position above the 50th percentile in labor-market pay, care must be taken to determine the sales jobs that qualify for the incentive opportunity set at that level, since there is a cost/productivity implication to doing so. All sales jobs may not have the opportunity to impact results at a level that justifies higher than median or 50th percentile market pay, as discussed later.

The role of a particular sales job in the sales process is the second consideration when determining if the incentive opportunity should be designed as a source of competitive advantage. It is not unusual today for customers to look to their suppliers to provide expertise that they once had on their internal staff. When companies look to their suppliers to provide a total solution, the sales job is both more complex and professionally demanding. This is because the salesperson often takes on the critical role of bringing together multiple resources—from internal functions and with external partners—to create solutions that provide significant value to customers. In such solution selling processes, the size of the incentive opportunity should recognize not only the importance of the sales role that the salesperson plays but also the profit margins that are likely to be realized through the effective sales efforts of these individuals.

A third consideration when determining if the incentive opportunity should be a source of competitive advantage is the performance expectations that employees in the sales job must meet. Two factors shape performance expectations—the number of measures used and the size of the performance goals (e.g., quotas). Generally speaking, the incentive opportunity varies based on the type of measures selected—for example, total sales volume, segmented volume by customer or product groups, profit margin—and the relative amount of "stretch" in the assigned performance quotes. Incumbents in sales positions that have significant "stretch" objectives annually would expect to be offered a significantly larger incentive opportunity—perhaps as much as 30 percent to 50 percent more than the median opportunity—to reflect the degree of difficulty in meeting aggressive performance expectations. In this context, aggressive performance expectations mean goals that could be 25 percent to 100 percent greater than assessed market opportunity. For example, if a market is growing at 6 percent and a company's goal is to take share from competitors, its performance expectation may be set at 9 percent (or, 50 percent greater than market). Thus, companies are willing to consider premium levels of incentive opportunity because the achievement of a "stretch" performance expectation contributes significantly to financial results and, in turn, to shareholder value.

2) Leverage associated with the incentive opportunity

The leverage associated with a sales incentive opportunity is the amount of "upside" pay earned at some defined level of performance above 100 percent. The objective of the upside pay opportunity is to motivate and reward salespeople for outstanding performance—that is, achieving results substantially above assigned goals or quotas. While the upside opportunity is available to all salespeople who overachieve target performance expectations, the upside/leverage pay is typically earned by the top 5 percent to 10 percent of the salesforce on a job-by-job basis. Thus, setting the upside or leverage pay opportunity can help a company realize its competitive business advantage because it provides a powerful incentive for salespeople to overachieve. When structured correctly, overachievement pay is a cost-effective approach to profitable growth because it is less expensive in the short term than adding sales staff.

The most common way to express leverage is as a ratio of the upside opportunity to the target incentive opportunity. For example, if the ratio is 3:1 for a particular sales job, and its target incentive opportunity is $10,000, the upside opportunity is $30,000 at some defined performance point above quota or goal. Typically, in business-to-business marketing environments, the leverage ratio for sales jobs falls in the range of 2:1 to 3:1. In business-to-consumer environments, the leverage ratio for sales jobs is based on the role of the job and may be as low as 1.5:1 for customer service-focused jobs to 5:1 for more complex roles in service industries.

Generally speaking, companies that successfully use the leverage ratio to create competitive advantage through the incentive plan set it at or greater than market levels as reported by industry surveys. This means that salespeople who overachieve earn more incentive compensation for their performance than salespeople in either direct competitors' or comparable sales jobs. To be in a position to offer overachievement incentive compensation at rates greater than the market, a company must be able to make a business case for doing so. Answers to the following questions are helpful in building that business case:

- From a profit perspective, can the cost structure of our business accommodate high incentive payments for high performance? If so, how much of the overachievement profit (e.g., over business-plan performance) is the company willing to share with salespeople who create that profit?
- At what ratio or level do our direct-product/service competitors and other competitors for salespeople set the leverage in their pay plan?
- How much personal impact do our salespeople have on customer decisions to buy our products or service over those of the competitors?

3) Plan type

There are two primary types of incentive plans used to motivate and reward the salesforce: commission plans and bonus plans. Either may be used in conjunction with base salary, or both may be used. A commission plan provides a percent share or dollar amount tied to sales dollars, product-unit sales or gross-profit dollars. While a goal or quota may be used in conjunction with a commission formula, commission programs support absolute measurement systems—the more of a product or service sold, the greater the incentive paid. Payment under a commission plan may be capped or uncapped. Bonuses are a percent of base pay, or a fixed dollar amount, for accomplishing objectives. These programs support relative measurement systems and always include a quota or goal—payout depends on performance against individual goals. Also, a salary-plus-bonus manages the amount of incentive payout to a preferred market rate while accommodating goal-based measurement. Like commission plans, payment under a bonus plan may be capped or uncapped.

Knowing when to use a commission plan or a bonus plan can be a source of competitive advantage for a company and its salesforce. This is because each plan type addresses different business objectives and drives different types of sales behavior. Commission plans reward individual effort and results tied directly to sales transactions. Payout based solely on a "deal" or a transaction is a common practice. Thus, commissions are used in some industries to promote new products and gain market share by winning new customers. On the other hand, bonuses are used in more complex sales environments where the goal is financial (volume, profitability, productivity) or nonfinancial (customer satisfaction). Payout is based on results relative to those goals.

While the amount of pay at risk is generally the primary determinant of behavioral impact, many factors influence the decision of which plan type to use in the sales compensation plan and whether the use of just one or both of them is appropriate. Commissions are more frequently used in transaction-oriented sales environments, or in environments focused on new business with a single market or product. In such a circumstance, there is relatively equal sales potential, and the results are driven by the seller. Bonuses, however, are generally used in an environment of slower or moderate growth (e.g., maturing industries with a focus on retention). In such a circumstance, the portfolio is typically complex, and territories do not have equal sales potential. Additionally, the ability to set reliable quotas has been verified, and the systems are in place to ensure that such quotas can be established.

4) Performance range

The performance range defines the parameters of the results for which incentive compensation is paid. The performance range confirms expected performance and establishes two other reference points: one below expected performance and one significantly above expected performance. It is common practice to define these three performance levels as follows:

- Threshold—The minimum level of performance that must be achieved before an incentive can be paid.
- Target—The expected level of performance (at which the target incentive opportunity is earned).
- Excellence—A level of outstanding performance, typically measured at the 90th percentile of all performance achieved by a salesforce. This is the point at which the defined leverage ratio, or upside incentive opportunity, is earned.

A company's approach to setting the performance range offers another opportunity to use the sales incentive plan as a source of competitive advantage. To do so, however, requires management to address and answer two of the toughest design decisions:

1) How much can the company afford to pay sales employees for below-plan performance?
2) How much is the company willing to pay sales employees for above-plan performance?

These performance points are used to establish a payout line or curve. While "threshold" and "target" have a clear impact on the payout, this is not necessarily true of "excellence." Payout may accelerate, decelerate or cease at this point—and that decision is one more facet that will impact the degree to which the plan acts as a competitive tool in the marketplace.

5) Terms and Conditions (Ts&Cs)

Underlying all sales incentive compensation plans are the critical rules that describe how the program will operate in a company. These are typically referred to as terms and conditions (Ts&Cs) or plan policies. The Ts&Cs document provides definitive answers to questions that arise about how the plan applies to eligible participants. The overall intent of the Ts&Cs document is thus to protect the company and the sales employees who participate in the sales incentive plan.

There are two major Ts&Cs categories:

- Definition and provisions that qualify a salesperson for participation in the sales incentive plan

- Definition and provisions of rules that determine how and when the results of a transaction are eligible for use in determining incentive payout, and that guide the allocation of sales results among resources who have participated in the selling process.

Because of the complexities inherent in these two areas, human resources and compensation must work with sales, finance and legal to ensure accuracy and adherence to all relevant rules, regulations and policies.

There are three specific areas of Ts&Cs that offer a significant opportunity to enhance the competitive advantage through the sales incentive compensation plan:

- **Definitions.** Care should be taken to avoid "jargon" in the document, but terminology associated with plan mechanics, plan elements and types of sales transactions or results should be clearly defined.
- **Employment Policies.** Because employment status impacts both eligibility and payout, there are several polices that should be clearly outlined in the document. These include the impact of employment changes (time off, new hires, terminations, promotions, transfers), the effect of ethics violations, how expenses are reimbursed, the salary adjustment program (if applicable) and eligibility for other programs (if any).
- **Sales Crediting and Performance Measurement.** The rules associated with how each performance measure is defined, tracked and reported, and the timing of crediting (including debookings or write-downs), are an essential element of the document. In this area, care must be taken to ensure that such rules are realistic and are not perceived as unnecessarily punitive.

The terms and conditions associated with the plan are frequently the deciding factor when a salesperson determines if the plan is "attractive and fair." Care should thus be taken to ensure that the Ts&Cs are relevant, clear and reasonable. Doing so supports the company's ability to use the sales compensation plan as a competitive lever.

Summary

Companies and their leaders—both sales and HR executives—should focus on creating and sustaining a competitive advantage through the sales compensation plan. Doing so increases the likelihood that business strategy and goals will be aligned with salesforce behavior, performance and rewards. However, in many companies the opportunity to create that alignment is missed because of the tendency to hastily "tweak" plans at the end of a current year for the next year. We identified five business benefits that companies realize when they not do take "shortcuts" and instead design their sales incentive compensation plans with competitive advantage in mind. We also explained the importance of understanding a company's business strategy and goals as they pertain to its competitive advantage. Finally, we identified and discussed the five elements of the sales incentive compensation plan that require design attention if a plan is intended to support a company's competitive advantage. Our goal has been to encourage plan designers—particularly HR/compensation professionals who participate in that design process—to take the initiative in helping their companies use the sales incentive compensation plan to create and support their competitive advantage.

Chapter 4
When Are Piece Rates Effective?
What Recent Studies Reveal
Robert L. Moore, Ph.D., Occidental College

Should workers be paid a fixed wage or be paid based on their output? Although piece rates may appear to be a "dinosaur" in U.S. business, recent studies have shown them to be quite effective in certain firms and industries (Lazear 2000; Paasche and Shearer 1999). Furthermore, they remain widely used in some occupations, such as sales, machinists and auto repair mechanics (MacLeod and Parent 1999, 187).

As early as Adam Smith, economists have considered piece-rate incentive plans as a classic example of so-called variable pay plans, in which compensation is based on some measure of the output workers produce. In addition to deriving the "optimal" structure of piece-rate plans, economists have analyzed their key advantages and disadvantages. They have also identified the conditions under which such plans are likely to be more profitable than hourly pay and offered suggestions for dealing with potential drawbacks.[1]

Nevertheless, it is only in the last 10 years that this economic analysis has been subjected to rigorous empirical tests. For example, the manufacturing firm Lincoln Electric Co. (HBS Case Study 1983) has perhaps the most notable success associated with piece rates. However, recent empirical work goes well beyond such case studies. Economists have applied sophisticated statistical techniques to new personnel data available from individual firms where piece rates, often as well as hourly wages, have been used. For reasons explained in this chapter, workers at such firms all perform fairly straightforward tasks that can be easily measured, such as installing auto windshields, manufacturing shoes, planting trees in British Columbia and "strip cutting" in the Midwest logging industry (Lazear 2000; Freeman and Kleiner 2005; Paarsch and Shearer 2000, 1999; Haley 2003). This relatively new empirical work sheds considerable light on the validity of the predictions of this economic analysis and the worker's sensitivity to the changes in incentive pay programs. Perhaps more importantly, such work also illustrates— using these real-world examples—what human resources practitioners might want to consider when deciding whether or not to adopt a piece-rate incentive plan to improve their company's profits.

This chapter's goal is to provide information about piece-rate incentive plans— with economists' analysis and empirical examples—to HR practitioners. The author hopes to provide a practical guide. Section I compares key advantages and disadvantages of piece-rate incentive plans to those of wage/salary plans, which is a discussion that is generally applicable to most incentive pay plans, and it also provides practical guidance about how to best deal with some of the key disadvantages. Section II outlines conditions under which piece-rate plans are most likely to be successful. Section III turns to the recent empirical evidence about how workers have responded to switching from wage-per-hour plans to piece-rate plans, and vice versa, in the real-world examples previously noted. Section IV summarizes the key implications of this work for practitioners.

Taken together, economists' recent empirical work clearly confirms their key predictions about how workers will respond to piece rates versus hourly (or salary) pay. Such evidence clearly refutes the claims of some sociologists and others who have argued that if incentives are "monetized," as in piece-rate plans, workers may actually reduce their output.[2] This evidence also provides quantitative estimates of the responsiveness of workers to changes in the incentives provided via piece-rate plans.

It is important to emphasize that the economic analysis and the empirical work lead to the conclusion that in general, piece-rate incentive plans are neither better nor worse than wage/salary plans. While the use of piece-rate incentive plans has, as predicted, increased worker productivity in the empirical work previously noted, an increase in productivity per se is not the same as an increase in profits. The various empirical studies, again taken together, illustrate this key point—profits (most likely) increased both with the switch to a piece-rate plan from a wage-per-hour plan in a major U.S. auto windshield installation firm in the 1990s, and with the switch from a piece-rate plan to a wage-per-hour plan by one of the last American shoe manufacturers, again in the 1990s. Thus, the key for practitioners is to try to understand under what specific conditions one plan will produce stronger profits than the other.

Key Advantages/Disadvantages of Piece-Rate Incentive Plans

Piece-rate incentive plans pay workers based on output, not on a measure of time or individual effort. For example, a manufacturing worker might be paid a set amount per item produced, or an agriculture worker hired to pick fruit might be paid a certain amount for each basket produced. Even the salesperson paid on a straight commission relying on the amount of product sold is being paid a piece rate (Lazear 1998, 99).[3]

There are two key advantages of paying on the basis of output produced. The first is sometimes referred to as the "incentive effect" in that it provides direct incentives to produce more, as opposed to simply showing up for work (Lazear 2000, 1347). As will be discussed in the next section, the incentive effect was the top executives' primary motivation for the Safelite Glass Corp., a large auto glass company, to switch the compensation plan for its windshield installers from an hourly wage to a piece-rate-plan.[4] The second advantage is piece-rate pay also provides a "sorting effect." It "encourages the good workers to stay and the bad workers to leave the firm." (Lazear 1998, 100). In some of the empirical work summarized in Section IIII, researchers have been able to carefully separate the changes in productivity that stem from these key advantages of piece-rate incentive plans.

While piece-rate incentive plans have other advantages, they also have some important disadvantages. Perhaps the major disadvantage in introducing almost any piece-rate plan is the increased risk to workers due to variations in output that are beyond the workers' control (Lazear 1998, 119). For example, due to a weather change, an auto windshield installer may find there are not as many windshields to install in a given month. Installers paid hourly will not suffer any change in earnings, but those paid solely on piecework will suffer a decline through no fault of their own. A similar situation could occur for a salesperson working on straight commission when there is a change in consumer tastes or an economywide recession that reduces the demand for the product the worker is trying to sell. Workers, especially those who are lower paid, will have more difficulty dealing with such variations in their incomes, given that expenses for such basics as food and housing are largely fixed.

Recognizing that its employees cannot tolerate variations in pay, especially when pay falls below a certain level, management can attempt to mitigate this increased risk to workers. For example, when Safelite switched from hourly wages to piece rates, it guaranteed workers their former hourly rate (HBS Case Study, "Performance Pay at Safelite Auto Glass" (A) 2001, 6). At the Lincoln Electric Co., full-time workers who had been with the firm for two years or more were guaranteed employment for at least 75 percent of the standard 40-hour week (HBS Case Study, "The Lincoln Electric Company" 1983, 7). As Edward Lazear notes (1998, 363), guaranteeing work is preferred to guaranteeing wages because it provides better incentives than simply showing up for work. Guaranteeing a basic hourly wage can also result in serious shirking (e.g., avoiding work), as was the case in the machine shop observed by Donald Roy (Roy 1952, 429).

A second potential disadvantage of piece rates is that they may give workers an incentive to skimp on quality. Piece rates may provide the wrong incentives when it comes to striking the appropriate balance between quantity and quality because it is often easier to measure quantity than quality (Lazear 1998, 116). There are ways to deal with this potential difficulty as well. For example, when Safelite experienced quality problems, it required workers to reinstall, without pay, defectively installed windshields and to pay for the replacement glass before other jobs were assigned to them (Lazear 2000, 1358). Lincoln Electric Co. also based workers' yearly bonuses partly on the "quality" of their work, as judged by their supervisor.

A third disadvantage is the significant cost that may be associated with measuring output. In addition, the firm also must determine the actual piece rate to use. The general principle derived by economists for how to set the optimal piece-rate structure may prove difficult to apply in some work situations (Roy 1952; Freeman and Kleiner 2005).[5] Similarly, when technology or product lines are changing frequently, firms that do not adjust their piece rates in response may face further difficulties. According to Freeman and Kleiner, executives may find there is a wide variety in workers' ability in differing jobs to earn, via piece rates, what they could earn at other firms (Freeman and Kleiner 2005, 309). Such a situation can lead to severe morale problems, as occurred in the machine plant described Roy (Roy 1952). In contrast, firms that pay hourly can usually adjust the production process without altering pay, even though they may still need to monitor effort or apply methods of production where the worker has no say in how much effort to put forth (Freeman and Kleiner, 310).

Conditions Where Piece Rates Are More Likely to Be Successful[6]

Economists have recently tried to delineate the specific conditions under which piece rates are more likely to be effective. First, as previously explained, piece rates are more likely to be effective when the costs of measuring output are low. The costs of measurement are lower when technology and product lines are not changing frequently; if they do change often, management has to spend resources ensuring the piece rate is adjusted appropriately. Second, piece rates are more likely to be effective when it is easy to determine the "quality" of the product, because the firm is more likely to set up the right incentives to balance quantity versus quality. Workers may let quality suffer when particular defects do not show up for several years. Third, because piece rates will attract the most productive workers and cause the least productive workers to leave, they are more likely to be effective among workers who have widely varying abilities rather than among those with very similar abilities. In addition, if hourly wages are used when workers' abilities vary widely, the poor workers will drag down the average wage for all, making it difficult to attract quality employees. Fourth, piece rates are more likely to be effective when workers' effort or performance is very responsive to increased pay. If increased pay does not result in increased effort, the incentive effect is obviously muted, and thus piece rates may not be justifiable. Fifth, when workers are more willing to accept the increased risk associated with variations in their pay that result from factors over which they have no control, piece rates are more likely to be effective. Sixth, piece rates are more likely to be effective when workers perform simple tasks. When tasks are complex, workers will tend to focus more on those that are directly measured and compensated, ignoring the others. Seventh, piece rates are more likely to be effective when workers are not highly dependent on others to produce the output; such dependence subjects workers to another source of variation in output over which they may have little control.

Results of Recent Empirical Work on Piece Rates

As noted in the introduction, it is only recently that workers' responses to piece rates versus hourly wages or salaries have been rigorously tested with new firm-level data. Perhaps the cleanest test comes from Lazear (2000), who was able to obtain personnel data in the 1990s from Safelite. Until 1994, workers who installed glass windshields were paid a straight hourly wage. During 1994 and 1995, Safelite's chief executive officer and president began to phase in a new compensation program based on the number of glass units the worker installed (a piece rate). It is important to note that Safelite had already implemented a sophisticated computerized system that automatically sent the customers' bills to their auto insurance carrier. Since it already measured the number and kind of units each employee installed, the costs of measuring worker output were not increased with the shift to the piece-rate pay program. Because workers complained that this program was an elaborate way of reducing their pay, Safelite guaranteed their previous hourly wage. The researcher also had a measure of a given worker's output under each pay program because the switch to the piece-rate program was introduced over time.

The switch to piece rates at Safelite had quite dramatic results. Productivity increased by 44 percent. Further, Lazear (2000) was able to statistically distinguish the pure "incentive" effect[7] (the increased productivity of existing workers) from the "sorting effect" (the increased productivity from attracting the more productive workers and the exiting of the least productive workers). Surprisingly, only about half of this 44 percent was the result of the incentive effect, with the remainder attributable to the sorting effect. In addition, the theoretical prediction that both the mean and variance of output should rise with the switch to piece rates was also confirmed. As already noted in the previous section, there was some evidence that the quality of the installed windshields had fallen (Lazear 2000, 1357).

Did profits increase as a result of this switch to piece rates at Safelite? Because compensation (and other costs) often increases, with the switch to piece rates, increasing productivity is not sufficient to conclude that profits must also increase. According to Lazear, it is likely that profits did increase for Safelite, because compensation increased about 7 percent, while productivity increased about 44 percent (Lazear 2000, 1357).

Two other recent studies used personnel data to focus more directly on how responsive worker effort was to differing piece rates. One study relied upon performance data from tree planters in British Columbia in 1994 (Paasche and Shearer 1999), and the other, modeled after the first, focused on loggers in a medium-sized firm in the Midwest United States from 1997 to 1998 (Haley 2003). Tree planters were paid exclusively by piece rate and received no guaranteed base wage. The firm paid more per seedling planted when the planting conditions were more difficult in order to induce the workers to accept the contract.[8] It is important to note that the output of the individual workers (the number of seedlings planted) was easily observable on a daily basis. The researchers found that "an increase in the piece rate of 1 cent (from a sample mean of 25 cents), would increase average daily output by 67 trees, holding planting conditions constant" (Paasche and Shearer 1999, 646). Stated in percentage terms, raising the piece rate by 4 percent increased productivity by about 8.5 percent.

The related study about loggers faced issues quite similar to those in the tree-planting industry. Like the tree planter, the strip cutter "performs simple yet physically demanding tasks: he fells, limbs, tops, measures, crosscuts, stacks and counts."[9] The output of cutters is easily measured, and cutters work independently. Further, logging in undergrowth or in timber with high limb retention requires more effort per log. To get loggers to accept contracts under such conditions, the piece rate must be increased, as was the case when the planting conditions were more difficult for the tree planters. The results indicated that a 1-percent increase in the piece rate (above its mean) results in about a 1.5-percent increase in productivity. In terms of logs cut, the results imply that raising the piece rate 1 cent above its 28-cent mean results in 36 more logs. These estimates are a bit lower than with tree planters, but qualitatively they are still quite similar, confirming that increases in piece-rate rewards result in higher productivity.

Another recent study (Paasche and Shearer 2000) focused on a different tree-planting firm in British Columbia, one that paid planters piece rates and fixed wages. It focused on the trade-off between quantity and quality. Because firms were fined by the government when trees were planted poorly, they were more likely to use fixed wages when working conditions rendered planting more difficult. Based on the workers who were paid under both pay plans, the authors estimated the incentive effect of piece rates and found that productivity increased about 22.6 percent. However, as predicted, quality suffered under the piece-rate plan, and the increase in well-planted trees was only about 14.3 percent (Paasche and Shearer 2000, 86).[10] The results confirmed that while workers are more productive under piece rates, quality falls (Paasche and Shearer 2000, 86).

Finally, the most recent empirical work on piece rates (Freeman and Kleiner 2005) examined the economic effects of a switch *from* piece rates *to* wages in one of the remaining U.S. firms in the shoe industry. Freeman and Kleiner found that this switch away from piece rates resulted in lower productivity of about 6 percent (Freeman and Kleiner 2005, 320). However, the *lower* worker productivity was accompanied by an *increase* in profits. Different human resources policies were introduced simultaneously with elimination of piece rates (and the introduction of hourly wages), including a "continuous-flow manufacturing system," work teams and a new safety program to reduce accidents and injuries (Freeman and Kleiner, 315-16).

Following the transition to wages per hour (time rates), pay and productivity fell, as did the number of grievances and worker compensation costs. The firm also more than doubled the number of styles introduced per year. On net, the relatively small loss in productivity was smaller than the cost savings associated with this substitution, so profits increased (Freeman and Kleiner, 323).

Conclusion

A review of the theoretical analysis of piece rates as well as recent empirical research suggests a number of key implications for HR and compensation professionals. First, recent empirical work clearly shows that incentives matter, and workers respond to them just as economists predicted. Further, the sorting effect of piece-rate incentive plans can be just as important as the incentive effect in improving productivity. Second, while relatively straightforward piece-rate incentive plans provide stronger incentives and result in higher worker productivity than wage and salary plans, there are definitely disadvantages to such plans. Those disadvantages include workers' increased financial risk, the increased costs associated with measuring worker output and the possibility of lower product quality. Such disadvantages may help explain why piece-rate incentive plans are not widely used in U.S. manufacturing. Third, the empirical results reviewed here demonstrate that profits can increase in some cases with the switch *to* piece rates (e.g., Safelite), but they can also increase with the switch *away from* piece rates (e.g., the last major U.S. shoe manufacturer). Fourth, and finally, to determine whether or not the switch to a piece-rate plan might improve their specific firm's profits, HR and compensation professionals will need to compare the conditions in their firms to the general conditions favorable to piece rates that this article outlined. They can also use the results of the empirical work described to estimate how their workers will most likely respond. If they conclude that such a switch is potentially profitable, they will need to consider the other policies outlined that can mitigate the disadvantages that inevitably accompany such a switch.

Footnotes

1. The economic analysis of variable pay versus fixed salary plans is only a small part of what has been referred to as "Personnel Economics," developed by economists during the last 25 years. It applies economists' analytical and empirical tools to the practical issues of how best to manage human resources inside the firm, including how to best structure promotions, as well as the incentive effects of pensions and hiring/firing decisions, among many others. It supplements the more general work of social scientists in the area. See Lazear, 1999, for more details.

2. See Lazear, 2000, 1347, who cites the claims of sociologists E.L. Deci and Mark R. Lepper in this regard. Prendergast (1999, 18) also refers to the non-economic literature, which argues that pay-for-performance can harm incentives and reduce productivity. Roy, 1952, 430, cites other sociologists to this same effect.

3. While economists consider sales commissions as a fairly straightforward form of a piece-rate plan, this chapter does not formally consider sales and how to set appropriate sales commissions, because this topic is addressed elsewhere in this book.

4. As John Barlow, Safelite CEO, responded to questions about productivity at Safelite: "Do the math. It takes an hour to put in a windshield, not including

travel time. If installers were on the clock for eight hours, but only putting in windshields for two and a half, what the hell were they doing the rest of the time?" (Harvard Business School Case Study, "Performance Pay at Safelite Auto Glass" (A) 2001.)

5. As outlined in Roy, 1952, as well as Freeman and Kleiner, 2005, when piece rates were set inappropriately, on some jobs— the so-called "gravy" jobs—it became easy for workers to meet the standard that would produce earnings comparable to other firms in the area, while on others—the so-called "stinker" jobs— it was almost impossible. Workers responded appropriately. On gravy jobs they "held back effort"—referred to as quota restriction by Roy, out of fear that the piece rate would be cut back if they produced, and earned, too much. On the so-called stinker jobs, workers also held back effort and were content to earn the guaranteed basic wage, just putting forth the minimum effort to avoid getting fired.

6. See Lazear, 1986, for a more complete and formal treatment of these considerations.

7. This measures the pure incentive effect, rather than the sorting effect, because it measures the increase in productivity for the same worker who was there prior to and then after the switch to piece rates. When it is averaged across all workers who stayed with the firm, the researcher obtained the increase in productivity due to the incentive effect in the aggregate. The remaining portion of the overall increase in productivity is then attributable to the sorting effect.

8. Planting conditions were more difficult when, for example, the soil was particularly hard, the terrain was not flat or where there was a lot of ground cover. See Paasche and Shearer, 1999, 654.

9. "'Felling' refers to cutting the tree down, and 'limbing' is the process of severing the limbs flush with the trunk. When the logger has limbed to where the tree is approximately 3.5 inches thick, the unmarketable crown is cut off, or ... 'topped.' Next the logger measures the limbless trunk into 100-inch lengths and crosscuts at the corresponding points. Finally, the logger stacks the logs into small piles. The only tools needed to successfully complete these tasks are a chain saw, a crude measuring device ... and physical effort." (Haley 2003, 882)

10. In addition, the authors calculate upper- and lower-bound estimates of this incentive effect of piece rates on productivity. The lower-bound estimate is of the order of an 8.8-percent increase in productivity, while the upper-bound estimate was calculated at a 60.4-percent increase in productivity. These results are less precise than in Lazear (2000) because the data are not as extensive.

References

Freeman, Richard B., and Morris M. Kleiner. 2005. The last American shoe manufacturers: Decreasing productivity and increasing profits in the shift from piece rates to continuous flow production. *Industrial Relations* 44(2):307 – 350.

Haley, M. Ryan. 2003. The response of worker effort to piece rates – Evidence from the Midwest logging industry. *Journal of Human Resources* 38 (4):881–890.

Harvard Case Study, 1983. The Lincoln Electric Co., 376–028, Boston, MA. *Harvard Business School*.

Harvard Case Study, 2001. Performance Pay at Safelite Auto Glass (A), Boston, MA. *Harvard Business School*.

Lazear, Edward P. 1986. Salaries and piece rates. *Journal of Business* 59 (3):405–31.

___, 1998. *Personnel Economics for Managers*, John Wiley & Sons Inc.

___, 1999. Personnel economics: Past lessons and future directions. *Journal of Labor Economics* 17(2):199–236.

___, 2000. Performance pay and productivity. *American Economic Review* 90:1346–61.

MacLeod, W. Bentley, and Daniel Parent. 1999. Job characteristics and the form of compensation. *Research in Labor Economics* 18:177–242.

Paarsch, Harry, and Bruce Shearer. 1999. The response of worker effort to piece rates: evidence from the British Columbia tree-planting industry. *Journal of Human Resources* 35(1):1–25.

___, 2000. Piece rates, fixed wages and incentive effects: Statistical evidence from payroll records, *International Economic Review* 41:59–92.

Pendercast, Canice. 1999. The provision of incentives in firms. *Journal of Economic Literature* March, 37:7–63.

Roy, Donald. 1952. Quota restriction and goldbricking in a machine shop. *American Journal of Sociology* 4:27–42.

Seiler, Eric. 1984. Piece rate vs. time rate: The effect of incentives on earnings. *The Review of Economics and Statistics* 66:363–76.

Chapter 5
Recognition Programs That Work

G. Michael Barton, SPHR, Trover Foundation

Recognition involves more than reinforcing positive work performance. Recognition is a commitment by the organization to its employees. This commitment is evident by the organization's willingness to recognize employees who make positive work contributions. Recognition is also a tool that can be used by astute leaders to create a positive working environment. The premise of recognition is that employees want to be acknowledged and valued for their contributions. It differs from the traditional incentive program that ties compensation to a certain performance level. Recognition aims to bridge the gap between performance and organizational culture. It does this by reinforcing positive workplace norms and behaviors. Almost all of the companies listed on *Fortune's* "100 Best Companies to Work For" have employed the use of recognition to build positive work cultures. Recognition is a key component of organizational strategy because it helps the organization focus on what is important. For example, a recognition program that focuses on excellent customer service will soon help build a culture that is customer friendly. Finally, a good recognition program helps impact the way employees feel about their workplace. It ultimately serves as a constant reminder to employees that their contributions really do matter.

Abraham Maslow's "needs hierarchy theory" provides a familiar model about how employee needs motivate behavior. Recognition fits into the "esteem" needs that employees strive to satisfy. According to Maslow's theory, esteem "includes self-esteem through personal achievement as well as social esteem through recognition and respect from others." Clayton Alderfer, an organizational behavior theorist, developed a companion theory of motivation to "overcome the (rigid) problems with Maslow's needs hierarchy theory." Specifically, Alderfer used three categories to describe human needs. These categories are existence needs, relatedness needs and growth needs. Relatedness and growth needs support employee recognition programs. Relatedness needs "include a person's need to interact with other people, receive public recognition, and feel secure around people." Growth needs "consist of a person's self-esteem through personal achievement as well as the concept of self-actualization presented in Maslow's model." Recent examples of how successful companies utilize recognition offer supporting evidence of its value. *Fortune's* list provides an annual testimony to the value of recognition. Figure 5-1 on page 69 looks at five companies from *Fortune's* list and how each has incorporated recognition into its organization. Notice the uniqueness and creative approaches each organization has brought to recognition.

The ranking on *Fortune's* list is shown in parentheses for each of the five organizations listed in Figure 5-1. The important point gleaned from this list is that recognition is a powerful component of culture. Yet with all its potential, some organizations still reject recognition's importance to success, and many organizations that claim to acknowledge the importance of recognition do a poor job of recognizing employees. Insincere and inappropriate recognition does more harm than good.

Some organizational leaders still see recognition as a "program of the month" with little value to the company's long-term strategy. These critics see recognition as having only a temporary value to employees and organizations. One only has to review some of the innovative programs offered in Figure 5-1 to conclude that this argument is flimsy at best. The Container Store has twice been the top company on *Fortune's* list. This author visited a Container Store in Atlanta and came away amazed at how much employees valued their jobs. Employees at this location cited the way they were recognized for their contributions as being important to their workplace perception. One employee told the author that he did not like to go on vacation because he missed his co-workers and the workplace.

Business Drivers

Figure 5-2 on page 70 lists the six key business drivers for recognition programs. These drivers can be used to track the success of the recognition program.

The drivers shown in Figure 5-2 provide a basis for objectively looking at the contributions of recognition programs to the organization. To remain competitive when recruiting and retaining employees, organizations must be tuned into the importance of recognition programs and how they can positively change an organization's culture. When employees realize that their contributions are important to the organization's success, they are more likely to see themselves as partners and embrace the organization's goals, mission and vision.

Figure 5-1:
Sample Approaches to Recognition

Organization	Recognition Type	Description
Genentech(1)	Celebration of milestones	Every milestone has a party and a commemorative T-shirt.
	Collaborative work assignments Open culture	Employees do not get assignments but get "appointments." The culture includes involving employees in the hiring process and playing "word buzz" bingo, which allows employees to check off boxes when trite buzzwords are uttered in meetings.
Wegmans Food Markets(2)	Puts employees first	Wegmans charters jets to fly new employees to the home office to be welcomed by the CEO.
	Employee training	Wegmans provides generous training programs for employees, and gave $54 million for college scholarships in 2005.
Container Store(6)	Safety	Drivers are rewarded for long service and safe driving records.
	Employee empowerment	Employees are empowered to resolve customer issues.
AFLAC(47)	Employee appreciation	Employee Appreciation Week is a seven-day party featuring food, concerts, movies, plays, a minor league baseball game, prizes and amusement-park outings.
Vanguard(60)	Spot recognition	Vanguard recognizes exemplary service with a $250 spot bonus award. The Vanguard Award for Excellence is awarded by a select group of "crew members."

Figure 5-2:
Key Business Drivers for Recognition Programs

Recognition

- Is a valuable tool for recruiting and retaining qualified employees
- Serves as a catalyst for improving customer service by reinforcing positive employee performance
- Rewards positive contributions to product and service quality
- Provides a method for recognizing improvements in productivity
- Positively impacts morale and loyalty to the organization
- Enhances revenues by keeping employee costs down, and increases profit potential by providing better products and services

Common Excuses for Resisting Recognition Programs

Still, there are skeptics that refuse to embrace recognition as an important program in motivating employees. Figure 5-3 on page 72 details some of the "common excuses" for not giving recognition and tips on how to overcome them. The bottom line is that senior leadership must embrace employee recognition as an important value to the organization.

Figure 5-3 helps organizations focus on how to overcome the negative propaganda often associated with recognition programs. Note that it is important to widely communicate these programs to all key stakeholders. The key stakeholders include employees as well as supervisors, executives, board members, and internal and external customers. Most of the excuses in Figure 5-3 can be overcome by properly designing and administering the recognition program.

Program Characteristics

In the remaining sections of this chapter, we look at the basic program characteristics that make up a recognition program and present a step-by-step process for communicating recognition programs. We also look at formal and informal recognition programs. Some formal recognition programs actually have many of the same characteristics as some incentive programs. The difference is that formal recognition usually ties to a specific organizational goal or initiative. Informal recognition programs are easier to administer and are generally more spontaneous than formal programs. Finally, we discuss the value of using public recognition to enhance the individual or work team's accomplishments.

To ensure the success of any recognition program, it is necessary to have senior leadership support and well-established guidelines in place. The following are six key characteristics of an effective recognition program:

1. Responsible Parties: It is important to name one individual to coordinate and nurture the recognition program. That person is responsible for the program development and ongoing administration of the program. The CEO *or a senior level executive* should identify who is responsible for the program's success. This creates a link to senior leadership support and tells the organization that recognition is highly valued.

2. Goals and Objectives: An effective recognition program must have a solid foundation framed with distinct and well-communicated goals and objectives. Example goals include the following:

- To increase customer satisfaction scores by at least 10 percent as measured by customer survey data.
- To achieve at least a 10-percent improvement in job satisfaction as measured by the employee opinion survey
- To reduce employee turnover by 15 percent.

There should be three to four program goals or objectives that reflect what the organization is trying to accomplish by implementing the program. The goals should be succinct and easy for all key stakeholders to understand. The organization should use the S.M.A.R.T. guidelines when establishing goals. These guidelines help determine in advance if the goals are specific (S), measurable (M), achievable (A), relevant (R) and tied to the success of the organization (T). To determine how recognition has directly impacted the goal, it is important to obtain data from the employee stakeholder on how specifically this component has impacted him or her. For example, when measuring the impact of recognition on turnover, the organization can use an "issue-oriented" survey. The issue-oriented survey consists of two to three questions, which makes its easy to administer and tabulate. The issue-oriented survey can be administered on the intranet or be sent to the employee's home. Exit interviews should also focus on how recognition may have impacted the employee's decision to leave the organization. Finally, the goals for the recognition program must become an integral part of the scorecard for the organization, the department and even the supervisor. This allows the organization to provide ongoing monitoring of the program's success.

3. Key Measures of Success: It is important to establish key indicators of the program early in its development. Key measures should be built around at least two or three strategic areas, such as the following:

- Financial
- Quality
- Service
- Performance

Figure 5-3

Common Excuses for Not Giving Employee Recognition

Excuse	How to Address the Excuse
"It's too expensive to offer."	• Most recognition programs cost less than 2 percent of the overall total rewards budget. • The cost of providing recognition is offset by reduced employee turnover and lower recruitment costs. • Recognition has a positive impact on quality, customer service, employee morale and employee productivity, which more than offsets the program cost.
"It has no long-term value to the employer."	• Recognition programs build loyalty and commitment from employees. • Recognition programs help establish the organization as a unique and innovative employer.
"Recognition leads to built-in expectations."	• Recognition should reinforce positive results. • Program expectations should be clearly communicated to all key stakeholders.
"It becomes a neverending process."	• For recognition to be meaningful, it must be an ongoing process and not a temporary approach. • It must be internalized by leadership and become an accepted approach to managing employees.
"It creates competition among employees."	• If communicated properly, recognition fosters a sense of pride and accomplishment.
"I feel uncomfortable giving or receiving recognition."	• Leaders should be trained in how to give recognition to employees. • Employees should be provided appropriate information about the recognition program. • Employee input should be solicited to help build a recognition program that is supported and meets the needs of those being recognized.

• Retention

• Attendance

• Job satisfaction/employee morale

The key measures should link to the program's goals and objectives. For example, the three identified goals discussed in the section develop goals and objectives would have the following key indicators:

• Customer satisfaction scores—These scores would be used to help determine if

Figure 5-3 *(Continued)*
Common Excuses for Not Giving Employee Recognition

Excuse	How to Address the Excuse
"The employee is already being paid for doing the job."	• Training and education with employees and supervisors that focuses on the importance of integrating recognition into organizational culture is key to overcoming this excuse. • All employees are paid a salary or wage for the work they do. However, organizations utilize a variety of rewards or payments to encourage desired behavior.
"Recognition should be reserved for the performance evaluation."	• Recognizing exceptional performance is both an important employee reward and a way of communicating a strong message to other employees about the organization. • Recognition is time-sensitive and should be provided as close as possible to the positive work contribution. • Continuous recognition of performance reinforces good work habits and gives employees a positive motivational tool.
"Creates confusion on what should be recognized."	• A good recognition program has detailed guidelines for what is to be recognized. • Program expectations should be widely communicated and understood by all key stakeholders.

Adapted from Recognition at Work, Second Edition. 2006. G. Michael Barton, SPHR. Scottsdale: WorldatWork Press.

the recognition program really did have a meaningful impact on customer service.

• Job satisfaction score—This score on the annual employee opinion survey can help determine the impact of recognition on morale. At my organization, we asked how recognition had impacted certain aspects of the employee's work life. We were surprised to learn that recognition was responsible for a 21-percent increase in job satisfaction.

• Turnover and job-vacancy rates—It is important to ask employees and job applicants how recognition impacts their willingness to remain or join the organization. Based on this feedback, both of these rates can be monitored as new recognition programs and approaches are implemented.

4. Easily Understood Eligibility Criteria: Program criteria should be easily understood by participants and key stakeholders. The program should avoid complicated formulas to determine recognition. Criteria should also be few in number and not an exhaustive list of requirements.

5. Cost-Containment Features: The recognition budget should be predetermined and should not be a moving target. For a program to have a long-term impact, the recommended funding level should be 1 percent to 7 percent of the total rewards budget. *This recommended funding is based on all components of the total rewards program that the organization actively supports as part of its overall total rewards strategy.* Note: When a recognition program is first implemented, the percent spent will often be below the recommended 1 percent to 7 percent range. However, to have a long-term impact, the organization must make a significant investment in recognition.

6. Program Communication: Communicating the recognition program involves a financial and time commitment on the part of the organization. Communicating to employees about the eligibility factors of the program and how the program will impact them is no small task. The organization must provide complete and current information about the recognition program. Several innovative communication approaches are available for the communication process. Media that can be used to communicate a recognition program include pamphlets and interactive voice presentations on the organization's Web site. To ensure the program meets the needs of the organization's employees, eligible participants should also be surveyed and asked for input about the program at least annually.

These characteristics provide a framework from which to build a recognition program.

Communicating Recognition Programs

Communication is the key element to the recognition program's success. A step-by-step process should be used to develop strategies for communicating a new recognition program.

Step 1: Answer the following questions before developing a communication plan:
- Who will be affected?
- What is going to be communicated (e.g., a formal recognition program, cash versus noncash awards, the recognition process)?
- Where are the stakeholders located who need to know about the program (e.g., multiple locations, all work shifts, specific departments, specific geographic areas)?
- How will the organization communicate the program to employees and key stakeholders?

Step 2: Identify steps that must be taken to communicate the recognition program.

Examples

- Develop the program's theme.
- Solicit input from key stakeholders about program communication.
- Identify key messages to send to stakeholders about the program.
- Develop program brochures and other communication approaches.
- Train leaders about the program.
- Send program announcements to all key stakeholders.
- Conduct meetings with employees.

Step 3: Identify action(s) to take.

Examples

- Work with the marketing department to develop a program theme.
- Conduct focus group(s) with key stakeholders to develop communication approaches.
- Review key program messages with senior leadership.
- Work with the marketing department and outside printing sources to develop program brochures.
- Establish a training program for organizational leaders.
- Send letters to all key stakeholders announcing the program's implementation.
- Meet with employees on all shifts and at all locations to provide program information.

Step 4: Establish expected outcomes.

Step 5: Identify the financial and people resources needed.

Step 6: Establish a timetable for completing the communication process.

This process should be used to develop a formal communication plan. The communication plan must be carefully integrated with program implementation. It is important to solicit support from all levels of management. However, the first-line supervisor is key to communicating the program. To ensure that a consistent message is provided to employees, "talking points" should be provided to all first-line supervisors. These talking points provide resource information that allows the supervisor to answer basic questions about the recognition program. Finally, communication about the program must be ongoing and presented in a number of different ways to employees. This approach ensures that the program is given the appropriate emphasis along with other total rewards programs. The next step is for the organization to determine if it wants a formal or informal recognition program. Some organizations have both formal and informal programs. We will take a look at both.

Formal Recognition Programs

According to Bob Nelson, author of *1001 Ways to Reward Employees*, a formal recognition program can simply be defined as a "predetermined program." But a formal recognition program involves making a long-term commitment to recognition. An important element for a formal recognition program is to focus on specific achievements such as significant contributions by the individual or the work team. A formal recognition program also has more well-defined program criteria than its informal counterpart. The program criteria must clearly define who is eligible and what types of performance or action(s) are eligible for recognition. The organization should encourage input from employees about the effectiveness of the program. This input should begin when the program goals are developed and should be extended to the ongoing administration of the program.

Finally, the types of rewards provided should be meaningful to employees. While the monetary amounts are lower in recognition programs than they are in incentive plans, the employee must still see the reward as having personal or financial value. For example, a day off with pay has significant personal and monetary value to employees who value spending time away from work. Formal programs can accomplish this goal by using either cash or noncash rewards. An example of a cash approach would be a small recognition bonus to an individual who handled a difficult customer concern. The cash award can take the form of a gift certificate or "weekend retreat" at an area hotel or recreational facility. An example of a noncash approach would be a certificate of recognition that is given to an employee publicly for exceeding certain performance guidelines.

The main point is that formal recognition programs should be flexible enough to address the needs of each individual employee. Some employees want public recognition, and the noncash approaches fulfill this need at little or no cost.

Designing a Formal Recognition Program

Designing a formal recognition program has some of the same requirements as an incentive plan. It is important that a step-by-step approach be followed when designing and implementing a formal program.

Step 1: *Establish monetary and program boundaries.* It is imperative to keep rewards meaningful while at the same time keeping the program within predetermined boundaries. Some program boundaries could include the following:

- Recognition will only be given for performance that is over and above established standards (e.g., excellent customer service).
- Cash bonuses will not exceed a certain amount for any one recognition event (e.g., $500).

- The program should enhance other total rewards programs such as cash incentive plans or base compensation.

Step 2: *Identify the behavior/performance to be recognized.* The program should spell out what behaviors and performance contributions are eligible for the recognition. Eligible behavior and performance may include the following:

- Performance/behavior that exceeds normal expectations (e.g., it is a given that all employees should direct customers to the proper location for service within the organization)
- Behavior that exceeds the supervisor's expectations
- Action(s) or behavior that enhance(s) the organization's image
- Action(s) or behavior that delight(s) the customer
- Improvement of a work process or development of a new approach to work problems.

Step 3: *Determine who does the recognizing.* The organization may want to develop a "matrix" similar to the one in Figure 5-4 to be used as a guide for who will be responsible for the recognition. The matrix identifies the primary decision maker in bold type, and the indirect decision makers are listed underneath. Indirect decision makers can recommend who should receive an award but do not have the final authority to grant it.

A recognition committee is comprised of key stakeholders within the organization who oversee the formal recognition program. In some organizations, the recognition committee presents all cash awards in order to track the money spent and to provide more public recognition. Noncash recognition can generally be approved by all levels of management within the organization.

Step 4: *Develop guidelines for communicating recognition to employees.* Some basic guidelines for communicating the actual recognition should be developed and distributed to those individuals responsible for recognition. These guidelines

Figure 5-4
Matrix

Noncash	Cash	Cash	Cash
	$400-$500	$200-$399	Less than $200
Sr. Leaders	CEO	Dept. Director	Supervisor
Managers	Sr. Leaders	Sr. Leaders	Managers
Board Members	Managers	Supervisors	Work Leaders
Rec. Committee	Supervisors	Work Leaders	Rec.Committee

Adapted from *Recognition at Work, Second Edition.* 2006. G. Michael Barton, SPHR. Scottsdale: WorldatWork Press.

provide leaders with "talking points" that can be used to present a consistent message about the recognition. Some communication guidelines include the following:

- Inform the employee, if permissible, who nominated him/her for the recognition.
- Provide a detailed description of the actual achievement or contribution.
- Cite the performance standard or work process where the employee exceeded expectations.
- Select an appropriate place and time to communicate the recognition to the employee.
- Be prepared to answer questions and discuss recognition in detail with the employee.

Step 5: *Document the recognition.* A "congratulatory citation" or similar document should be used to detail the employee recognition. The congratulatory citation should identify what took place, the person(s) involved in the achievement, how the employee was successful, when the action occurred and where it happened. The congratulatory citation will be placed in the employee's personnel file. It should also be used in conjunction with the employee's performance evaluation to help highlight positive contributions made by the employee during the period for which he or she is being evaluated.

Step 6: *Establish guidelines for reinforcing positive behavior and desired performance.* Useful guidelines include the following:

- Establish performance and recognition standards and communicate them to employees.
- Leave something tangible with the employee (e.g., cash or noncash award).
- Conduct the recognition as close to the desired performance as possible.
- Refer to the recognition when conducting the employee's performance evaluation to reinforce the importance of the positive contribution(s).
- Solicit feedback from the employee during and after the recognition process.

These steps help employees and leaders regard the program positively. For the program to be seen as effective and viable, it must be seen as a stable tool that has the same impact as any other total rewards program. For example, recognition can be effectively tied to the employee performance evaluation. It can also be used to expand achievements that were already recognized by incentive and even base compensation (e.g., congratulatory citations, public recognition and noncash approaches).

Informal Recognition Programs

Informal or spot recognition programs reward employees and have fewer program criteria than formal approaches. Informal programs are relatively easy to implement and administer, and are useful in reinforcing positive work behaviors on the spot. They have the ability to respond quickly to organizational goals such as obtaining excellent customer service scores. The key elements of an informal recognition program do resemble some of the elements previously discussed for formal approaches. The major difference is that informal programs generally are more spontaneous and much easier to develop. The emphasis for an informal approach is to provide immediate recognition rather than focusing on formal program criteria. The organization must still be careful when implementing an informal approach. It must still be seen as a credible program by employees. Some of these key elements are incorporated into the design of the program, which is discussed in the next section. Two important elements to emphasize before the design process are financial limits and program responsibility. It is important to develop financial limits before the program is implemented, even though dollar limits are low for informal approaches because noncash awards are used almost exclusively. It is also imperative to establish who has the responsibility for managing the program. The responsibility can be given to the human resources department, a recognition committee or a program coordinator. The important point is that assigning responsibility avoids the perception that an informal program is merely a collection of "thank-you notes" and "feel good" merchandise.

Spot recognition has the unique quality of having elements that fit both a formal and informal program. It provides immediate recognition, much like an informal program, but still has definitive structure, like a formal program. Trover Foundation has an excellent example of a program that bridges both formal and informal recognition. It is called the "gold card" program. Employees who exhibit excellent customer service are rewarded with a "gold card" from their supervisor or the customer. The gold card is essentially a "thank you" for performing excellent customer service. The gold card is returned to the human resources department and used as part of the employee's performance evaluation. The employee who receives a gold card becomes eligible for a monthly drawing. This monthly drawing is held in the employee cafeteria during lunchtime. The lucky winner receives a check for $500, which is net of income taxes. This program has built excitement and continues to receive high marks from employees on the annual opinion survey.

Designing an Informal Program

Informal programs are much less structured and more spontaneous compared to formal approaches. They are referred to as "in the moment" programs that reward positive behavior as it occurs. However, informal programs should still have structure and meaningful guidelines. There are six important steps to follow when designing an informal program.

Step 1: *Define the program's purpose.* The purpose does not have to be complicated but should simply state what the program is trying to accomplish. A common example would be: "The purpose of the informal recognition program is to recognize meaningful employee contributions that can be readily observed and immediately rewarded."

Step 2: *Determine who will be eligible.* Generally, all employees are eligible to participate in an informal program. The senior leadership team and sometimes department managers are often excluded from the program. Since these programs are relatively inexpensive, it is a good idea to include as many employees as possible.

Step 3: *Establish program expectations.* The expectations should be built around areas that the organization is seeking to improve. Examples include customer service, organizational morale, team development and productivity. Sample expectations are as follows:

- Increase management visibility with employees and provide them with a tool to reward positive work performance.
- Provide a positive work environment that recognizes employees for their contributions.
- Provide a method to recognize employees who provide excellent customer service.

Step 4: *Define what behavior and actions are eligible for recognition.* An informal program should not be a "giveaway program" that recognizes meaningless contributions. The recognition should focus on meaningful contributions, such as when an employee exceeds expectations on a project or work assignment. Exceptional behavior and performance should be the major reasons why supervisors recognize employees. However, using an informal approach allows the supervisor to recognize those performance areas that do not fit neatly into a formal program.

Step 5: *Identify the types of recognition approaches to be used.* Most informal programs use small cash awards, recognition certificates, merchandise or some other token that employees value. The following items are a representative sample of what is often found in an informal program:

- Thank-you card from the supervisor
- Gift certificates
- Small cash bonuses (generally less than $50)
- Movie tickets
- Pizza party
- Articles in the employee newsletter
- Free parking spot
- Personal recognition from the CEO
- Flower or balloon bouquets.

It is important to identify what items are available to use for recognition. The number of items is not as important as how well each item or approach will be accepted by the employee.

Step 6: *Match informal approaches to the organization's culture.* The recognition should reflect what is important to the organization's culture. For example, if the culture is mature and conservative, a more traditional approach such as certificates of appreciation may be appropriate. A younger organization may prefer gift certificates and public recognition.

Public Recognition

Some employees want to be recognized for their achievements publicly. This adds to the recognition and enhances its potential for motivating the employees. Trover Foundation's "Gold Card" program has proven to be an excellent way to recognize employees publicly for their service to the customer. The problem is that some employees do not like to be recognized publicly and in fact are embarrassed by any public display. It is important for the individual who is doing the recognition to know what the employee prefers. The best way to find out is to ask. Employees will be honest about their preference for public recognition. There is one more caution about publicly recognizing teams for their accomplishments. Some team members are "social loafers." Social loafers "piggyback" on the accomplishments of their team members. However, the social loafer does not do her or his share of the work. When presenting a team incentive publicly, the rest of the team may feel cheated if the social loafer is also allowed to be recognized for his or her lack of meaningful contribution. To prevent social loafing, it is important to have monitors in place that can track both group and individual contributions. For example, dividing the work into measurable contributions can ensure that everyone contributes equally. Social loafing should be discussed up front with the team, and slackers should be penalized. Employees want to be recognized for meaningful contributions. Public recognition that is aimed at the expected level of performance does little to enhance the value of the achievement. In fact, this type of "one-size-fits-all" recognition can turn off other employees who feel slighted by this insincere approach.

If it is determined that public recognition is valued by the employee, it is important to follow some specific guidelines for conducting the public recognition. It is imperative to select the appropriate place, time and audience for the public recognition. Figure 5-5 on page 83 provides specific guidelines that should make public recognition more meaningful.

Public recognition can be used to reinforce other total rewards programs. For example, incentive awards can be given publicly, depending on the employee and the culture. Specifically, group incentives can be distributed publicly, along with appropriate celebration and testimonials from organizational leadership. This can add to the enjoyment of the accomplishment if all employees understand their roles and eligibility for the total rewards program. The service awards banquet is an example of a formal recognition program that is generally appreciated by long-term employees and their families. This type of public recognition is a way to thank the employees and their families for their dedication to the organization.

Finally, public recognition has the advantage of giving the honored employee his or her "15 minutes of fame." This is the only opportunity for most individuals to receive formal recognition. For this reason, the organization has a responsibility to the employee to ensure that the recognition fits his or her needs.

Keeping Recognition Programs Fresh and Fun

The program must adapt to the changing needs of the employees in order to retain employee enthusiasm. Most of the companies on *Fortune's* list incorporate fun and excitement into their recognition programs. Some of these organizations have incorporated recognition with other total rewards programs to address specific needs of the employee. Trover's "Gold Card" program takes both a formal and informal approach to recognition. This program focuses on the individual and provides a financial reward as well. Some organizations go beyond the scope of what a traditional recognition program offers. These organizations "bundle" recognition with financial and personal rewards in order to emphasize certain financial and quality objectives. Keeping the program fun and exciting is important. Tips for keeping the program exciting include the following:

- Adding new components to the program at least annually, if possible.
- Tailoring the program based on feedback received from employees (e.g., what do they see as important to them for recognition?).

Figure 5-5:
Guidelines for Conducting Public Recognition

Select an appropriate time and place for public recognition.

- Use departmental or group meetings to publicly celebrate the recognition.
- Hold the meeting at the beginning of the employee's workday. This allows the employee to savor the recognition throughout the workday.
- Allow enough time to appropriately recognize the employee.
- Recognition should be as close to the achievement as possible so it is fresh in the employee's memory and to those who attend the public recognition.
- Avoid negative locations when conducting the recognition. Some examples may include the supervisor's office, the employee's work area, especially if it is congested and busy, or a public location that may have a heavy traffic flow.

Written recognition

- Select a widely read organizational publication such as a newsletter or circulating memorandum.
- Focus on the specifics of the employee's achievement. This will build credibility with the individuals who are reading about the accomplishment.
- Cite the performance standard or organization goal that was exceeded, if appropriate.

Web site recognition

- Incorporate pictures of the individual employee in his or her work setting.
- Use graphics, if appropriate, to illustrate the impact of the employee's achievement on the organization and the department's productivity.
- Describe in detail the employee's achievement, such as who was involved in helping the employee, what happened to the organization as a result of the achievement, and when and where the achievement occurred.
- Post the achievement on the Web site for at least 14 days so employees and other Web site users can have an opportunity to read about the accomplishment. This also extends the employee's "15 minutes of fame" when colleagues and loved ones read about the achievement.

Communicate the recognition clearly and enthusiastically

- Choose positive statements to communicate the recognition (e.g., "I appreciate the long hours and quality of work you put into this project").
- If the recognition is given in a meeting, use positive facial expressions to reinforce the verbal message.
- Written public recognition should be active rather than passive in tone. Descriptive language will add to the recognition and excitement.

Encourage input from the employee

- This allows the employee to thank others and include them in the recognition process.

- Think creatively in designing new recognition approaches. An example would be a "point system" approach that allows employees a chance to earn a weekend retreat, or perhaps a "casual Thursday" to recognize employees for their commitment to a project.
- Celebrate! Recognition comes alive when we celebrate the individual and group achievement of our employees.

These tips, along with the willingness to adapt the program to the needs of the employee and the organization, keep it meaningful to everyone involved.

Conclusion

This chapter has summarized how to develop a recognition program. It has examined the important elements of formal and informal recognition approaches. It has also looked at the importance of ongoing communication to employees about recognition. In the final analysis, any recognition program will be effective only if it is used on a regular and consistent basis. The importance of training supervisors on how to effectively recognize employees cannot be overstated. Some supervisors simply have a difficult time recognizing employees for positive contributions. To overcome this difficulty, supervisory training must focus on how to recognize, when to recognize and where to recognize. The "how to" should focus on what to say to employees to make them feel good about the recognition. The "when to" must focus on the timing of the recognition. For example, when recognition is given to the employee early in the work shift, it has the power of making the employee feel good all day. The "where to" involves choosing private or public recognition. If private recognition is chosen, the supervisor must be careful that the employee does not see the location as threatening. For example, some employees may view the supervisor's office as a place "where people are fired rather than praised." If public recognition is used, it must match the personal preferences and needs of the employee.

It is up to the organization to integrate recognition into the total rewards program. This is no small task. Senior leaders must commit enough financial resources to the program. This financial commitment includes the program rewards, communicating the program and supervisory training. No program will be successful if it is not communicated continuously. Communication helps keep the program fresh and exciting. It also gives it "top of the mind awareness" with all key stakeholders.

Finally, what makes an organization unique is its reputation for valuing and recognizing its employees. Recognition programs can help organizations create an exciting place for employees to work. These programs signal to employees that their accomplishments really do matter.

Resources

Barton, G. Michael. 2006. *Recognition at Work*, Second Edition. Scottsdale: WorldatWork Press.

McShane, Steven L., and Mary Ann Von Glinow. 2003. *Organizational behavior*. 2nd ed. New York: McGraw-Hill.

Nelson, Bob. 1994. *1001 Ways to Reward Employees*. New York: Workman Publishing.

Bonuses for Teams and Operations

Chapter 6
Team Incentives
Robert J. Greene, Ph.D., CCP, CBP, GRP, SPHR, GPHR, Reward $ystems Inc.

The increased use of teams as an approach to organizing work has called into question whether compensation strategies and programs devised for job-based organization structures work as effectively for teams. A critical first step in developing effective compensation strategies and programs for a "team" is determining the type of team that the strategies and programs are being developed for. There are three basic types of teams: work (process) teams, project teams and parallel teams.

Work (process) teams are organizational units that perform the work of the organization on an ongoing basis. Membership is relatively permanent, and members work full-time in the team—it is their organizational role (job). The team member role description is simple—do whatever needs to be done at the time. As a result, it is generally beneficial to have each member acquire and develop the knowledge, skills and behaviors required by the work of the team (crosstrain). Examples of a work team would be a production team that builds a product/subassembly or a customer service team that services a group of assigned customers.

Project teams consist of a group of people assigned to complete a one-time project. The members typically have well-defined roles and may work on specific phases of the project, either full-time or in addition to their other responsibilities. They often have different occupations. Most often they report to a project manager relative to their work on the project, rather than to their regular manager. An example would be a cross-functional team that is using concurrent engineering to develop a new product.

Parallel teams (a.k.a., task forces) consist of people assigned to work on a specific task in addition to their normal role. The term "parallel" suggests that task force work is carried on while the regular work continues, and members are almost always assigned to a task force on a part-time and temporary basis. Members typically have different occupations and work in different parts of the organization, although employees in the same occupation or the same organizational unit could evaluate ways of improving a process or project while doing their regularly assigned work. Parallel teams can be very similar to project teams, depending on the nature of the assignment, the duration and the degree of involvement. Membership on a safety team would be considered a parallel team activity even though it was extended in duration, while participation in a complete redesign of a safety program would be likely to be considered a project-team activity.

The type of team is critical when considering how employee roles are designed and how performance is defined, measured, managed and rewarded. Since the different types of teams have differing objectives, require different types of members and ask for different commitments, it is reasonable to assume that the performance and rewards-management strategies that will be effective will be different for each type of team.

Incentives for Work (Process) Teams

Work teams perform organizational work, operating as a unit with defined objectives. Team members have as their primary role doing the work assigned to the team. Although "do whatever needs to be done at the time" sounds like a strange role description, it actually fits the nature of the work. Members are generally expected to acquire most or all of the knowledge and skills required to perform all of the operations performed by the team.

Individual base pay rates for team members are usually administered within the salary structure used for the rest of the organization, although a structure could be created just for the team roles. Pay rates and pay actions can be based on performance, progress in achieving competence or a combination of both. One approach to administering base pay is to define specific skills or skill sets associated with the work of the team and to establish a process for testing mastery of each of the skills/skill sets. This approach is called "skill-based pay." Pay rates are progressed as individuals learn more skills, which is consistent with the philosophy that a multiskilled member of a work team is more valuable than someone with only a single skill. Another approach to base pay administration is merit pay, which progresses pay rates based on individual performance in the assigned role. Both of these approaches have rich literatures of their own and will not be discussed here.

Using base pay as the sole source of team member rewards may limit the effectiveness of a team. Since base pay level is tied to individual performance or skill mastery, it can promote the wrong mindset and behavior. Performance actually manifests at the team level, so it is a questionable practice to focus on individual performance alone. Also, it may be very difficult to determine individual contributions, and attempting to do so may put individuals in competition with each other for pay increases rather than encourage cooperative and supportive behavior. For these reasons, many organizations are using variable pay programs for work teams, in order to provide the motivation to achieve team objectives. Used in conjunction with base pay programs, the incentive programs can encourage members to align their efforts to maximize team performance.

The use of team incentives in conjunction with a skill-based base pay system has been proven to be successful in balancing team member focus between individual performance and team performance. One of the great dangers in implementing skill-based pay for team members is that employees may be motivated to become "full-time students" and be reluctant to forego skill training just to perform the work needed to produce team results. A similar danger exists with merit pay, which can cause team members to compete for fixed-sum pools. Complementing merit pay adjustments with some form of team incentive plan reduces the individual focus, since other team members are bound to apply social pressure for each employee to contribute to the overall result as well as perform well individually.

One of the most heralded models for group or team incentives is "gainsharing." The primary objective of this approach is to encourage workers to do what needs to be done better, cheaper and/or faster by providing contingent awards that share the gains in productivity. This type of incentive program is discussed in Chapter 7.

A widely used term for other types of work-team incentive plans is "performance-sharing." In today's service-oriented environment, performance factors such as customer satisfaction, innovation, quality and other qualitative measures have become as important as the cost and output numbers often used in gainsharing plans. As a result, there is a trend toward using multiple criteria to define performance for use in team incentive plans. Standards and measurement scales are assigned to each criterion, as are relative importance weights. Overall team performance is then used to determine the incentive funds available, and these funds are typically distributed in an egalitarian manner (equal percent of base pay, equal dollar amounts, equal amounts per hour worked, etc.). An example of a "performance-sharing" incentive plan for a customer service team is shown in Figure 6-1.

A "scorecard" such as this one fits an environment where the team members are handling transactions that are relatively straightforward and standard in nature. In this case, the performance criteria have been determined to be of equal impor-

Figure 6-1
Sample Project Plan

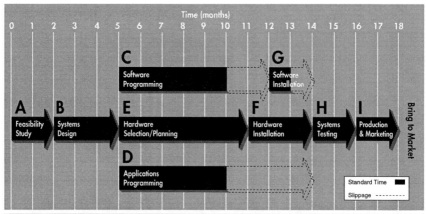

Segment	Milestones	Standard Time/Slippage	Incentive Criteria	Eligible
A	Present feasibility study to management	2 months/0	Timeliness	Project staff
B	Complete systems design	3 months/0	Timeliness/quality/cost	Systems staff
C	Complete software programming	5 months/2 months	Quality/cost	Software staff
D	Complete applications programming	5 months/4 months	Quality/cost	Applications staff
E	Complete hardware section/planning	6 months/0	Timeliness/quality/cost	Operations staff
F	Complete hardware installation	3 months/0	Timeliness/cost	Operations staff
G	Complete software installation	1 month/1 month	Timeliness/cost	Software staff
H	Run successful systems test	2 months/0	Timeliness/quality/cost	Project staff
I	Produce/market system and deliver to market	2 months/0	Timeliness/quality/cost/ sales of product/product acceptance	Project staff

tance to "success" and are equally weighted. This particular plan could fit a call center that takes highly structured inbound orders that originate from a defined customer base. If a significant amount of influence on the size of the order were to be possible, there should be a criterion that tracks the size of the order. In such a case, there would have to be a viable process for determining the level of customer satisfaction, perhaps a survey done shortly after the transaction among a random sample of customers. The measurement level chosen here is aggregate team performance. The assumption is that orders are taken by whoever is available to do so. It could certainly be argued that individual incentives could be used instead of team incentives, particularly if individual transactions could be tied to specific employees.

In contrast to the customer service team example, a research team consisting of members from different occupational specialties that is attempting to develop a new technology would probably best fit an incentive plan based on aggregate results. Since no member would have the knowledge to achieve the desired results without the knowledge of the others, it becomes very difficult to decide how much each member contributed. Selecting the appropriate level at which performance should be defined, measured and rewarded is critical to the effective use of incentive compensation.

Incentives for Project Teams

The life of many professionals consists of a mosaic of overlapping projects rather than the performance of specific duties associated with a defined "job." Persons in occupations not typically thought of as "professional" are increasingly working in a project-focused manner due to changes in organizational structures. Project teams are being used to design and refine key business processes that extend laterally across the organization. Given the increasing prevalence of project work, it is important to examine performance-and rewards-management strategies used for project staff members.

Projects are generally defined by the desired end results, project timelines and milestones along the way to project completion. Because they are of limited duration and are "one-time" in nature, projects lend themselves to being managed using a formal framework. Building a new plant or laboratory and installing an enterprisewide IT system are endeavors with a definable end result. Given the magnitude and complexity of such projects, there is a need to plan, execute and evaluate the work performed to produce the result. Software packages are readily available today that enable users to keep track of materials, people and capital at every step along the way. Project management itself has become an occupation.

Figure 6-1 on page 92 illustrates a project plan used to create a computer software product and bring it to market. The planning method used by the software firm is referred to as the critical path method (CPM) because it breaks the project into segments and determines the resources and time required for each segment. The segments along the horizontal line in the center of the diagram are said to fall along the "critical path," which means they must be completed during the allotted time or the project will be late. Other segments not falling on the critical path have slippage built in, which means there is more time available than it will take to perform the work and therefore they can be scheduled more flexibly. For each segment in Figure 6-1, performance standards are established that typically utilize quality, cost and/or customer-satisfaction criteria in addition to timeliness.

The role of individuals in a project will vary. Some individuals may participate only in one segment, others may be involved in several segments at once and project management may be involved throughout the project. Some personnel assigned to a particular project may work on other projects or their regular jobs simultaneously. Therefore, one of the key considerations in compensating project-focused personnel is to match the basis for appraising their performance and determining their rewards to the work they perform. Another key consideration is when performance is measured and when it is rewarded. This should occur at a time that fits the work cycle and when performance metrics are available and meaningful.

The project-focused environment raises unique administrative issues. Project managers who are expected to evaluate work may not be the people to whom project personnel report on a day-to-day basis. For people who do not work full-time on the project, two or more supervisors or project leaders may be responsible for evaluating their performance and helping to determine their rewards. As a result, the following occur:

- Project managers have to evaluate people who may have been with them only a short time.
- Unit managers have to evaluate people who technically report to them but who frequently move from one assignment to another, often dropping out of sight for extended periods.

In addition to employees who work on projects only part of the year, there are employees who are on a project longer than a year and whose "permanent home" no longer is clear. If the original supervisor is expected to look after these employees, some mechanism must be in place to ensure that pay levels and career progression do not suffer. When people are assigned to project staffs without a clear plan for their future utilization, employees can become the in-house equivalent of expatriate workers without a home country and with no repatriation plan.

The software firm's incentive strategy for the project illustrated in Figure 6.1 provides a framework for developing incentive programs for each of the project segments and for the overall project. Each segment is designed to have one or more milestones, with performance objectives developed for each segment and at each milestone. Rewards can then be tied to performance on each segment. In this illustration, four different types of performance criteria are used:

- *Timeliness* measure—completion date versus schedule
- *Efficiency* measure—actual cost versus budget
- *Quality* measure—performance versus standards
- *Customer satisfaction* measure—customer reaction versus expectations.

The criteria used and their relative importance vary by segment.

Once performance criteria, criteria weighting and performance standards have been established, the project-segment incentive programs work as "performance versus predetermined objectives" incentive plans. Because the firm in question subscribes to a management-by-objectives philosophy, this incentive strategy represents a good fit with the organizational context. In organizations with a more laissez-faire culture, this discipline must be developed, at least for employees assigned to project teams.

The annual compensation targets assigned by the software firm are fairly typical and illustrate the relationship of base pay, incentive and total direct compensation targets. (See Figure 6-2.) For those involved in more than one project, each person's incentive opportunity is allocated to the specific incentive plan(s) he or she participates in to add up to the established annualized incentive opportunity. (See Figure 6-3 on page 96.) Incentive-award determination can be based on individual or group (segment) performance, or a combination of both. The mix between individual and group incentives should be based on the degree of interdependence among participants. A scale can be used to guide determination of the appropriate mix. (See Figure 6-4 on page 98.) This decision requires a subjective judgment based on the specific context for each project segment. These judgments can be made by management, by the staff or through joint determination, but it is critical for the process to be consistent with the prevailing culture and to be viewed by employees as equitable across the project.

In this particular software organization, some of the systems analysts and programmers were not eligible for incentives while performing regular job assignments (when not on project status), and this created a serious issue. Because there was money at stake, employees competed to participate in project work, and it was clear that much of the competition was dysfunctional. It is not hard to imagine that people whose skill, knowledge or interests may not fit the project require-

Figure 6-2
Sample Targeted Compensation Levels

Organizational Level	Base Pay	Incentive Target	Total Direct Compensation
Manager	$80,000	30% of base pay	$104,000
Senior Systems Analyst	$50,000	20% of base pay	$60,000
Programmer I	$25,000	10% of base pay	$27,500

Figure 6-3
Sample Incentive Opportunities

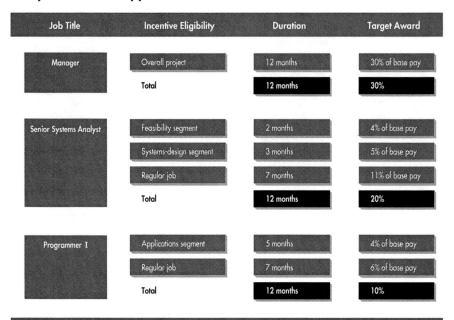

Job Title	Incentive Eligibility	Duration	Target Award
Manager	Overall project	12 months	30% of base pay
	Total	**12 months**	**30%**
Senior Systems Analyst	Feasibility segment	2 months	4% of base pay
	Systems-design segment	3 months	5% of base pay
	Regular job	7 months	11% of base pay
	Total	**12 months**	**20%**
Programmer I	Applications segment	5 months	4% of base pay
	Regular job	7 months	6% of base pay
	Total	**12 months**	**10%**

ments still would be convinced that the incentive opportunity was too good to pass up and would apply considerable pressure on management to assign them to the project.

Many organizations have recognized yet another motivation issue: how to provide incentives that encourage those working only on some project segments to focus on the overall success of the project. This is commonly handled by including these staff members in an incentive plan for the entire project, even though they only participate in a portion of the project. Target award levels can be allocated to both project work and other work, based on the relative time spent on project work. This type of overarching incentive plan provides a common "magnetic north" for all participants in the project, and it calibrates the compasses of each person and unit to the overall objective.

Integrated incentive plans that cover the entire project should include project segment leaders/managers and any staff members responsible for ensuring that the segment's inputs and outputs are compatible with those of other related segments. When project performance cannot be measured meaningfully until the marketplace has "voted" on the quality of the product, some type of sales or customer-satisfaction-driven incentive plan may be the most appropriate rewards vehicle. One approach is to create a venture-participation plan using a formula based on sales, the number of units sold or percentage of sales volume in excess of a threshold amount (such as the investment in the project) to determine award levels. Another approach is to create an ownership plan using phantom-stock or book-value calculations to determine awards. Both approaches would involve the selection of a reasonable period after project completion during which participants could share in results. Obviously, care should be exercised to ensure that open-ended formulas do not generate unreasonable windfall earnings. On the other hand, denying a fair share of value added may dim the allure of future projects to those who could be critical to project success.

When projects demand staff from different occupations and functions, it is often necessary to use different management structures. The information technology (IT) network representative on a cross-functional design team may administratively report to an IT manager, but the person's work will be directed by someone designated as the project manager, thereby creating the dreaded "two boss" scenario. This scenario is dreaded because performance and rewards management systems are under the control of line direct-reports, who may know little about how well an employee performed on the project. The other management challenge is that project staff members often work on the project part-time while they continue in their "regular jobs." This raises the critical issue of how their performance is measured: based on project performance, based on performance in their "regular job" or based on a combination of the two. It is admittedly difficult to get direct-report managers to do effective appraisals and do them on time, but attempting to get two or more managers to coordinate their efforts to do joint appraisals is even harder.

When project incentives are used, the question arises as to whether overall results or individual contributions (or both) should determine awards. Much of this should depend on the degree of interdependence of the work. If someone contributes to a project by doing separate, stand-alone specialist work, it may be appropriate to reward him or her at least partially based on individual performance. On the other hand, measuring and rewarding performance at the team level may be advisable.

For organizations without formal incentive plans, it may still be advisable to recognize contributions to projects with monetary rewards. If a "spot bonus" or "performance award" program is in place, project contributions can be recognized using existing mechanisms. If incentives and performance awards are not available, perhaps the organization should ask itself if this is a realistic and viable strategy in an era where project success often has a major impact on organizational success.

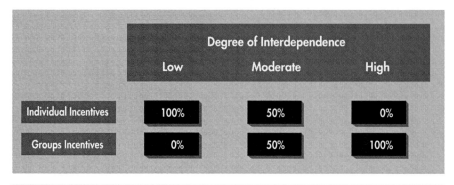

Figure 6-4
Determination of Individual - and Group-Incentive Mix

	Degree of Interdependence		
	Low	Moderate	High
Individual Incentives	100%	50%	0%
Groups Incentives	0%	50%	100%

An increasingly frequent challenge relating to project teams is that members may not be collocated and may be occupationally and culturally diverse. Technology has made "global relay teams" possible, which capitalize on time differences by passing work around the globe to project members. However, when occupation and culture cause communication issues, this approach can be very difficult to administer effectively. Even when translation software enables language differences to be addressed, not all work is formulaic in nature, and it may require subjective interpretation of words and meanings. This is a truly daunting challenge if very dissimilar cultures are involved. For example, if Asian members of a team assume all decisions will be consensual, made only after considerable dialogue, while American members use a "go forth bravely" individual decision-making approach, the probability of conflict or misunderstanding is high. And if substantial team incentive awards are at stake, the intensity of the conflict can be so great as to erode the effectiveness of the team.

Incentives for Parallel Teams

Parallel teams can be task forces or standing committees, as stated earlier. An example of a standing committee would be a safety team that was assigned the task of monitoring safety programs and tracking safety statistics. Participation in a task force is rarely considered a substitute for the "day job," and membership is both temporary and part time. Task forces are increasingly being used to evaluate existing systems and processes, to select new technology and to improve existing products. Too often they are considered to be a free resource by the organization, since it is rare for additional compensation to be expended on members. This belief that this work is free is delusional, because time, energy and resources expended on task-force work are not available for the ongoing work of the organization.

Task forces are often not managed well, or even managed at all. People are assigned (or volunteer) and are given a vague mandate such as "take a look at on-site day care and see how much it would cost and if it would give us a competitive edge in attracting and retaining call-center operators." Without a well-defined set of objectives, a timeline and an agreement on the financial and time resources available, the task force is apt to guess at how the task should be done. Contributions to task-force work are often ignored when performance is measured and rewards determined, thereby sending the message that doing this work well is nice but not critical. And very often members are selected (or volunteer) who have no experience working with each other and who may not have the interpersonal skills to work effectively. A questionable approach is to have people who are not fully occupied or who are not performing critical work named to participate, since they will not be missed on their regular job. Their skills may not fit the work of the task force.

Steps that can be taken to increase task-force effectiveness are: 1) clearly define why the task force is being formed and why its work is needed, including the work to be done and the expectations (timelines, performance criteria and standards); 2) select competent members; 3) gain commitment to the objectives of the commissioning party; 4) define and commit resources (time, money, information, staff support, rewards available); and 5) provide an effective modus operandi (authority structure, training, relationships). These steps are very consistent with the guidelines mentioned earlier for managing other types of teams, and they make the point that resources are consumed by task forces and it is worth it to manage them well.

When task forces are assigned important work that requires considerable investment of time, it becomes problematic when these contributions do not have any impact on performance evaluation or rewards. The author was interviewing a key executive in charge of the entire logistics chain in an organization who pointed out that she was (rightfully) working on three major task forces involved with implementing new technology. She concurred that her participation was absolutely necessary but pointed out that the task-force work was consuming 60 percent or more of her time ... and yet her performance on her "full-time job" was the sole basis for determining her performance rating, salary action and incentive award (and probably her career progression). She made her point.

Task-force work, when significant, can be folded into performance and rewards management in the same manner as in the example cited earlier of the systems analyst who worked part-time on the project and part-time in the regular capacity. It seems a mistake to ignore it, since this sends the message the work is not important or that it is not valued. On the other hand, occasional task-force participation may be rewarded with recognition or nonmonetary rewards, such as dinners or even afternoons at an event celebrating the contributions of those who have contributed. If the organizational culture supports celebration of contribution, and if the organization has developed the skills to do it well, appropriate recognition can be motivating and rewarding, and it can also bring about better dissemination of the work of the task force throughout the organization. It is also possible to use task-force work as a career-development tool. "Stretch" assignments can be made that can help people develop new skills, and "out of occupation" work can increase understanding of how different bodies of knowledge and occupational perspectives can be used to produce more robust solutions.

Other types of parallel teams are standing committees such as safety committees and teams formed to provide counsel to management, such as GE's "workout" teams. Although there is often a fine line between parallel and project teams, project teams are typically more structured and require a formal project plan to control and coordinate the work. Project teams also utilize different staffs to perform the work for different segments of the project.

Recognition can be used in lieu of financial awards, particularly since it could be argued that people used time that theoretically should have been spent on other organization business and that the salary provided compensation. For decades, 3M has had a provision that anyone can spend 15 percent of their time pursuing something they believe will lead to a productive result. If this type of sanction is provided, there may be no need to build any other formal mechanisms into the performance- or rewards-management programs.

Integrating Team Incentives with the Total Compensation Strategy

There are two concerns relative to effectively integrating team incentives with other forms of compensation: *alignment and balance.*

Alignment of the motivation provided by team incentives with the total compensation strategy and with the focus the organization wants team members to have is a fundamental requirement for team incentive effectiveness. If team incentives motivate members to achieve team objectives but result in less than optimal results at the larger unit/organizational level or at the business-process level, they become dysfunctional. Therefore, it may be necessary to consider how team performance can improve business-process performance and/or overall performance and to add measures to the team incentives to ensure performance is enhanced elsewhere in the organization when the team is judged as performing at a high level.

Balance between team incentive-award potential and other forms of compensation is also required in order for team incentives to be effective. For example, if there is both an organizationwide incentive plan and a team incentive plan, the relative reward potential should be determined in a way that provides balanced motivation. If a profit-sharing plan is unlikely to pay out more than 3 percent to 5 percent of base pay while the team incentive target is 15 percent of base pay, it is unlikely that team members will have much concern about organizational results, and they will more likely focus only on team results. At the other end of the spectrum, if individual incentives can generate much higher awards than the team incentive, balance may be lacking between the emphasis placed on individual performance and the emphasis on team performance. It is therefore necessary that a model be constructed that establishes the relative role played by individual, team and organizational performance, and that the incentive programs provide balanced motivation.

Conclusion

Teams are varied in their nature and in the commitment they require. It seems appropriate that rewards for team members vary in a manner that reflects the nature and scope of their work in teams. Full-time permanent membership in a work team argues for measuring performance in a manner that reflects both individual contributions and team results. Tying rewards and/or recognition to both is appropriate.

Participating in a project argues for measuring and rewarding performance on that project, particularly if the period is of long duration or if the commitment is a significant part of the person's time. Performance and rewards/recognition may also be based on the permanent assignment and may be based on a combination of project and job performance.

Service on a task force (parallel team) is typically of shorter duration or requires a relatively small time commitment over an extended time frame. As a result, it may appropriately not have an impact on an employee's performance appraisal, salary action or incentive award. Other forms of recognition may be more appropriate and be adequate. However, given the increasing prevalence of task forces and their increased scope and complexity, the organization should consider treating them in a manner similar to projects.

Team participation often requires a focus on the aggregated results rather than on individual performance. Expecting members of a team whose sole reward is in the form of merit pay to act in an unselfish, cooperative and noncompetitive manner may be unrealistic. Limited salary-increase budgets can make for individual competitiveness and undermine the team fabric. Work teams rewarded solely on the basis of individual performance appraisals are difficult to manage and often do not operate with the "do whatever needs to be done at the time" mindset necessary for effectiveness.

Therefore, using variable compensation programs that reward team results can reduce competitiveness at the individual level. Salary actions can still be used to reward members for developing skills/knowledge and for excelling in their work. Complementing salary actions with team incentives can reward both individual striving and contribution to team results.

Organizations using teams should consider direct compensation strategies that ask for, measure and reward all of the behaviors that will result in effectiveness. They should also recognize contributions of teams to the organization through appropriate recognition. Recognition can be in the form of small monetary rewards or non-monetary rewards such as gifts, celebrations and public acclamation. Team contributions can also be a factor in career progression for those who demonstrate their ability and willingness to work with others to make them more effective and to contribute to organizational success.

Chapter 7

Scanlon Principles and Processes: Building Excellence at Watermark Credit Union

Dow Scott, Ph.D., Loyola University Chicago
Paul Davis, Scanlon Leadership Network
Chuck Cockburn, Watermark Credit Union

This case study demonstrates that the use of Scanlon Plans (i.e., gainsharing) is not restricted to manufacturing companies, and that it can substantially contribute in the financial services industry. The fundamental principles of this participative management system are discussed as they are being applied at Watermark Credit Union.

In the late 1930s, Joe Scanlon developed a plan to save the struggling steel company for whom he worked and for the employees he represented as the president of his local steelworkers union. What was eventually called the "Scanlon Plan" was quickly recognized as an effective means for employers and employees to work together for the benefit of both. During World War II, Scanlon became acting head of the steelworker's research department, where he pioneered labor-management cooperation in a variety of industries. This collaborative approach caught the attention of Douglas McGregor, a professor at Massachusetts Institute of Technology (MIT) who was advocating participative management as a means to increase company innovation and productivity. McGregor brought Scanlon to MIT as a lecturer, where he taught and encouraged students and faculty to examine this extraordinary management idea. One of Joe Scanlon's students, Carl Frost, spent 30 years at Michigan State University (MSU) working with "Scanlon Companies" and teaching students about the Scanlon Plan. Another student, Frederick Lesieur, who became a Scanlon Plan consultant, remained closely aligned with MIT.

Because of its strong academic roots at MIT and MSU, the Scanlon Plan is one of the most rigorously examined and improved-upon set of leadership principles and business processes used today. The Scanlon Leadership Network, an association of companies with Scanlon Plans, provides leadership in the development and implementation of these plans, and has been a repository of knowledge since it was formed in 1964. The Scanlon Leadership Network represents companies ranging from those with 50 employees to multinational corporations with thousands of employees. The network has helped organizations in manufacturing, transportation, health care, retail, communications, warehousing and a variety of other industries implement Scanlon Plans. Although the Scanlon Principles (i.e., Identity, Participation, Equity and Competence) remain the same, the way these principles are implemented has become diverse and incorporates state-of-the-art management systems, which may include lean systems, Hoshin's policy deployment, high-involvement teams, Deming's quality management and Six Sigma. The companies applying these principles represent some of the most profitable and best places to work in the United States. So why does the Scanlon Plan, according to *Training* magazine (Lee 1999), remain "Businesses' Best Kept Secret"?

"The 20th century has been a hothouse of management fads ... In the meantime one truly big idea has bubbled along since the 1940s, never receiving the accolades we regularly bestow on more modest insights. And it's surprising considering this one has all the elements of a blockbuster. Its watchwords read like an abstract of 50 years' worth of business hot buttons: employee participation, management-labor cooperation, collaborative problem-solving, teamwork, trust, gainsharing, open-book management and servant leadership."

The reasons for the lack of awareness include the following:

- The Scanlon Plan is purposely not trademarked, and so consulting firms and publishers have no economic motive to promote the plan.
- It is challenging to implement and demands capable leaders.
- It is not branded consistently because companies who implement this Plan are encouraged to find a name for it reflecting their values, and others have a natural desire to rebrand it and promote it under their own name.

The authors believe a way to help managers learn about the Scanlon Plan is through case studies of organizations successfully using the Plan. Watermark Credit Union is a midsized financial institution that embraced Scanlon just two years ago. Following is its story.

Watermark Credit Union's Challenge

Watermark Credit Union, then Seattle Telco Federal Credit Union, was chartered in 1938 when the United States was still enmeshed in the Great Depression.

Originally the credit union served King County telephone company employees and their families. Today, Watermark's eight branches serve more than 70,000 members, and Watermark has assets in excess of $450 million. By all measures, this organization has enduring success and has been well managed. Watermark's senior management team and board are convinced that the company must become much larger and better-capitalized to remain competitive in the fast-changing financial services industry. In the last decade, more than 50 percent of banks and credit unions have either merged or closed. Many of these institutions lacked the resources to keep up with technology, provide competitive products and services or meet regulatory requirements. Watermark management believes the credit union must grow to at least $1 billion in assets with a capital ratio of at least 10 percent by 2012. This requires assets to double and an even-faster growth rate in capital. To achieve these goals, productivity must improve (i.e., the expense-to-asset ratio). Reducing this ratio from 4 percent to 3.5 percent, for example, would save more than $2 million annually.

Faced with this challenge, Watermark determined that the Scanlon Principles and Processes would be the best vehicle to accomplish these goals. Executives recognized that a collaborative effort with all employees involved would be required. Because the credit union implemented a Deming philosophy in the prior five years, management believed the organization was well prepared to successfully introduce a Scanlon Plan. Deming's emphasis on teamwork, open communication, process improvement and creating an excellent work culture fit perfectly with the Scanlon Principles.

Watermark's Application of the Scanlon Principles and Process

The Scanlon Principle of Equity requires a company to balance the needs of its key stakeholders. For most Scanlon organizations, key stakeholders include investors, customers and employees. Some Scanlon organizations also include suppliers and their community as key stakeholders. Scanlon philosophy believes change is "a given," and it is a fundamental duty of leadership to help the organization change. Scanlon Principles and Processes can be seen in the philosophy of Watermark, in the process Watermark used to develop its plan and in the final plan it created.

The investor provides the capital for operating the organization and is one of the three key stakeholders. Investors want to receive a fair return on their investment and assurance that their investment is secure. Unlike many private organizations, Watermark does not have stockholders (i.e., investors), but capital is required, and that capital is held by the organization. Watermark's board and senior managers make judgments as to how best to invest that capital.

The second important group of stakeholders is Watermark customers (i.e., credit union members). Even though members have an ownership stake in the success of the organization, their primary interest is having access to quality financial products and services at a competitive price. There are many other forms of financial institutions that want their business.

The third group of stakeholders is employees who want to be paid fairly for their competencies and for the contribution that they make to Watermark. Employees also want a work environment where their contribution is respected, their jobs are secure and opportunities exist to improve their skills and position in the organization.

For an organization to survive in the long run the needs of these stakeholders must be balanced, but to flourish, these needs must be integrated to support all stakeholders. GM and Ford are public examples where this balance was unachieved, resulting in a serious decline for these companies. Until recently, both were known for high wages not only for production workers, but also for management. They also provided good returns for investors. Today, their debt is considered "junk" status. Both failed to serve their customer needs. Quality was not as good as in Japanese auto companies, especially those that practiced lean methods developed by Toyota. Cooperative labor relations (learned from Scanlon) and quality methods (learned from Deming) provided a foundation that allowed the Japanese companies to produce better cars at lower cost, using less space, and with better supplier relations. Ford and GM have made significant gains in their production processes, but their efforts may prove to be too little too late.

The Scanlon philosophy recognizes that productivity improvement and innovation are not the exclusive purview of management, engineering or research and development, but must come from all employees within the organization. However, to tap this potential, employers must provide employees with an opportunity to participate or contribute their ideas. In addition, employees must have the information and competence to participate intelligently, and they must have a compelling reason to participate. Research and more than 60 years of experience indicate that innovation and productivity improvement are direct results of engaging employees, and capturing and implementing their ideas.

Finally, the Scanlon Principles and Processes seize the inevitability of change and transform this inevitability into a competitive advantage. Recognizing that every person is in the process of becoming either more competent or less competent, developing the necessary tools to improve competency is a central mechanism for coping with the changing customer needs, technologies and mandates from society.

Scanlon Plan Fundamental Principles Implemented at Watermark: The EPIC Plan

The Scanlon Plan has four fundamental principles that provide a foundation for living the Scanlon philosophy and creating extraordinary performance outcomes. As is evident from the Watermark case, these principles are specifically adapted to meet organizational needs. The Scanlon Principles are interdependent, and thus, require implementation as a whole rather than step by step or in a specific sequence.

Identity

The "Identity" principle asserts that each organization must have clarity of purpose and offer a unique set of services and products to survive. Each person in the organization must understand the business and how he/she contributes to its success. As a result, management must not only educate employees in the technical requirements of their job, but also help employees understand the wants and needs of customers, the strengths and weaknesses of competitors, and the contribution that investors make to the organization's success. Without this basic organizational knowledge, employees will be unable to make meaningful contributions to the success of the business.

Creating an identity is an educational process beginning with an organization's history, mission and goals, and external mandates under which the business must operate. The identity section of Watermark's plan was developed to explain the credit union's vision and why there was a compelling need to change to reach that vision. This became a tool for helping employees understand the Scanlon Principles and Processes. The plan's Identity section describes:

- The history of the credit union movement and Watermark
- Watermark's business strategy, board of directors and organization structure
- How capital affects the credit union, customers (i.e., members) and employees
- Why Watermark needs to change to survive.

In conjunction with developing the Identity section of the Scanlon Plan, management is committed to creating a transparent business model where financial and operational information is available and is explained to employees.

Participation

Watermark follows a traditional Scanlon Process for obtaining employee input. The system is designed to solicit input and solve problems at the lowest possible level, while sharing and integrating ideas for improving productivity companywide. Two committee types work in tandem to solicit suggestions and facilitate implementation of suggestions. Every department elects a two- to five-member "review committee" responsible for evaluating, responding to and processing suggestions received from its area. Appointed department managers or supervisors lead the review committees. Every Watermark employee is represented by a review committee and is given the opportunity to provide input and influence decisions.

The second type of committee is the "screening committee," which reviews all suggestions forwarded by the review committees. The committee prioritizes, approves and oversees implementation of suggestions that fall outside of the review committees' authority. The screening committee is comprised of a mix of appointed and elected members. Senior management appoints members based on the potential member's expertise; review committees elect members to represent different constituencies throughout Watermark. Both review processes give careful consideration to employees' leadership and technical competence. At no time does the number of appointed members exceed the number of elected members, ensuring employees and management have equitable representation.

The review committee and the screening committee are empowered to form improvement teams that conduct research or implement an approved suggestion. Improvement teams are chartered for a fixed period with a beginning and ending date. Improvement teams practice the, "Plan, Do, Check, Act" cycle, introduced by Deming. The committee that charters the team monitors the team's work.

Suggestions focused on business innovation and improvements are routed through an evaluation process to obtain approval for implementation and to monitor suggestion implementation. Consistent with Deming's management philosophy, Watermark has eliminated all individual incentives. Employees, therefore, do not receive any individual payment for making suggestions. The financial reward (as will be described) results from actual productivity improvement or innovations that provide a financial return for Watermark. Because all employees share in the financial return from suggestions, it is in every employee's best interest to help develop and implement a suggestion regardless of who initially made it.

To facilitate employee involvement, a full-time coordinator position has been added to hold all participants accountable for EPIC Plan responsibilities, to serve as liaison between management and staff, and to facilitate committees and employees in accomplishing EPIC goals.

Equity

Equity is defined as a fair and just return among key stakeholders, i.e., the organization, its members and employees, for the investments they make in the organization. Balancing the interests of these stakeholders is critical to the long-term success of a Scanlon Plan. Equity does not mean "equal" in a Scanlon organization. It would be impossible to create equal returns for each stakeholder because each has a different need and makes a different contribution.

Watermark recognizes the interests of these stakeholders:

- The organization (i.e., investor as represented by the elected board) wants growth and financial soundness, which is represented by capital, to ensure the continued existence of the organization.
- Members (i.e., customers) want competitive prices, quality service and a long-term relationship with the financial institution.
- Employees want job security, competitive wages and benefits, involvement and the opportunity to share in the credit union's profitability (Watermark's EPIC Plan 2005).

Although Scanlon companies use performance measures including labor-cost saving, EVA, profit, earnings and waste reduction, Watermark chose a traditional gainsharing formula which tracks its productivity and rewards employees for improvements. The gainsharing formula is a productivity ratio of operating expenses that employees can affect (e.g., compensation and benefits, supplies, telephone expenses and software/hardware maintenance) divided by gross income (e.g., loan, investment and fee income). Improvement in the gainsharing formula is based on a rolling quarterly average of the three most recent years. All full-time, part-time and temp-to-hire employees are eligible for earned gainsharing bonuses. The gainsharing bonus pool generated by productivity improvement is divided evenly (50 percent for each) between the organization (i.e., the credit union) and employees. Eighty percent of the employees' share is paid out each quarter, with 20 percent held in a reserve account. The payout to individual employees is based on a percentage of their earnings during that quarter. No exempt employee receives more than the highest amount paid to a nonexempt employee.

The reserve account's purpose is to offset any year-end deficit (i.e., productivity is less than the three-year rolling average) and to focus employees on annual performance goals. If at the end of year, a surplus is in the reserve account (company performance improved during the year), the balance is divided among employees, as per the gainsharing formula. If, however, a deficit occurs (overall performance improvement has declined), the loss is deducted from the reserve and the organization writes off any amount not covered. The reserve fund is set to zero for the upcoming year. Everyone at Watermark, including the CEO, is eligible to receive a bonus from Watermark's Scanlon Plan.

The design team invested considerable time developing a performance measure that was reliable and valid, and would provide timely feedback to program participants. Watermark is committed to making financial data available to all employees in an understandable form.

Competency

This principle is based on the belief that continuous improvement requires continuous learning. The Scanlon Principles recognize that operating in a more flexible and proactive work environment requires employees to have broad-based job skills, stronger interpersonal competencies and fundamental understanding of how the business operates (i.e., business literacy). For employees to contribute ideas that have the potential of increasing productivity, they must be more knowledgeable than employees in traditional organizations. Watermark provides numerous development opportunities including tuition assistance, access to an online university, internal training on Scanlon principles and the EPIC Plan, on-the-job training, software skills training, supervisor and management training, Deming training and leadership development.

Implementation

The Scanlon implementation process has proven to be one of the most engaging and effective change processes in business. This process is designed to do the following:
- Adapt the Scanlon Principles and Process to meet specific needs of the company.
- Help employees understand the specific features of the plan.
- Build employee and management commitment to the Scanlon Principles and Processes.
- Build internal competency.
- Develop a written plan documenting how the Scanlon Principles and Processes will be practiced.

The implementation process starts at the top and cascades through the organization. It relies on employee involvement in the development of the plan and multiple secret ballot votes to assess commitment during the design and trial period. As is described in this paper, Watermark followed the implementation process that has been refined and tested in numerous organizations during the last 60 years.

Leadership Exploration and Commitment

The senior leaders at Watermark first learned about the Scanlon Principles and

Processes and the Scanlon Leadership Network through their CEO, Chuck Cockburn, who studied Scanlon at previous organizations. After adopting Deming's Total Quality Management philosophy, instituting the Scanlon Process seemed an obvious next step for supporting the Watermark management team's aggressive growth goals. The leadership team studied Scanlon-related articles and attended a meeting where it met with the president of the Scanlon Leadership Network and a local Scanlon consultant to learn more. In that meeting, the need to pursue a Scanlon Plan became obvious to all, as was made clear through a secret ballot vote. The vote had two questions: (1) is there a compelling need to change, and (2) should Watermark try to develop a Scanlon Plan? The senior team unanimously affirmed both questions. After receiving support from top management, Watermark's CEO drafted Watermark's "mandate for change" to document for management and staff why change is inevitable and should be embraced rather than avoided.

The exploration of the Scanlon Plan was expanded to other management team members. At this stage, the top leadership team, not outside consultants or trainers, explained the Scanlon Principles and the reason that senior management believed that this plan was essential to Watermark's future success. All levels of management had an opportunity to vote to implement a Scanlon Plan. Watermark managers unanimously offered their support and voted to proceed.

Employee Exploration and Commitment

After the management team voted to proceed, the mandate and the Scanlon Principles and Processes were explained to all Watermark employees in small group meetings. Once this information was presented, employees were asked if the implementation process should continue by chartering a design team to draft a Scanlon Plan customized for Watermark. More than 80 percent of all Watermark employees voted to proceed with the implementation process with the understanding that once the plan was designed they would have an opportunity and responsibility to approve the plan.

Proposal Development and Approval

The design team consisted of 14 members: six members appointed by the CEO based on specific expertise needed to develop the plan and eight elected employees who represented a cross section of Watermark employees. For five months, the design team developed its plan, which became known as the "EPIC Plan." This name was chosen in recognition of the four Scanlon Principles and because it symbolized the journey to excellence upon which the company embarked. To keep employees informed of its progress, the design team shared the minutes from each of its meetings. When the plan was completed, it was presented to all employees one week prior to the employee vote. Employees were asked to submit any questions to the design team in the week before the off-site, all-employee conference meeting where voting took place. At the meeting they were provided the opportunity for additional discussion prior to the vote.

On Oct. 10, 2005, employee commitment to the EPIC Plan was demonstrated when more than 85 percent of the employees voted in favor of implementing the plan. The board of directors unanimously approved the plan on Nov. 18, 2005.

Plan Implementation and Review

Upon the EPIC Plan's approval, Watermark began the implementation process, with a set start date of Jan. 1, 2006. As part of implementation, Watermark developed courses to educate employees about the principles and process of the EPIC Plan. This approach ensured that each person was skilled and knowledgeable about the plan. All staff received training on the following:

- Scanlon history and EPIC Principles
- The suggestion system
- An introduction to business literacy.

In addition, all team and committee members received training in the following:

- Active team participation
- Leading and working in teams
- Reviewing and screening committee roles and responsibilities.

For many companies with a Scanlon Plan, a trial period of one to two years is often an integral part of the implementation process. This period allows for the plan to be tested and fine-tuned before a final-approval vote. In any change effort, skeptics often have good reason to be skeptical. In the Scanlon implementation process, skeptics are given a chance to see the plan in action before they vote. In most Scanlon organizations, this is the final vote, where others continue to vote to renew their plans either when major changes are required, or after a scheduled renewal date.

Rather than implement its EPIC Plan for a trial period, Watermark built a review process into its plan. For the first two years, the EPIC Plan is reviewed every six months, and annually thereafter. It is now in the beginning stages of the first review. The suggestion system is processing an average of 29 suggestions per month. A bonus was paid in one of the two quarters that have passed since plan implementation. Training programs have begun to help employees understand the EPIC Plan and become more competent at their jobs. The "fairness committee" (a nonunion grievance procedure) recently was developed and is in the implementation stage.

Challenges and Opportunities

The Scanlon Plan's success is contingent upon the development of a collaborative relationship among three critical stakeholders, i.e., employees, owners and members. Leadership must become more universally shared throughout the organization, with the understanding that leaders serve the organization and the employees who report to them. With this type of stable, caring leadership, Scanlon Plans can produce extraordinary performance and commitment. Watermark is committed to perpetuate this "servant leadership" style of management.

Maintaining employee interest and commitment to the EPIC Plan presents a challenge. Watermark is working out how to prioritize the vast number of suggestions submitted through its EPIC Plan. To help identify the suggestions with the greatest impact, the screening committee developed a prioritization matrix. Queued suggestions are scored in the matrix, and the suggestions with the highest score will have the greatest impact. The matrix is made public so employees are kept informed about why certain suggestions are being worked on rather than others. Senior management realizes that employees need to be kept in the communication loop to maintain a high level of involvement. Additionally, senior leadership remains committed to integrating the Scanlon values and methods into the everyday operations of the business.

In summary, management believes that implementing a Scanlon Plan will enable Watermark to use the untapped knowledge, creativity and resourcefulness of its employees. Employees will participate in making decisions and suggestions. They will learn that they can make a difference, and they will share in the gains realized. Employees will be able to align their goals with the company's goals and view themselves as stakeholders. The productivity increase will result in the lower expense-to-asset-ratio needed for Watermark to achieve its long-term plans for growth and profitability.

First published in *WorldatWork Journal*, Second Quarter 2007

Section IV
Long-Term and Equity Incentives

Chapter 8

Procter & Gamble's Balanced Approach to Long-Term Incentives

Gibson J. Bradley, Procter & Gamble
Blair Jones, Sibson Consulting
Clare Hatfield, Sibson Consulting

The fallout of the 2004 proxy season is a widespread de-emphasis on stock options. In their place, companies are either fully or partially adopting restricted stock or long-term cash plans, perceived to be more politically correct for these times of increased shareholder activism, a volatile economy and the imminent move toward the expensing of options.

A recent survey of early proxy filers for 2003 revealed that nearly one third were increasing the use of restricted stock for executives, in some cases partially or totally substituting restricted stock for options (Meyer, 2003). At lower levels, eligibility for options is also being tightened. Even where options remain, a pullback in participation and opportunities is evident across global locations, as some multinational companies move toward adopting more locally competitive incentive practices in their overseas operations.

There are many reasons for this shift. However, these reasons may not always reflect balanced consideration of both internal and external factors. A 2003-2004 survey of stock option practices of more than 350 U.S. public companies conducted jointly by Sibson Consulting and WorldatWork showed that changes to stock option practices in a period of 18 months have been driven primarily by external concerns relating to effects on shareholders and anticipated accounting changes. Internal considerations relating to attraction, motivation and retention of talent are less likely to be major factors in such decisions. (See Figure 1 on page 118.)

Another recent Sibson Consulting survey of 23 consumer products companies confirmed this trend. More than 70 percent cited option expensing as a reason for their decision to change global equity programs, but only 24 percent cited talent-related concerns (Sibson 2004).

Figure 1
Factors Leading to Change

External Factors	2002		2003	
	Minor Factor	Major Factor	Minor Factor	Major Factor
Concern about the effects of option program on shareholders (dilution, overhang, etc.)	35%	32%	25%	56%
Anticipated accounting changes (e.g., FASB options earning charge)	Not asked in 2002 survey		25%	52%
Effects of public accounting scandals	15%	2%	38%	7%
Internal Factors				
Value of options in attracting and retaining employees	31%	41%	52%	30%
Value of options in motivating employees	30%	42%	50%	31%

However, one has to wonder, if companies were to step back and take the time to pursue a thoughtful approach to long-term incentives (LTIs) rather than rushing to respond to the multitude of environmental forces, then perhaps companies, participants and shareholders could be better served. In some cases, shareholder alignment is deteriorating as organizations appear to lose sight of the goal of LTIs, namely to align employees' interests with the long-term performance of the organization, not to deliver short-term rewards. Taking the longer-term view, options actually may be very suitable for many organizations that currently have depressed share prices but good longer-term prospects for growth.

Therefore, instead of following the "wisdom of the crowd" and pursuing the next big LTI idea, organizations should take a broader perspective and consider the long-term implications of LTI changes on the workforce, the organization and its shareholders. Procter & Gamble (P&G) is one company that bucked the trend of discarding stock options just because other companies have done so. Instead, management considered what role LTIs, and specifically stock options, should play for its people in the future, in the United States and abroad, by using P&G business and people strategies as the basis for a balanced, full-scale review of its global LTI practices.

Taking a Holistic View of LTI Design

The fundamental reason for employing LTIs at any level in any organization is to align the interests of participants and shareholders, with the goal of achieving the long-term business objectives. In the authors' experience, retention is of secondary importance, as top talent can usually be acquired for the right price. The overarching aims for LTIs must be prominent at all times. Failing to base changes to LTI practices firmly on the company's specific business and talent needs, i.e., to attract, retain and motivate employees to achieve the business' objectives, will lead to suboptimization. Therefore, the most effective approach to LTI plan design is to look to the underpinning of the broader shareholder equation, which seeks to balance business and organizational strategy, talent implications, values and principles and financial impact. (See Figure 2). This is the approach that P&G chose to follow: Addressing all these considerations as well as the external competitive landscape allows an organization to consider the myriad factors making up its own, unique situation in order to invest in LTIs for the largest return.

This article also explores how P&G applied this approach in its examination of global LTI practices. The company applied two fundamental compensation principles in guiding the review; to pay competitively and to support the business strategy. To accomplish this, P&G conducted a comprehensive review of its global LTI practices over a period of several months. The review, conducted in partnership with Sibson, encompassed the internal factors shown in Figure 2, balanced against an extensive competitive assessment conducted by another major global consulting firm. The study also included a tailored study of planned future LTI changes at peer companies. This "future scan" ensured current competitive data was interpreted in the context of future market direction.

Figure 2
Key Considerations to Balance in LTI Design

Business and Organizational Strategy	Supportive of the business strategy, organizational principles and culture
Talent Implications	Supports the attraction and retention of required talent
Values and Principles	Fair for both shareholders and for participants
Financial Impact	Aligned with financial responsibility to shareholders

Business and Organizational Strategy
Align Proposed LTI Practices with the Strategic Business Direction

It would be a fair bet that any successful organization has actively adjusted its business strategy to some degree in the last few years as it moved toward new markets, merged or matured from a startup to a more established operation. P&G was no exception. Four years ago, it realigned the business under global brands and sharpened its focus on providing the highest value to customers. In doing so, the company set itself on a path to spark further product innovation and deliver record growth in both established and developing geographies. The strategy has paid off. During the last three years, P&G has delivered shareholder returns of 81 percent, achieved EPS growth of 125 percent and increased net sales from $40 billion to $51 billion.

Considering that the goal of any LTI plan is to lead and/or support the strategy as it changes, strategy should be the key driver and ongoing reference point for any plan changes. An organization must ensure that each area of design and mechanics is linked to the business strategy, as outlined in Figure 3 on page 121.

Linking plan design to the business strategy aligns participants' motivation with the strategic imperatives of the business. Communication about the linkage can then be used to reinforce the strategy and clarify the intent of the LTI vehicles. For example, a young outsourcing business was acquired by an investor who wanted to drive significant growth before an anticipated future exit. The new CEO switched from a cash-based LTI to a phantom equity plan. The CEO reinforced the link between the plan and the business strategy at quarterly communication meetings with staff, explaining the business strategy, the impact of individual performance on the value of the company and resulting rewards from the LTI plan based on performance. The clear communication increased motivation and drove the behavior required to achieve the business strategy by increasing understanding of how the business operated.

Align Proposed LTI Practices with the Organization's Culture, People Strategy and Rewards Strategy

In addition to the business strategy, LTI design must align with the organization's people strategy. Typically the people strategy reflects the business strategy (e.g., an investment bank with an aggressive growth strategy is likely to have a strong performance-oriented culture and rewards framework), but also contains more direct detail about how the organization wants to interact with its employees. Figure 4 on page 122 highlights some of the key questions that help in this analysis.

Figure 3

Aligning Plan Mechanics With Business Strategy

Design Element	LTI Design Considerations
Eligibility	• Is the plan focused on the individuals who will be key to the organization achieving its goals?
Performance Measures	• Are the performance measures of the LTI plan the best quantifiable measures of the key strategic drivers of the business, e.g., if the strategy is to outperform a peer index, are LTI awards linked to the organization's performance against that peer index? • Do the measures send the right messages about what's important?
Performance Period	• Is the performance period aligned with the timeline of the strategy, e.g., for returns to investors, or the achievement of specific business goals?

Target Setting	• Do the LTI plan targets reflect the objectives outlined in the business strategy on the following dimensions:
	  - Relative versus absolute
	  - Versus plan/budget; standard or improvement over prior year
	  - Use of thresholds
	  - Modification of goals midterm.

Award Size/Funding	• Are award opportunities commensurate with the degree of performance increase required to achieve the strategy, i.e., the bigger the required step-change in business performance, the bigger the award opportunity should be for executives who successfully drive that performance?

When P&G revisited its global LTI designs, it carefully examined its people strategy to ensure that the revised LTI plans would reflect the company's "build from within" approach to talent management and the need for mobility of key people across the organization. Management also wanted to maintain the company's stature as an "employer of choice" by offering attractive, competitive opportunities for long-term wealth creation across all global locations.

Talent Implications

Any changes to LTI practice need to reference the people strategy, as outlined

Figure 4

Aligning Plan Design With People Strategy

People-Strategy Considerations	LTI Design Considerations
Talent Profile	• Who are the people that the company needs to achieve its goals? - What is their profile? - Where will they come from? - What skills will they need to be successful?
Culture	• How well do the compensation vehicles align with the culture the organization is trying to perpetuate or create?
Pay Prominence	• What role does pay, and specifically LTIs, play in the people strategy? • Will LTIs increase/decrease in prominence under the proposed arrangements?
Receptivity to Change	• How do participants typically respond to change? • What is the risk of change at this time? • Do participants like/value the current LTI design? - Would participants most likely recommend tweaking or whole-scale redesign?
View of Current Design	• How would a change in the compensation program change the employee value proposition?

above, to ensure that rewards are focused on attracting and retaining those employees who have the most impact on driving the organization's performance.

To assess whether LTI plan changes will cause turnover or demotivate participants, the organization needs to analyze the differences in the rewards deal offered to employee populations under the previous LTI plan versus the proposed plan. Sibson's 2003 Rewards of Work study shows that the reasons people join and stay with a company are broader than compensation alone, including the full range of reward offerings, often referred to as the employee value proposition (EVP). (See Figure 5 on page 123.) In changing LTI practices, a company is potentially changing two key areas of its EVP, direct financial rewards and affiliation. Analysis of the impact on the direct financial component needs to include comparisons of levels of LTIs under the new plan versus the old plan for the population as a whole and for different segments, and also whether the rewards are competitive.

Figure 5
The Employee Value Proposition (EVP)

Affiliation analysis should consider the role of pay in the culture, e.g., whether the LTI plan changes have an impact on affiliation by introducing or removing ownership opportunities.

P&G approached the talent issue by focusing on the impacts on different groups' EVPs, e.g., different salary bands, employee groups and key growth geographies. By conducting a comprehensive analysis of both the overall impact and impact by segment, P&G was able to fully understand the implications of any changes on critical populations.

Values and Principles

An organization's LTI plan must be perceived as fair both for participants and, as increasingly publicized, for shareholders.

For participants, this means ensuring that LTI practices are aligned with the rewards strategy; they are equitable and clearly communicated. The plan should adhere to a clearly articulated rewards strategy, which allows the board and management to make decisions about pay levels and plans within a mutually agreed upon, transparent framework that is operated in the interests of both employees and shareholders. Employees should be aware that the reward strategy is the basis for their compensation levels. Any changes to plans or practices should continue to adhere to the guiding principles that employees understand and expect. For example, as mentioned previously, one of P&G's guiding principles was to pay competitively and fairly across all global locations.

Equity across different areas of the business is a key consideration in global organizations. With LTI participants in more than 70 countries, P&G needed to ensure that its new LTI practices were perceived to be fair worldwide. This involved balancing the need to pay competitively in each location with the need to ensure the right degree of calibration across global P&G teams and the right level of individual recognition. Accordingly, the LTI design team addressed three questions: Will any changes affect the desired degree of employee mobility across countries? Might any changes affect collaboration across business units and geographies? Are top performers and other key individuals receiving rewards commensurate with their contributions?

Both the philosophy and rationale behind the plan and its mechanics should be clearly communicated to participants. Clarity about the rationale behind the plan can increase participants' understanding of the business strategy. Clearly communicating the mechanics of the plan can ensure that employees have line of sight, and understand how their actions impact the business and, in turn, their incentive payouts.

P&G's approach was to cascade communication about the new compensation arrangements and the rationale underlying these changes to the entire organization. (See Figure 6.) The communication goal was to share the facts with employees on an "adult-to-adult" basis, outlining the strategic business rationale for the compensation plans, including the thorough analysis behind the plan design.

Figure 6
A Cascade Communication Process

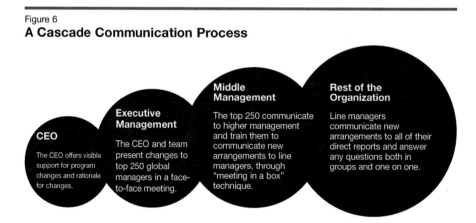

CEO
The CEO offers visible support for program changes and rationale for changes.

Executive Management
The CEO and team present changes to top 250 global managers in a face-to-face meeting.

Middle Management
The top 250 communicate to higher management and train them to communicate new arrangements to line managers, through "meeting in a box" technique.

Rest of the Organization
Line managers communicate new arrangements to all of their direct reports and answer any questions both in groups and one on one.

Communication cascaded from the top of the organization: management had ownership for communicating the implications to its teams. The result was a better understanding of the business strategy that the incentive plans supported and increased buy-in among all levels of employees affected by the new compensation arrangements.

One of the best ways to objectively examine the fairness of LTI plans from a shareholder perspective is to measure how closely historical LTI practices have aligned with shareholder interest by analyzing the relationship between pay and performance. This analysis plots actual historical incentive-payout levels against shareholder returns to analyze the degree to which past total pay levels have aligned with performance (equity with long-term performance, annual incentives with annual performance) and thus are defensible with varied constituencies. The stronger the correlation between shareholder returns and payout levels, the better the alignment with the returns delivered to shareholders and employees. The analysis can help determine whether elements of compensation are appropriately structured to ensure future pay alignment and consistency with the compensation philosophy (e.g., target pay levels, mix of pay components, leverage of variable pay programs).

Financial Impact

Once an organization has begun to narrow down potential LTI vehicles and practices based on the first three considerations, the alternative designs need to be evaluated for financial impact.

Financial impact encompasses the economic costs of the proposed LTI plan, including the impact on cash flow, dilution and unwanted turnover. It also includes the accounting costs and impact on the profit and loss statement (P&L) at year-end. While financial impact is an extremely important consideration, companies too often focus on financial impact to the exclusion of the factors discussed, as the widespread move away from options in response to the anticipated requirement for expensing options attests.

Companies can gauge what is reasonable in terms of financial impact by analyzing what is affordable for the company and for shareholders. The first step is to thoroughly analyze the sensitivity of the proposals under different business-performance scenarios. These might examine possible maximum payouts if performance expectations are exceeded; target total payout cost to the organization; and comparisons of total payouts and the associated dilution with historical and peer LTI expenditures.

P&G fully explored all of the financial implications of different design alternatives, but balanced the findings regarding financial impact with all of the other considerations discussed, which ultimately led to an LTI design that was financially responsible and responsive to the company's business and people needs. This balanced approach was key to the program's ultimate acceptance by participants.

As a final consideration, it is becoming increasingly common for shareholders to have the final say in whether LTI practices are acceptable. Approval can be explicit, e.g., the requirement to gain shareholder approval of all equity grants, or implicit, such as shareholders expressing their opinions about management decisions, including pay practices.

Shareholder acceptance should be discerned as part of the LTI design review and analysis. Most major commercial investors have guidelines that detail their expectations and preferences for the businesses in which they invest. These guidelines may outline views on risk, debt or the key measures of the organization's health that they want to see preserved. They may also contain expectations relative to shareholder dilution through equity plans and other incentive design preferences. By considering investors' views and presenting a business case and financial impact for the plan proposals, an organization can win over its shareholders. Investors are likely to approve a plan that is designed to drive performance improvement and yield tangible results.

Finding the Balance

Balancing all of the considerations that impact LTI design can prove challenging. The following four steps identify the critical success factors for LTI redesign.

1. Create a scorecard to balance all of these considerations and present the overall picture. An effective way to consider all of these factors is to set them out in a summary scorecard. P&G used such a scorecard to measure the potential effectiveness of different design alternatives against each key consideration. (See Figure 7 on page 127.)

2. Be cognizant of any unintended consequences of your chosen design. In addition to examining strategies, talent, values/principles and financial impact separately, organizations must remember that these considerations form a "seesaw" where each area impacts the others. For example, an organization that leans toward saving money from a financial perspective may have implications on the levels that can be offered to specific individuals and, hence, talent strategies. Therefore, the analysis must consider the intersections and impacts of each factor upon another.

3. Explore any variations in impact on different populations. Organizations must consider whether proposed practices affect different levels within the organ-

Figure 7

P&G's Balanced Scorecard for Long-Term Options

Consideration	Key Concerns and Questions
Business and Organizational Strategy	• Does the solution support our business strategy? • Does the solution hinder the company's ability to manage the business globally? • Are we restricting our ability to maintain our "build from within" culture? Are we compromising our goal to be an employer of choice?
Financial Impact	• What are the financial and economic costs in comparison to our current program? • How are changes likely to be viewed by shareholders? Do they align with investor's guidelines?
Talent Implications	• What is the impact of the changes on the employee value proposition for different employee groups across geographies? • How exposed is the business to the loss of key talent, especially in key geographies? • Will the change impair employee mobility across locations? • Might any changes affect collaboration across business units and geographies?
Values and Principles	• Are the changes consistent with the company's values and principles? • Are the changes consistent with the guiding principle of paying competitively and fairly across all global locations? • Do the changes support and reinforce those principles that are the foundation of the compensation strategy?

ization in different ways. If so, the design must reconcile these differences. For global organizations, the issue may hinge on how to achieve their strategic objectives while offering different LTI levels across different geographical areas.

4. Consider longer-term implications and needs. Finally, it is important to consider what is right for the organization, its employees and shareholders, not only in the short-term but also in the immediate future, to minimize the chance that practices will need to be revisited again soon.

Final Thoughts

The current environment represents challenges and opportunities related to LTI design. Companies can position themselves to address the challenges and take advantage of the opportunities by taking a holistic approach to the LTI design process, incorporating not only traditional design considerations such as competitive practices and financial impact but also the internal considerations such as business imperatives, culture and values that make each company unique. In so doing, companies can be more assured of solutions better customized to their specific circumstances, better manage against unintended consequences and lay the stage for a well-supported implementation.

The process P&G engaged in did just this, highlighting the following key success factors:

- Avoid overweighting competitive trends and underweighting your internal business and talent needs in your review and decision processes.
- Use a rigorous and thorough fact base to build confidence and help ensure a given solution makes sense for your company.
- Use systemic review framework to support tough decision-making.
- Bring the CEO and senior leadership team to the point of decision by involving multiple progress reviews.
- The CEO and senior leadership team need to take a visible role in decision-making and rollout to reinforce how any changes support the business and organizational strategy.
- Even in the event of a takeaway, a principled and value-based approach allows for "adult-to-adult" conversations.

Ultimately, P&G came to a design that was aligned with its business and people strategies, responsive to its specific talent needs, consistent with the companies' values and still financially responsible for shareholders. In the end, being true to your company's unique business and talent needs—while staying cognizant of external trends—is the only way to develop effective compensation plans, and if done right, can lead to compensation designs that create competitive advantage.

First published in *WorldatWork Journal*, First Quarter 2005

Chapter 9
Restricted Stock: The Option to Options?
Donna Stettler, Deloitte

The Financial Accounting Standards Board (FASB) unanimously agreed April 21, 2003, that options should be recognized as an expense on the income statement. Subsequently, the FASB has met several times, including Sept. 10, 2003, when it agreed to delay issuance of an exposure draft to the first-quarter 2004, with a final statement of accounting standards expected to be released in third-quarter 2004. So, even though an effective date has not been discussed formally, companies no longer are asking themselves if expensing stock options will be required, but rather, how the rules will be applied and what the potential charge to earnings will be.

Companies and compensation committees already are weighing the benefits provided by stock option programs against the potential charge to earnings. Requiring stock options to be expensed effectively neutralizes the plain vanilla stock option's big advantage (historically, no cost and a tax deduction for the company) and is prompting companies and their compensation committees to consider the appropriateness of incorporating other forms of equity compensation into their long-term incentive programs.

While the looming charge to earnings in and of itself is a formidable factor to reckon with, companies also are facing intense pressure to examine their stock option programs from several other fronts. The public, investor groups and regulators are all voicing loud criticisms of executive compensation packages in the wake of corporate scandals, declining share prices and high-profile bankruptcies. Employees also are taking a more critical look at stock option awards. With so many of their awarded options underwater, they are no longer seen as an attractive compensation tool.

In light of this increased scrutiny and the high probability that companies will be required to expense stock options in the near future, restricted stock has been gaining popularity among compensation committees, institutional investors and corporate executives. Companies like Microsoft, Amazon.com, Cendant, Exxon-Mobil and American Express have announced their intent to use restricted stock more extensively.

The following overview sheds light on why companies are contemplating restricted stock as either a substitute for, or in addition to, stock options for their long-term incentive opportunity and describes the various types of restricted stock available.

Restricted Stock's Somewhat Troubled Past

Restricted stock, in its most common form, awards an employee a number of shares with restrictions placed on the holder's ability to sell or transfer the shares. These restrictions lapse with the passage of time—usually three or four years. After that time, the employee is allowed to hold or sell the shares free and clear of any restrictions. Generally, the only risk to the employee is the possibility that he or she leaves the company prior to the lapse of the restrictions. It is precisely this "guarantee" of value, regardless of stock price performance, that historically has brought heavy criticism down on restricted stock and bolstered the popularity of stock options. Remember, options only deliver value to the employee if the stock price increases from the date of grant, assuming the stock option's exercise price is equal to the fair market value (FMV) at date of grant.

Restricted Stock's More Promising Future

Although restricted stock still has many critics and has been described merely as "pay to stay" or "pay to breathe" compensation, there are several reasons why restricted stock is being considered as an option to stock options:

Known and immediate value. Unlike stock options, whose value is calculated using the somewhat complex Black-Scholes model, the value of restricted stock can be calculated simply by multiplying the current stock price by the number of restricted shares granted. While some argue that the restrictions placed on the shares should be taken into account, there is little question by all parties that the restricted stock has value at time of grant. And, unlike an option, restricted stock retains some value even if the stock price declines after date of grant.

For example, if an employee received restricted stock with a $15 FMV, he or she owns something with some immediate value. Even if the stock price falls to $10, the employee's award still has a $10 value. If the employee received stock options with an exercise price of $15 and the stock price drops to $10, the options are worthless and provide zero value.

Undisputed earnings impact. For financial statement purposes, the expense associated with restricted stock is straightforward and measured at fair value at grant date. The fair value of restricted stock is measured by the number of shares awarded multiplied by the FMV of the stock at the time of grant. In contrast, most companies currently base the stock option expense calculation on the Black-Scholes methodology, even though, at the time the article was written, the FASB had not finalized the valuation methodology used to calculate the expense. The Black-Scholes calculation requires the input of several variables, some of which the company has flexibility in selecting (such as the assumed expected life of an option). This flexibility may result in inconsistent cost calculations applied across companies. Thus, the use of restricted stock would seem to result in greater equity compensation cost to all parties and more accurate intercompany comparisons.

Number of shares required. Due to its greater per-unit value, restricted stock requires fewer shares than stock options to deliver long-term incentive opportunity to employees. This makes restricted stock very attractive to companies that are either running out of shares in their equity reserve or already have very high overhang (potential shareholder dilution from equity-based grants to employees).

Consider the case in which a company would like to provide an executive with $100,000 in long-term incentive opportunity. The impact on the shares reserved for use in a shareholder-approved equity plan would vary based on the strategy used to deliver this long-term incentive opportunity value. Assuming the current stock price is $10 and there is a Black-Scholes value of 45 percent of FMV, or $4.50, the company would need to grant 22,222 stock options ($100,000 divided by $4.50). However, given the same facts, the company would only need to grant 10,000 shares ($100,000 divided by $10) of restricted stock. So, for companies reaching their equity reserve ceilings, restricted stock awards may extend the life of company equity pools.

If the awarded restricted stock carries no risk of forfeiture other than continued service over time, then the dollar grant value could be reduced from $100,000 to reflect the reduced risk and guaranteed value. Reducing the grant value from $100,000 to, say, $70,000, would require the company to grant only 7,000 shares ($70,000 divided by $10).

Real stock ownership. Restricted stock creates real stock ownership at the grant date. Conversely, stock options only create ownership at exercise—often several years after the option is awarded. Even though recipients may not sell or transfer their awarded restricted shares until the restrictions lapse, they still own the shares and are encouraged to think and act as owners immediately at grant date. Contrast this with stock options: At the grant date, employees receive only the opportunity to exercise the option and receive the shares at some future date. Psychologically, restricted stock provides employees with a greater feeling of ownership than stock options and also is a better motivator of positive long-term behavior.

Retention. Despite the negative connotation surrounding the phrase "pay to stay," this may be precisely what certain companies require. Restricted stock provides companies with a powerful retention incentive, especially during periods of business and/or economic uncertainty when stock prices are falling and stock options may be underwater. Remember, restricted stock always will have some value, even in situations of slow or negative stock price movement. As mentioned, restricted stock generally is granted with the vesting based on a number of years. So, while all an employee needs to do is remain with the company for a number of years to receive full benefits of the award, this may be the company's simple goal.

With all of its positive attributes, companies can no longer avoid considering restricted stock as an option to stock options simply because of a generalized black mark placed by certain critics. While it is true that restricted stock without performance criteria can be considered "pay to stay," this article demonstrates that more than one type of restricted stock exists, and companies need only look to their business needs and objectives to determine which type is right for them.

The Many Types of Restricted Stock

With all of the attention given to time-based restricted stock, many might not know that more than one type of restricted stock exists. Companies have the choice and flexibility of basing the vesting of restricted stock on employees remaining with the company for a certain number of years, or linking the granting and vesting with achievement of one or more pre-established goals. There are five types of restricted stock strategies:

- Time vested
- Performance accelerated
- Performance vested
- Performance granted
- Restricted stock units (RSUs).

Time-Vested Restricted Stock

This is the most common form of restricted stock. As the name implies, these shares vest based solely on the passage of time, from the possibility that the recipient may leave the company prior to the shares vesting. For example, MyCo grants 5,000 shares of restricted stock to Mary with a current FMV of $23 per share. All

Pros and Cons of Time-Vested Restricted Stock
- High perceived value to employee
- May be perceived as pay for stay by institutional investors
- Strong retention incentive, especially during periods of uncertainty
- Does not require a minimum level of performance for participant to receive value
- Easily understood and administered
- Undisputed value for P&L purposes

of the 5,000 shares vest at the end of three years (i.e., cliff vest). In this example, Mary will receive her 5,000 shares three years from now, assuming she remains employed with MyCo.

Time-vested restricted stock delivers some value upon vesting, regardless of company, individual or stock price performance. This is why time-based restricted stock receives the most criticism as being merely pay for stay versus pay for performance. Some companies further strengthen the retentive value of time-vested restricted stock by imposing stock-retention requirements on the restricted shares until retirement.

Performance-accelerated Restricted Stock

Like the time-vested strategy described above, these shares also generally vest after a specific number of years; however, vesting may be accelerated if the company achieves certain pre-established goals. Because the vesting of the shares may be accelerated, the original vesting is usually longer (e.g., seven years), rather than the three to four years typically attached to time-vested restricted stock. For example, MyCo grants 5,000 shares of restricted stock to Mary with a current FMV of $23 per share. The 5,000 shares vest at the end of seven years, but vesting may

Pros and Cons of Performance-accelerated Restricted Stock
- High perceived value to employee
- May be perceived as pay for stay
- Significant handcuff
- Does not require a minimum level of performance for participant to ultimately receive value
- Ties compensation to pre-established performance goals
- Requires establishment of long-term performance goals
- Undisputed value for P&L purposes
- Lower perceived value; therefore, lower motivational value than time-vested stock
- More difficult to understand

be accelerated if MyCo's earnings per share reaches $2.50.

So, with performance-accelerated restricted stock, if performance goals are not achieved, participants will receive their shares at the end of the original vesting period (e.g., seven years), with the only requirement being that they remain employed with MyCo. From a company and shareholder perspective, there is at least a longer time required for the participant to remain employed (higher retention value than the typical three-year cliff vesting of time-vested restricted stock). There also is stronger alignment with shareholders by accelerating vesting based on achieving a pre-established goal.

Performance-Vested Restricted Stock

In this case, shares only vest if the company achieves certain pre-established goals. Unlike the time-vested and performance-accelerated restricted stock strategies described above, performance-vested restricted stock is not guaranteed to vest at some established point in time. So, for example, Mary's 5,000 shares will vest in five years if earnings per share (EPS) is $2.50; four years if EPS is $2.60; or three years based on an EPS of $2.70. If MyCo does not achieve an EPS of at least $2.50

Pros and Cons of Performance-vested Restricted Stock
- Vesting only occurs if company achieves pre-established goals
- Lower perceived value; therefore, lower motivational value than time-vested stock
- Ties compensation to stock price appreciation and pre-established performance goals
- Much more volatile impact on earnings than time-vested because the final value (charge) of the award is based on the number of shares earned and the stock price at the end of the performance period
- Links compensation to the creation of shareholder value; requires establishment of long-term performance goals
- Less dilutive than time-vested restricted stock
- More difficult to understand

within five years from date of grant, Mary's 5,000 shares of restricted stock will never vest. Performance-vested shares, therefore, provide the strongest alignment yet with shareholders' interests.

Performance-Granted Restricted Stock

Shares are granted based on the attainment of certain pre-established goals. The shares awarded often vest based on the passage of time. Like the performance-vested shares, the performance-granted shares are based on performance and,

Pros and Cons of Performance-Granted Stock
- Stock only granted for achievement of pre-established goals
- Lower perceived value; therefore, lower motivational value than time- and performance-vested stock
- Ties compensation to stock price appreciation and the attainment of pre-established performance goals
- Requires establishment of long-term performance goals
- Links compensation to the creation of shareholder value
- More difficult to understand
- May be less dilutive than time- or performance-vested restricted stock

therefore, also provide a strong alignment with the interests of shareholders. Using our example, at the end of, say, a three-year period, Mary could receive 3,000 shares of restricted stock if MyCo's EPS is $2.50, or receive 4,000 shares if EPS is $2.60 or 5,000 shares if EPS is $2.70. Once Mary has received the appropriate number of restricted shares based on EPS performance, the link of compensation to shareholder value creation could be further strengthened by applying time-based vesting restrictions on the earned shares.

Restricted Stock Units (RSUs)

Restricted stock units (RSUs) are an unfunded company promise to deliver shares to the participant at a future date; the value of an RSU is equivalent to the value of a company share. Essentially, RSUs may be substituted for actual shares of company stock in any of the restricted stock types described above. For example,

Pros and Cons of Restricted Stock Units (RSUs)
- Ability for participant to defer taxation, thereby eliminating the need to sell shares or borrow to cover the taxes
- If company becomes insolvent, deferred units are worthless and so is the stock
- Allows participant to maintain full number of shares for a longer period of time because a portion of the award does not need to be sold to cover taxes upon vesting
- Risk that the ordinary income tax rates will increase substantially over the deferral period
- Links compensation to the creation of shareholder value
- No ability to sell units during deferral period (i.e., no liquidity)
- Strengthens link to shareholders as participants are unvested for a longer period of time

instead of granting 5,000 shares of restricted stock to Mary that vest in three years, MyCo could grant Mary 5,000 RSUs that vest in three years. The tax consequences, however, can be very different. Restricted stockholders recognize tax at the time the restrictions lapse. For RSUs, however, the recognition of taxable income does not occur until the shares are received. And most holders of RSUs elect deferral of payment (must be in company stock) beyond the scheduled vesting date, such as retirement.

To illustrate, assume Mary has received 5,000 shares of restricted stock that vest on Jan. 1, 2006. Mary has little control over the date the restrictions lapse and will recognize ordinary income tax on Jan. 1, 2006. Alternatively, if Mary were a senior executive who wants to defer owning the stock and paying the taxes to beyond 2006, RSUs would be the appropriate strategy. The company would grant 5,000 RSUs to Mary, which are scheduled to vest three years later in 2006, and will be distributed to Mary at retirement. Now, even though the original restrictions will lapse in 2006, taxes will not be due until the RSUs are received at retirement.

RSUs provide flexibility to defer taxation beyond the vesting date without extending the restrictions—something that would probably not be acceptable to all participants, due to the continued risk of forfeiture. See "Accounting and Taxation of Restricted Stock" for further discussion of the tax implications of RSUs, as well as the tax and accounting implications of each of the restricted stock types discussed in this article.

What Type of Restricted Stock Is Right for Your Company?

This article has presented five types of restricted stock strategies, each of which can be designed to fit your company's purposes. The ideal restricted stock alternative depends on your individual company's objectives. Companies will, of course, prioritize their objectives based on the current economic and industry environments. Consider Company A, which may be in a turnaround situation and needs to ensure retention of key employees for a period of time. Here, time-vested restricted stock may be the best choice. This strategy will provide employees with a known value that they will only realize if they remain with Company A for three years. Company B may be introducing a new product line and wishes to encourage senior executives to grow and develop the products. Company B could grant executives performance-vested shares that will vest based on achievement of growth and profitability goals.

Figure 1 on page 138 illustrates how each of the different types of restricted

Accounting and Taxation of Restricted Stock

Accounting. The forced adoption of SFAS 123, Accounting for Stock-Based Compensation, would not only put stock options on a more equal footing with other equity alternatives, but also would neutralize most of the accounting differences among the various types of restricted stock awards. Under APB 25, Accounting for Stock Issued to Employees, and SFAS 123, time-vested, performance-accelerated and performance-granted restricted stock are accounted for in the same manner. These types of restricted stock are subject to "fixed" plan accounting, which means that the FMV of the shares on the grant date is amortized over the applicable service (vesting) period.

If the vesting of the shares is tied to performance, "variable" accounting applies under APB 25, and the cost is marked to market each quarter until vesting. Thus, the total cumulative charge will be based on the value of the shares at the vesting date. Under SFAS 123, however, the value for a performance-based award is estimated at grant based on management's expectations of the number of shares that will vest. The total amount of expense recognized is based on the number of shares that ultimately vest, but the value of the shares at the date of grant is utilized and not adjusted with changes in the market.

Dividends paid in cash on stock, whether restricted or not, are charged to retained earnings.

Tax. Because the shares are subject to significant restrictions, the tax code provides that the employee is required to recognize income only when the restrictions lapse, unless an IRC Section 83(b) election is made, which accelerates taxation to the date of grant. The amount of income recognized is equal to the FMV of the shares on the vesting date, or grant date under the 83(b) scenario. Dividends paid on restricted stock are treated like compensation until the restrictions lapse. The tax consequences of the various types of restricted stock are fairly straightforward but offer very little flexibility in terms of timing.

RSUs are taxed for federal income taxes (and self-employment taxes, for those independent contractors with awards) when they are distributed, not at vesting; FICA is due at the vest date. The amount of compensation is equal to the FMV of the shares on the distribution date. Any dividends paid during the deferral period are considered wages and are subject to withholding (similar to restricted stock). Acceleration of taxation to date of grant under IRC Section 83(b) is not available for RSUs because they are not considered property for tax purposes.

stock meets certain typical high-level corporate objectives for long-term incentives. It does not include RSUs because they may be substituted for any type of restricted stock.

Figure 1

How Restricted Stock Meets Corporate Objectives

	Type of Restricted Stock		
Key Objective	**Time Vested**	**Performance Vested/Granted**	**Performance Accelerated**
Retention	Fully Meets Objective	Partially Meets Objective	Partially Meets Objective
Link pay to performance	Does Not Meet Objective	Fully Meets Objective	Partially Meets Objective
Minimize P&L Impact–APB 25	Partially Meets Objective	Does Not Meet Objective	Partially Meets Objective
Minimize P&L Impact–SFAS 123	Partially Meets Objective	Partially Meets Objective	Partially Meets Objective
Tax efficient	Fully Meets Objective	Fully Meets Objective	Fully Meets Objective
Minimize dilution/ share usage	Fully Meets Objective	Partially Meets Objective	Fully Meets Objective

● Fully Meets Objective ● Partially Meets Objective ● Does Not Meet Objective

Awarding Restricted Stock in Lieu of Stock Options

The main question is: How much? If a company previously granted an employee $100,000 of long-term incentive opportunity in stock options, should that employee now receive $100,000 of restricted stock? The answer depends on the type of restricted stock involved.

If a company awards nonperformance-based restricted stock to replace some or all of the stock option-based, long-term incentive opportunity, it would not be appropriate to award the same grant date value for several reasons:

- Time-vested restricted stock has immediate value and a relatively low risk of becoming worthless.
- Stock options only provide value if the stock price increases. Restricted stock is valuable, to some degree, even if the stock price stays flat or drops.
- Stock options often require a much longer time horizon than restricted stock (e.g., three to seven years depending on stock price appreciation) to provide comparable value to restricted stock.

Companies, therefore, must balance the downside protection and certain "guarantee" of value provided by nonperformance-based restricted stock with the greater upside potential and riskiness associated with stock options.

Figure 2 illustrates the "downside protection zone" (years 0 to 3) provided by restricted stock and the greater upside opportunity (years 3 to exercise) provided by stock options. This illustration is based on granting 1,000 stock options in year 0, versus 300 shares of restricted stock with a current FMV of $30 and a compounded annual growth rate (CAGR) of 12 percent. Based on these assumptions, the grant of 300 shares of restricted stock yields more value than the 1,000 stock option grant until approximately year 3. After that "break even" point, the 1,000 stock-options provide an increasingly higher value due to the higher number of equity units awarded (1,000 versus 300).

Figure 2 also indicates that some amount of discount to the award value is required to offset the downside protection value provided by restricted stock. This protection only exists with nonperformance-based restricted stock. In determining the size of the award, companies must reflect on the guarantee/risk balance between restricted stock and stock options, as well as between the various types of restricted stock. Figure 3 on page 140 illustrates the varying degree of risk, as perceived by the employee, associated with each equity type.

Awards of performance-vested or performance-granted restricted stock would not need to be discounted for the "guaranteed" value because the employee is not guaranteed to receive the award, and this type of equity has an associated risk element similar to stock options. If time-vested or performance-accelerated

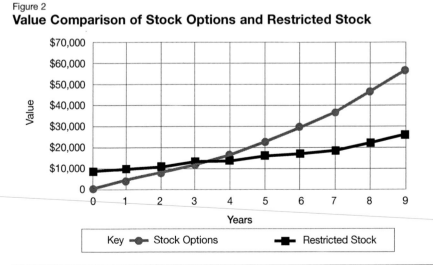

Figure 2
Value Comparison of Stock Options and Restricted Stock

Figure 3
Employees' Perception of Risk

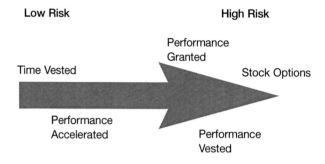

restricted stock were used, however, it would not be appropriate to award the same grant date value as under stock options. Rather, the value should be discounted to reflect the guarantee of value provided by these restricted stock strategies.

Restricted Stock and Stock Options—Working Together

With so many publicly traded companies granting so many stock options for so many years to so many people, it is unrealistic to think that stock option programs will be abandoned completely. Of those companies already granting or considering granting restricted stock, very few are utilizing solely restricted stock for their long-term incentive. Most companies still see value in using stock options and are awarding approximately 25 percent to 50 percent of the long-term incentive opportunity in restricted stock, with the balance of the opportunity awarded in stock options. Stock options will remain an important part of LTI programs for a long time to come. While it is true that companies and their compensation committees are reviewing the various restricted stock strategies, it is more as a supplement to their existing stock options programs, rather than a substitute.

Companies contemplating adopting a restricted stock program should consider performance-granted or performance-vested restricted stock as they more closely align the interests of shareholders and executives than time-vested strategies and eliminate the pay-to-stay connotation broadly applied to restricted stock.

First published in *WorldatWork Journal*, First Quarter 2004

Chapter 10
Who Moved My Options?
Stéphane Lebeau, Akamai Technologies Inc.
Robert Todd, Akamai Technologies Inc.

Editor's note: The co-authors wish to recognize the editorial contribution of Christian Laniel, a senior adviser in compensation for Canadian National who specializes in the design of compensation and incentive programs.

Restricted stock and restricted stock units (RSUs) are hot topics, made more salient by a harsh economic environment and the almost certain guarantee that public companies will expense options. The bellwether Microsoft, among others, reinforced this trend by announcing that it would abandon stock options in favor of restricted stock for its broad-based equity programs.

Restricted stock is a major shift from the 1990s, when options were the rage and employees willingly would trade their cash bonuses for options. Some even accepted a reduced salary. Back then, nonpublicly traded entities went a step further by implementing phantom stock plans to attract talented employees and retain them.

What's happening? Is equity-based compensation radically changing? Are options becoming obsolete as restricted stock takes center stage?

In the best-selling book *Who Moved My Cheese?* by Spencer Johnson, M.D., cheese (options) is running out, and the time has come for the mice to look for a new food supply (equity compensation). In reality, many companies have been quick to start their journey back into the equity maze, searching for fresh sources of equity compensation. Who can blame them? Who wants to be likened to Hem, one of the book's "littlepeople" who denies and resists environmental change only to risk starvation?

Adaptation is key to survival, but many companies enter the maze blindly following the leader to a new source of equity compensation without evaluating their own needs. The source in this case, restricted stock (or its close cousin, the RSU), may prove hard to digest. The shift to exclusive restricted stock use may be as unhealthy as the unilateral use of stock options in the past. Can this one source meet everyone's needs?

This article guides readers through the maze of equity-based compensation by exploring equity use at organizations in three distinct development phases: startup, in transition and mature. Equity choices from employees' perspectives will be examined, followed by key compensation principles to determine the appropriate equity vehicle.

Startup Phase

Startups are fragile and require large capital investments in the form of public offerings, warrants, debt, preferred stock and partnerships. Their need to generate cash to fund the business plan through operating and investment activity is paramount. Corporate tax deductions generally are not of utmost concern, as most companies in their infancy do not generate income. Because investors focus on growing sales, increasing market shares and surviving until the next cash infusion, earnings per share (EPS) is a long-term goal. Startups also have high price volatility due to thin trading volume, high risk of failure and lack of proven success.

Options Ideal for Startup Phase

Stock options generate cash upon exercise to help fund the business plan. Using equity preserves working capital for the startup, which can be used for other operating activities. The exercise of an option triggers a capital investment in the company (equal to the option strike price) and a transfer of capital to the employee (compensation) by the marketplace. While an accounting charge to earnings may apply under SFAS 123, the effect on cash flow to the company is positive after payment of the option strike price and the subsequent corporate tax deduction. SFAS 123 provides rules for estimating a fair value for stock-based employee compensation using Black-Scholes or other prescribed valuation methods.

Stock options can be granted in larger numbers than restricted stock because their lower theoretical value allows the company to grant more options than corresponding shares of restricted stock, providing substantial upside for the employee. For this reason, startup companies often have a relatively high overhang, but the benefit of using larger grants to attract and retain talent outweighs the potential dilution impact. Overhang is defined as outstanding stock options and warrants, plus the remaining options available to be granted, divided by the total shares outstanding.

The startup company's goal of retaining and motivating employees may be compromised, however, if the security's market value falls below the strike price of the options. This problem has led many companies to think creatively in dealing with their underwater options.

Restricted Stock Not Well-Suited for Startup Phase

Restricted stock is issued to employees at a minimal price, such as $0.01 per share, so it generates a compensation expense on issuance under APB 25 and SFAS 123. (APB 25 provides for the intrinsic-value expense recognition of stock-based employee compensation.) This means that restricted stock does not generate cash like stock options, and it adds to the startup's loss (numerator) on issuance that will be diluted only when the restrictions lapse when the company is in a loss situation. If options are granted at fair market value (FMV), the expense is zero because the difference between the strike price and the FMV is zero.

For the company and the employee, restricted stock can be more difficult to comprehend than stock options, starting with the possible cumbersome obligation for the employee to write a check for at least $0.01 per share to the company for "consideration" of the shares. The restricted stock recipient also has 30 days from the date of grant to file an 83b tax election with the IRS, which represents a very complex and risky tax-planning decision. The impact for the employee of such a decision is explored in more detail in the section titled "The Employee Perspective," page 147.

If the employee forgoes the 83b election, the company needs to decide "how" the employee will pay the tax obligation under the lapse of restrictions. Startups generally don't have cash reserves or positive shareholder equity, so they cannot use internal treasury transactions to help facilitate the payment of the employee's tax liability. These companies must rely on market makers to help facilitate the sale of a portion of these restricted shares to generate cash to pay the withholding taxes due as the restrictions lapse.

Price volatility is a cause of concern with restricted stock use in this development stage. If the startup's securities are thinly traded on the market, the sale of a share lot for withholding purposes could be detrimental to the price. Additionally, a low price coupled with a small amount of share vesting and brokerage fees could cause the value of the award to the employee to be greatly reduced.

Restricted stock units (RSUs) or phantom stock will not increase the number of shares outstanding until issuance, but they face the same tax withholding and expense issues as restricted stock awards and may not be appropriate for this development stage.

In-transition Phase

Companies moving from startup to mature often have to perform a difficult balancing act. On one hand, they must conserve cash and show steady and growing positive cash flow to demonstrate the health of their business plan. On the other hand, they must pay close attention to shares outstanding and the impact on EPS growth as the business reaches profitability and the equity vehicles used to compensate employees and management directly impact both of these financial measures.

Stock Options Preferable for In-Transition Phase

Stock options are preferable for the in-transition phase for the same reasons noted under the startup period. There is an element of stock options, however, that takes on its full importance in the transition phase. Stock options generate cash upon exercise that contributes to funding the business plan without diluting EPS on issuance. Overhang, potential dilution of shareholder's equity and other market forces often limit this source of capital.

At this stage, the company may want to consider granting nonqualified versus incentive stock options (ISOs) because ISOs do not generate an automatic tax deduction for the company and such deductions grow in importance as the company reaches profitability. The company can assure a tax deduction by issuing nonqualified options because those options are taxed on the date of exercise and the spread between the exercise price and market price is automatically added to the employee's wages. With ISOs, the company must trust the employee to report back the disqualifying disposition. The company will receive no tax deduction if the ISO remains qualified, but will still benefit from the cash generated by payment of the exercise price.

Restricted Stock: Akin to Cash-funded Vehicles

The stock price may be less volatile in the in-transition phase than in the startup phase, and trading volume should be higher, assuming the company is showing steady growth and a stronger balance sheet. The more predictable the price movement and volume become, the more attractive restricted stock appears for retention purposes. The use of restricted stock, like options, conserves cash by substitution. Employees sometimes are paid less salary or receive equity grants in lieu of cash bonuses. Restricted stock is attractive to employees because the risk of value loss is lower. As long as the security is publicly traded, the security always will be worth something.

Restricted stock is more akin to cash-funded programs than other equity vehicles for several reasons. Employees cannot defer taxation because they cannot choose when the restrictions will lapse. The lapse of restrictions is like the automatic exercise of nonqualified stock options from the employee's point of view. The corporate expense structure is very similar to cash programs from an accounting perspective, but there is a double hit to shareholders. Not only do shareholders fund the program through cash purchase of the shares, but these additional shares also dilute the percentage of their ownership interest. The company presumably benefits by saving the "cash" that would have been spent on compensation, but unlike options, the company will not receive additional cash. The balancing act continues with the company's need to increase free cash flow without sacrificing steady EPS growth.

In contrast, RSUs or phantom stock will not increase the number of shares outstanding until issuance. Because of this deferral and the resulting ability for a company to better manage the full financial impact at a later date, RSUs may be more appropriate for this development stage than pure restricted stock. RSUs are very similar to nonqualified stock options except for the timing of the receipt of shares. An RSU holder can defer receipt or vesting of the shares for a specified predetermined period of time, but this feature is not common in broad-based distributions. Imagine tracking 10,000 employees and their deferral notices. Pass the smelling salts!

Mature Phase

Mature-stage companies have a different set of issues than startup and in-transition companies. Their main issues are growth and relative stock price appreciation. A company that is mature is more likely to have positive EPS and positive cash flow. Mature companies are described as predictable, stable and safer than less seasoned companies. These companies are the cruise liners in the capital ocean. They are hard to maneuver, slow and steady, difficult to sink and stable. They also are less thrilling, as a matter of taste, than the sexy speedboat startups or in-transition pleasure boats, because ballistic growth and catastrophic drops in stock price are more unlikely.

The mature company offers its investors preservation of capital, but lower risk translates to lower expected reward. However, the mature company can transfer wealth to employees and shareholders in many ways. Excess cash reserves can buy shares on the open market, and the company can either retire the shares or use them to fund employee equity programs. If the company retires the shares, shares outstanding decrease and ownership interests of current shareholders increase. There also would be fewer shares to divide a dividend payment. If the company funds the employee equity programs with these shares rather than issuing new shares, the number of shares outstanding will stay the same rather than increasing, which also benefits shareholders.

Stock Options Lose Appeal for Mature Companies

Stock options are attractive because they offer more leverage. Companies can grant employees a higher number of options than restricted stock at an equivalent dollar value because each option's cost is lower due to the risk of the stock's market price falling below the option's strike price (out of the money). They also communicate a better message to shareholders that employees' wealth will be created in proportion to the company's success. On the flip side, stock options lose some of their appeal because of the lower potential stock price appreciation associated with mature companies, and the increasing shareholders' concerns over high overhang and dilution.

Restricted Stock and RSUs Are Preferable in Mature Phase

When issuing restricted stock, the company could finance the employee tax withholding through treasury transactions to reduce the price risk and broker's fees inherent in open market transactions. The company would simply buy the withholding shares directly with excess cash and place the net shares in the employees' accounts. The cash then would fund the withholding obligation. This is a definite advantage for mature companies with cash and positive shareholder's equity over their rivals with less capital resources.

Mature companies can provide larger salaries and richer benefits to attract employees. Established companies often are more stable and offer greater job security. The downside to security and muted risk is the fact that the stock price may not be as exciting. Restricted stock is ideal for employees at mature companies, because even if the price does not move, it is still worth something. If the company pays dividends, restricted stock can be another cash transfer mechanism to the employee. Restricted stock often has voting rights that can help management when seeking shareholder approval. Mature companies may value cash or restricted stock incentives more highly than options because of these vehicles' lower sensitivity to changes in market price.

The company also could issue RSUs to avoid increasing dilution; this would not entitle the employee to dividends or voting rights. The employee would not need to write a check for the consideration of the shares and, in some cases, the shares could be deposited upon vesting in a "net" transaction that would avoid brokerage commission and open market transactions to satisfy tax-withholding requirements. This considerably lessens the administrative burden for both the employee and the company. RSUs also could be settled in the form of cash in lieu of shares to avoid the dilutive effect of share issuance.

The Employee Perspective

Employees know that equity can provide an additional opportunity to participate in the rewards of the business. Depending on the employees' risk tolerance, they will readily accept positions that pay a combination of cash and equity in favor of similar positions at competing firms that rely solely on cash compensation. The more risk-tolerant people—those with lower security needs—tend to be at startups and in-transition companies.

In mature companies, employees generally regard equity as gravy. The main entrée (salary) pays the bills; the side dishes are retirement savings benefits, health insurance, vacation time, etc. The employee loves gravy, but does not count on it for sustenance. This is an important demographic distinction, and one may wonder if these organizations are competing for the same talent after all.

In all business-development phases, equity does the following:

- Provides employees with an additional opportunity to participate in the rewards of the business
- Aligns employees' hopes and desires more closely with shareholders
- Encourages a win-win situation

Options draw a line in the sand that says: "If you help move the price above this line, you will be rewarded. But if the price goes below this line, you will receive nothing." Restricted stock draws a line in the sand that says, "If you help move the price above this line, you will be rewarded. And if the price drops below this line, you will still receive something for your effort." Employees would certainly prefer the less risky restricted stock on face value, but restricted stock has its own set of complexities.

The average employee does not comprehend the complicated tax scenarios inherent in each equity vehicle. Many don't realize that restricted stock requires an immediate tax-planning decision. The 83b election allows employees to demonstrate their confidence in the future stock price appreciation by making an advance tax payment within 30 days of issuance to the IRS based on FMV on the date of grant. This election is the only opportunity employees have to influence the timing of their tax event. The risks in making the election are twofold. First, that they will terminate employment and never receive the "property" for which they prepaid taxes. Second, that the FMV of the property will drop, causing them to pay more taxes upfront. There is no IRS refund mechanism.

This tax decision can affect the potential value of the shares awarded. If there is price appreciation and the employee remains employed, the 83b election offers substantial benefits. If the company wants to remove the risk of this decision from the employee, it can issue restricted stock units instead. RSUs are not 83b eligible, but the employee would lose the possibility of voting and dividend rights.

The employee cannot control the timing of taxation for restricted stock except by making an 83b election. The employee, however, can control the timing of income recognition for stock options. This is an important equity vehicle feature of options that may be overlooked by both professionals and novices. The delivery of value to the employee is greatly influenced by the tax treatment of each type of award.

Figure 1 on page 149 shows the value of a $10,000 award and the tax effects for different equity vehicles. We assumed a Black-Scholes adjusted value of $3.25 for stock options issued at a FMV strike price of $5. Restricted stock was issued at $0.01 per share at that time. To illustrate what happens when the stock price falls below the strike price, we also assumed a two-year decline in the stock price from $5 to $3, followed by a gradual climb in value.

The value to the employee drops significantly when no 83b election is made. In the first two years, the forfeiture risk, coupled with the declining stock price probably, would cause the employee some added stress. The advance tax payment can be a significant investment for many employees. The retentive value of the restricted stock ends when it becomes 100-percent vested. But, assuming the employee holds onto the net shares, the stock options have twice the value of non-83b restricted stock, with the gap widening with each year's rise in price. Compensation professionals can appreciate the retentive advantage of options and the additional leverage they can provide over restricted stock granted at an equivalent value.

Tax filings can be an additional sticking point for employees who will need to track the "basis" in the shares left over from each restricted stock lapse. When they file their taxes, they will report the "tax" sale in section D of their Form 1040. When they sell the remaining shares, they will need the basis to calculate the capital gain on the sale for each lot. If the restricted stock vests frequently over the course of the year, this can add up to several lines of activity for tax selling and then again for any employee-directed sales. This is confusing, and most employees probably will require professional tax advice.

Determining the Appropriate Equity Vehicle

The first step in identifying the appropriate equity vehicle is determining the organization's needs. Organizations develop and change over time. Figure 2 on page 150 summarizes company sensitivities in each of the development phases.

The second step in identifying the most appropriate choice is understanding the characteristics of each available equity vehicle. (See Figure 3 on page 150.) Stock

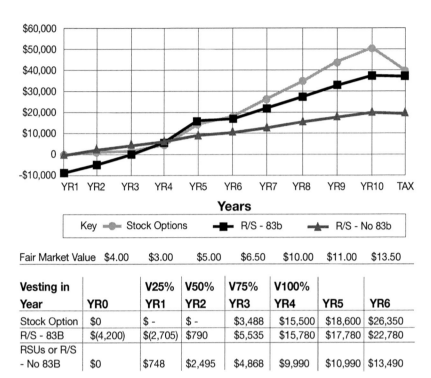

Figure 1

Potential Value of $10K Award for Various Equity Vehicles

Fair Market Value	$4.00		$3.00	$5.00	$6.50	$10.00	$11.00	$13.50

Vesting in		V25%	V50%	V75%	V100%		
Year	YR0	YR1	YR2	YR3	YR4	YR5	YR6
Stock Option	$0	$ -	$ -	$3,488	$15,500	$18,600	$26,350
R/S - 83B	$(4,200)	$(2,705)	$790	$5,535	$15,780	$17,780	$22,780
RSUs or R/S - No 83B	$0	$748	$2,495	$4,868	$9,990	$10,990	$13,490

R/S = Restricted Stock

options, restricted stock and phantom stock meet the organization's developmental needs in different ways. Each one is a substitute for cash, but some are more leveraged or risk tolerant than others.

In addition to the risk/reward cash trade-off, retention is a key benefit of equity. The retention factor increases with a corresponding rise in market price. Restricted stock is more "price" tolerant and may provide greater retention benefits to employees than options when the stock's price is in periods of low growth or decline. Companies can add performance measures to the equity grants, further correlating their vesting to the achievement of important corporate milestones, but this has an impact on EPS charges and the retention factor.

Stock options are more leveraged than restricted stock, because a greater number of options may be granted for the same economic value at any given price. But such a benefit comes with a high price. With stock options, shares are used at a more rapid pace, and shareholders today are less inclined to approve additional

Figure 2
Company Sensitivities in Development Stages

	Cash Conservation	Cash Generation	Tax Deduction	EPS Charges
Startup	High	High	Low	Low
In-transition	High	Medium	Medium	High
Mature	Low	Low	High	High

shares for employee equity plans.

The slower stock price appreciation of mature companies makes equity use less attractive to broad-based employees. No equity compensation vehicle is able to anticipate all macro/micro economic variables and perfectly reward employees for their efforts and results. Forces outside the company's control can influence the equity vehicle's value delivery to the employee. These market forces include interest-rate changes, corporate scandals, disruptive technologies, market perception, etc., that can unduly benefit or harm the employee's equity compensation package. A rising or sinking tide displaces all ships.

Compensation professionals must remain flexible and adapt quickly to environmental changes while avoiding the lemming syndrome. In tough times, it is the compensation professional's goal to design pay plans that separate the chaff from the wheat, and induce those titans to stay and fight rather than jump the ship. In some cases, cash may become the lowest-cost compensation vehicle in light of dilution and overhang concerns.

Figure 3
Characteristics of Equity Compensation Vehicles

	Cash Generation	Tax Deduction	EPS Charges	Dilution
ISO Option	Yes, on exercise	No, unless disqualified	Yes & no, fixed	Yes, on exercise
NQSO Option	Yes, on exercise	Yes, on exercise	Yes & no, fixed	Yes, on exercise
Restricted Stock	No, unless FMV	Yes, on vesting	Yes–fixed	Yes, on issuance
Restricted Stock Units	No	Yes, on vesting	Yes–fixed	Yes, on vesting

Final Thoughts

Many companies have expressed alarm and fear that SFAS 123 will be the demise of stock options and other equity-based incentives. Option-issuance abuses often are mistakenly regaled in the press as the norm rather than the exception. Companies will continue to issue options because of their leverage, cash-conservation and cash-generation qualities. Employees also expect them if they accept less cash and more risk at a young company. Restricted stock will become more prevalent among larger enterprises as the expense treatment of options lessens the differences between the two vehicles and price stability and cash position make the vehicle more attractive.

Performance stock-option issuance will generate the same expense under SFAS 123 as stock options without performance criteria. This should encourage companies to include performance measures in making grants that might have been excluded because of variable accounting requirements under APB 25. Many times, the performance-vesting schedule includes a cliff-vest feature to avoid variable accounting, which would not be necessary if SFAS 123 were adopted. Performance measures could benefit shareholders and lessen the likelihood of dilution of shareholders' equity without a corresponding positive achievement in company performance.

RSUs may offer some advantages over restricted stock. The financial administration is easier than with restricted stock, as no cash or shares change hands between the company and employee at the time of grant.

Although the move toward expensing options has called their use into question, they clearly have advantages over restricted stock in many circumstances. There are many varieties of equity "cheese," and the trick is in settling on the right recipe for the occasion. Research, education, and consulting colleagues and industry professionals will help ensure your batter is properly mixed. We cannot all be great cooks right away. It is only through experimentation that we can discover the secrets of sweet success.

First published in *WorldatWork Journal*, First Quarter 2004

Chapter 11
The Changing Requirements for Equity Compensation
Linda Zong, CCP, CBP, GRP, Deloitte Consulting LLP

Together with other accounting and tax rules and standards, the American Jobs Creation Act (AJCA) of 2004 and the Sarbanes-Oxley Act 2002, FAS123(R) ushered in a new era for equity compensation by invoking radical changes in equity-based compensation among employers. As a result, both public and nonpublic companies must understand the implications of these new rules and regulations for different types of equity compensation programs and proactively act to reconsider and restructure their existing equity compensation mix.

Key Provisions of New Accounting and Tax Rules

Under APB25 (Accounting Principles Board Opinion No. 25) adopted in 1972, no compensation expense exists for time-based vesting options granted at fair market value and for an employee stock purchase plan (ESPP) qualifying for favorable tax treatment under Section 423 of the Internal Revenue Code (the "Code") of 1986, as amended (Cooley Godward 2003). Also, in 1993, Congress enacted the Internal Revenue Code (IRC) Section 162(m), prohibiting companies from deducting certain forms of compensation for a company's five highest-paid executives on their tax returns. The exemption status from IRC Section 162(m) makes stock options granted with qualifying features an attractive vehicle for companies delivering incremental compensation while maintaining the employer's tax deduction (PricewaterhouseCoopers 2005).

FAS123(R), issued in December 2004, requires a public entity to use a grant-date fair-value-based methodology to measure the cost of share-based payment awards received in exchange for employee services. That cost will be recognized during the period that an employee is required to provide service—the requisite service period (usually the vesting period). A public entity will initially measure the cost of share-based awards per its current fair value and remeasure the fair value of that award at each reporting date through the settlement date. Changes in fair value during the requisite service period will be recognized as compensation cost during that period. Companies can choose the "modified prospective application" (MPA) transition method or the "modified retrospective application" (MRA) transition method for adopting the FAS123(R) standard.

On March 29, 2005, the Securities and Exchange Commission (SEC) released Staff Accounting Bulletin No. 107 (SAB107) to provide guidance on key provisions of FAS123(R), including the choice of one of several valuation methods such as a "lattice" (for example: binomial) or a "closed-form" (for example: Black-Scholes) valuation model as long as the method meets the requirements of the standard.

Figure 1 on page 154 illustrates the principal differences between APB25 and FAS123(R).

Simultaneously, the American Jobs Creation Act of 2004 adds a new section to

Figure 1
The Principal Differences Between APB25 and FAS123(R).

Key Provisions	APB25	FAS123(R)
Scope	Applies to instruments issued to employees	Applies to instruments issued to employees and nonemployees (except under ESOPs)
Measurement Method for Equity Awards and Liability Awards (Public Company)	Intrinsic value	Fair value
Recognition Period	Service period/vesting period	Requisite service period
Measurement Date	"Fixed accounting"—grant date; "variable accounting" or cash settlement—deferred measurement usually until date of exercise/settlement or resolution of contingencies	"Equity-classified"—grant date; "liability-classified"—measured at fair value each reporting period until date of payment or settlement
Modifications	New measurement date established, potential for variable accounting	Incremental value of new award over old award, and unamortized compensation cost for old award during the remaining requisite service period
Option Pricing Model	Does not apply	No specific model preferred; closed-form model (for example, Black-Scholes), binomial and simulation models are acceptable
Option Pricing Inputs	Does not apply	Exercise price, current price, expected life, expected volatility, expected dividends, risk-free rate
Taxes	If the tax deduction exceeds book compensation cost, the resulting windfall tax benefit is credited to APIC. If the deduction is less than book compensation cost, the resulting shortfall is debited to APIC to the extent of the pool of previous windfall tax benefits. Otherwise the shortfall is charged to income tax expense. Because most awards did not generate book-compensation cost under APB25, shortfalls were rare (PricewaterhouseCoopers 2005).	Same as APB25 except that shortfalls more likely to occur due to the charged compensation cost

the Internal Revenue Code as Section 409A (Inclusion in Gross Income of Deferred Compensation under Nonqualified Deferred Compensation Plans). The new section is similar to the Sarbanes-Oxley rule in the tax world for nonqualified deferred compensation, which is now subject to tax when vested, unless a company meets specific requirements for timing of deferral elections, distribution and funding. The IRS indicated in Notice 2005-1 that incentive stock options, qualified ESPPs and restricted stock awards are exempt from the provisions of Section 409A. Most stock options granted at fair value subject to Code Section 83(b) and void of deferral features will be exempt from the IRS rules as well.

In addition, Sarbanes-Oxley Section 302 on financial reporting disclosure requires the company to characterize and document the new rules' impact on earnings due to the potential material effects on financial reporting incurred by FAS123(R) and the AJCA deferred-compensation tax rules. Also Sarbanes-Oxley Section 404 requires an ongoing internal control system to address the use of valuation methods, recognition of share-based payment cost, identification of deferred tax assets and tax provisions, the data-quality assurance process and the reward program administration procedures (Deloitte Consulting 2005(1)). If implemented or administered incorrectly, stock plans can result in internal controls violations due to an improperly classified balance sheet, P&L and equity accounts, as well as costly correction measures and fines for tax, social insurance, securities currency exchange and data privacy noncompliance.

FAS123(R) and Other Rules Implications for Equity Compensation

Under FAS123(R), most rewards are classified as an equity award, except for the SARs settled in cash or cash-unit plans and phantom stock, which are classified as a liability award. The equity-classified award will be measured only once on the grant date and not remeasured unless the award is modified, while the liability-classified award will be remeasured at the end of each reporting period, at fair value, until settled.

Stock Options

A stock option is considered an equity appreciation value award under FAS123(R). Compensation cost is based on the award's fair value (on the grant date, estimated per a valuation model). The fair value equals the expected value on the grant date multiplied by the number of options expected to be vested. The number of options to be earned is revised each reporting period.

In terms of tax treatment, with incentive stock options (ISOs), the employee does not pay regular income taxes at the time of exercise, but needs to hold shares at least one year from the date of exercise and two years from the grant date to receive special tax treatment by treating the spread as an adjustment item for Alternative Minimum Tax purpose. With Nonqualified Stock Options (NQSOs), the employee will be taxed on ordinary income earned that equals spread at exercise. The reason these options are called "nonqualified" is that they do not qualify for special treatment of ISOs. The employee must report ordinary income when the option is exercised.

Restricted Stock/Restricted Stock Unit (Settled in Shares)

Restricted stock or stock-settled restricted stock units (RSUs) are considered an equity full-value award under FAS123(R), with compensation cost based on the common stock price of the underlying share on the grant date.

For service-based and performance-accelerated plans, the charge equals the fair value at the grant for the vesting period. For a performance-based plan, the charge equals the fair value at grant multiplied by the number of shares expected to be earned. The number of shares to be earned is revised each reporting period.

An employee receiving restricted stock awards is not taxed at the time of the award unless an election under Code Section 83(b) has been made to accelerate the tax paying upon receipt of restricted stock and avoid potential recognition of ordinary income when forfeiture restrictions lapse. Service-based and performance-accelerated restricted plans may be subject to Code Section 162(m) deductibility limitation. Performance-based restricted plans may qualify as performance-based compensation not subject to 162(m) deductibility limitation.

Stock Appreciation Rights (SARs) (Settled in Shares)

FAS123(R) implications and tax obligations for stock appreciation rights (SARs) settled in shares are similar to those for stock options.

Performance Share or Performance Unit (Settled in Shares)

Performance share plans are incentive plans in which shares of company stock are awarded to incentive participants only if certain companywide performance criteria are met, such as earnings-per-share targets. Performance unit plans use the current value of stock to develop a dollar allocation rather than a stock award based on the participants' contribution to company performance. The goal of performance shares or units is to provide an explicit incentive for employees to focus their efforts on maximizing shareholder value. FAS123(R) implications and tax obligations for a performance share or a performance unit are settled in shares and are similar to those for restricted stock or restricted stock units settled in shares.

Employee Stock Purchase Plan (ESPP)

Under an Employee Stock Purchase Plan, employees can purchase company stock at a discount to its fair market value. An ESPP is considered an equity full-value award under FAS123(R). Generally speaking, an ESPP will not incur an accounting charge to the company if the company provides a discount of 5 percent or less to employees, generally allows most employees to qualify to participate and does not provide any option features, with the exception of two enrollment features.

With qualified Code Section 423 ESPPs, employees are not taxed at the time the shares are purchased, employees are taxed only when the shares are sold. Depending on if the shares were held for the required holding period, a portion of the gain may be taxed as capital gains or as ordinary income.

Stock Appreciation Rights (SARs) (Settled in Cash or Cash-Unit Plans)

SARs settled in cash or cash-unit plans are considered liability appreciation value awards under FAS123(R). The compensation cost is measured at the end of each quarterly reporting period using a variable fair-value accounting until final measurement of the liability at the "intrinsic" value is settled in cash.

The tax obligation for the SARs is settled in cash or a cash-unit plan and may require that cash payments received by employees be treated as ordinary income.

Emerging Trends in Equity Compensation

Various surveys reflect the emerging trends in equity compensation under this new FAS123(R) environment. The noticeable trends include the decline in the use of stock options, the more prevalent practice of restricted stock/unit plans and performance-based equity plans and more sophisticated usage of employee stock purchase plans. A majority of companies use a combination of equity vehicles such as the omnibus incentive plan, stock options, restricted stock and performance-based plans as primary long-term incentive plan tools.

Figure 2 on page 158 illustrates the key summary findings on the employer actions regarding equity compensation programs (Deloitte Consulting 2005 (2), Mercer 2005 and PricewaterhouseCoopers 2005)

Broad-Level Stock Options Are Reduced

The most prevalent reaction to the mandatory stock options expensing requirements in the new accounting regulations is to scale back the grant level of the stock options. The Deloitte survey indicated that 75 percent of respondents are reducing the number of options granted. The Mercer survey indicated that 54

Figure 2

Employer Action on Equity Compensation Per Survey Results

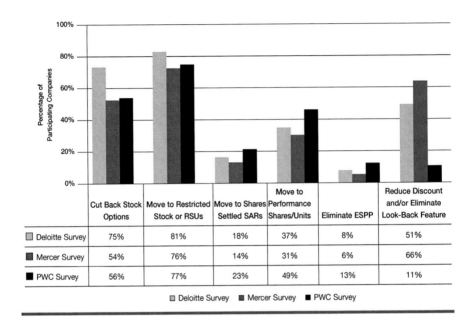

	Cut Back Stock Options	Move to Restricted Stock or RSUs	Move to Shares Settled SARs	Move to Performance Shares/Units	Eliminate ESPP	Reduce Discount and/or Eliminate Look-Back Feature
Deloitte Survey	75%	81%	18%	37%	8%	51%
Mercer Survey	54%	76%	14%	31%	6%	66%
PWC Survey	56%	77%	23%	49%	13%	11%

☐ Deloitte Survey　■ Mercer Survey　■ PWC Survey

percent of U.S. publicly traded firms are changing eligibility, participation or award levels of broad-based stock options. Likewise, the PWC survey indicated that 56 percent of the total sample companies would reduce stock option grant levels.

Restricted Stocks or Share-Settled Restricted Stock Units (RSUs) Become More Popular

The Deloitte survey indicated that 81 percent of the responding companies who are considering an alternative equity-based compensation plan use either time-based restricted stock/units (45 percent) or performance-vested restricted stock/units (36 percent). The Mercer survey showed that 76 percent of the responding companies made changes or planned to change to restricted stock in the last two years, with 40 percent of the companies opting for service-based restricted stock and 36 percent of the companies opting for performance-based restricted stock. Similarly, the PWC survey revealed that 77 percent of the survey's participating companies planned to move to either restricted stock plans (37 percent) or restricted stock unit plans (40 percent).

SARs Settled in Shares Are Expected to Increase

Historically, stock appreciation rights (SARs) rarely were granted due to their unfavorable accounting treatment under APB25. The use of stock-settled SARs is expected to increase because fewer shares will be issued and more shares will remain in the plan's share reserve, available for future issuance. The Deloitte survey showed that 18 percent of the responding companies planned to move to share-settled SARs. The Mercer survey indicated that 14 percent of the participating companies made changes or planned to change to share-settled SARs in the last two years. The PWC survey showed that 23 percent of the surveyed companies planned to move to stock-settled SARs. In addition, the Frederic W. Cook & Co's. 2005 Top 250 Long-Term Incentive Grant Practices for Executive Survey tracked the increased use of SARs at FAS 123 companies (10 percent) that voluntarily implemented "fair value" accounting for share-based grants versus non-FAS123 companies (1 percent). It serves as a clear sign for the future direction of SARs usage by employers under the FAS123(R) environment.

Performance-Based Long-Term Incentive Plans Have Become More Prevalent

Many companies will incorporate a performance element into option plans. Thus, performance, contingent stock options and performance-accelerated stock options emerge as alternative options. Performance-based restricted stock and performance shares or performance units settled in shares will increase as well. The Deloitte survey said that 37 percent of respondents were changing to performance-granted stock plans, with 24 percent to performance-granted restricted stock/units and 13 percent to performance-granted stock opportunity. The Mercer survey showed that 31 percent of the participating companies made changes or planned to change to performance shares/units plans in the last two years. The PWC survey said that 49 percent of the surveyed companies considered moving to performance-based equity plans.

Employee Stock Purchase Plans (ESPPs) Will Scale Back Slightly, with Revised Features

Although most current ESPPs will incur compensatory cost, various survey results indicate that only a small percentage of responding companies plan to eliminate them (8 percent per Deloitte, 6 percent per Mercer and 13 percent per PWC). Most employers choose to reduce the discount and/or eliminate the ESPPs' look-back feature (51 percent per Deloitte, 66 percent per Mercer and 11 percent per PWC). As long as employee stock purchase plans are modified with a lower discount rate and by eliminating a look-back feature to avoid compensatory cost, they continue to serve as popular equity compensation programs since many employers cut stock option grants to lower-level employees.

In summary, Figure 3 on pages 162 and 163 illustrates a primer for equity compensation, with a description of the various types of share-based compensation plans addressed by how they are structured, the FAS123(R) treatment for their compensation cost, the U.S. taxation implications, the pros and cons of each type and the predicted trend of their prevalence in the foreseeable future.

Employers' To-Do List
Transitioning to the Share-Based Payment Standard FAS123(R)

Most companies need to understand the new disclosure requirements under FAS No. 123(R) and estimate the FAS123(R) fair-value and compensation cost associated with each equity compensation plan. In response to the latest regulatory changes and shareholders, companies need to do the following:

- Choose a proper measurement method.
- Distinguish liability presentation from equity presentation of the share-based payments.
- Make changes not only in plan design but also in the actual language of plans and grant agreements.

Expensing Stock Options via Option-Pricing Model

To deal with the regulatory impact of the new rules on the stock options, companies need to make sound assumptions about the expected term and volatility—the two most difficult inputs to determine, and the most significant drivers of option value. They need to make these assumptions regardless of the option-pricing model companies choose.

Reducing/Eliminating/Accelerating Stock Options or Modifying Stock Options Terms

Companies' options include the following:

- Choose to reduce or eliminate stock option participation or the number of shares granted.
- Accelerate unvested underwater option or shorten option term.
- Modify the terms of the existing stock option plans to reduce FAS123(R)-incurred compensation cost.

Adopting Restricted Stock/Restricted Stock Unit (Settled in Shares) Program

Companies should follow the practices of leading companies to move from stock options to restricted stock or performance-based restricted stock units. These two types of full-value awards help companies better manage share usage and plan dilution.

Implementing a Broad-Based Share-Settled SAR Program

The use of stock-settled SARs is expected to increase because stock-settled SARs offer many advantages to companies using fewer shares and leaving more shares in the plan's share reserve, available for future issuance. Thus, under FAS 123(R), stock-settled SARs are an attractive alternative to stock options. Companies could consider adopting a new cashless exercise by exchanging existing stock options for stock-settled SARs.

Adding Performance-Share or Performance-Unit (Settled in Shares) Program

The FAS 123(R) makes performance-based restricted stock awards or share-settled performance unit plans more popular. The performance plan design's critical elements are the right participation levels and the performance criteria. Companies should introduce the proper performance targets in equity compensation plans, particularly for senior executives, and assess the implications of market versus performance conditions.

Modifying The Employee Stock Purchase Plan

Companies do not have to eliminate the employee stock purchase plans entirely, partly because companies already scale back the stock option grants to lower-level employees. Nevertheless, companies do need to modify their plans to make the plans less expensive by reducing the discount and eliminating the look-back feature.

Reducing or Eliminating Cash-Settled SARs, Cash-Settled RSUs or Cash-Settled Performance Units

Due to the variable cost calculation under FAS123(R) and the 409(A) election requirement for deferral feature, companies should reduce or eliminate granting of SARs settled in cash, cash-settled RSUs or cash-settled performance unit plans.

Developing a Holistic Mix of Long-Term Incentive Plans (LTIPs)

Companies must grasp the pros and cons of each equity compensation type under the FAS123(R) environment and re-evaluate the total compensation mix, including the cash and equity compensation. They must take this step to do the following:

Figure 3

The Changing Requirements for Equity Compensation

	At-the-Money Stock Options (Nonqualified) with Service Condition	Incentive Stock Options (Qualified)	Discounted Stock Options	Premium Options	Restricted Stock or Stock-Settled RSUs
Description	Options with exercise price equal to stock price at grant date; vest based on continuous employment over specified time period	Same as nonqualified at-the-money stock option except for special tax treatment if the option complies with IRC requirements	Stock options with exercise price less than stock price at grant date	Options with exercise price set higher than grant-date stock price	Grant of shares (restricted stock) or promise to issue shares (RSUs) upon completion of service condition
Classification	Equity	Equity	Equity	Equity	Equity
Award Type	Appreciation	Appreciation	Appreciation	Appreciation	Full Value
FAS123(R) Treatment	Expense based on fair value at grant and number of options that vest, recognized over vesting period	Same as nonqualified at-the-money stock option	Same as nonqualified at-the-money stock option; fair value higher than at-the-money option, but generally increase is less than discount amount	Same as nonqualified at-the-money stock option except lower grant-date fair value	Expense based on grant-date fair value of stock and number of shares that vest, recognized over vesting period
U.S. Taxation	(1) Employee: taxed ordinary income tax on exercise equal to spread; (2) Employer: deduction equal to employee's income	(1) Employee: ISO holders do not pay regular income taxes at the time of exercise if no disqualifying disposition occurs; subject to capital gains tax at sale of shares; (2) Employer: No deduction unless disqualifying disposition	(1) Employee: taxed at vesting because discounted options are treated as deferred compensation under IRC Section 409A; (2) Employer: Deduction equal to employee's income	Same as nonqualified at-the-money stock option	(1) Employee: subject to tax at vesting based on stock price on that date; may elect under IRC Section 83 (b) to be taxed at grant date; (2) Employer: Deduction equal to employee's income when taxed
Pros	(1) Employees may receive substantial gain from well-timed exercise without shareholder gains; (2) easily qualifies for IRC Section 162(m); (3) can be issued to employees and directors	Same as nonqualified at-the-money stock option except employee may receive capital gains treatment instead of being taxed as ordinary income	Same as at-the-money option except provides rewards even if stock price declines; employee may perceive that discount has more value than increase in fair value measured for FAS 123(R)	No value to employee unless stock price rises above premium; increases motivation; reduces FAS 123(R)'s fair value	(1) Employees share upside and downside of share price (2) receive dividends; (3) dilution not as great as options
Cons	(1) Employees do not share the downside risk; (2) overhang and dilution issues; (3) FAS123(R) accounting removes its previous advantages; (4) little retentive effect in falling market	(1) Same as nonqualified at-the-money stock options; (2) employer generally has no tax deduction unless disqualifying disposition; (3) can only be issued to employees	Unfavorable tax treatment for employee under IRC Section 409A	Employee may demand more options to make up for perceived reduction in value	(1) Employees realize value even if stock price declines; (2) not deductible under 162(m) unless performance based; (3) may be viewed as giveaway by shareholders
Trend Predicted	Decrease	Decrease	Decrease	Flat	Increase

Figure 3 *(Continued)*

The Changing Requirements for Equity Compensation

	Stock-Settled SARs	Performance Shares/Units with Performance Conditions	Performance Shares/Units with Market Conditions	Employee Stock Purchase Plans (ESPPs)	SARs (Settled in Cash or Cash-Unit Plans)
Description	Employee receives stock equal to intrinsic value at exercise; otherwise identical to nonqualified stock option	Restricted stock or units that vest based on time-based vesting plus attainment of non-stock-price-related performance conditions (e.g., revenue or EPS)	Same as performance shares with performance conditions except with targets related to stock price increases or tying stock price to an index	A program that allows employees to purchase company stock at a discount to its fair market value	Same as stock-settled SARs except intrinsic value at exercise paid in cash
Classification	Equity	Equity	Equity	Equity	Liability
Award Type	Appreciation	Full Value	Full Value	Full Value	Appreciation
FAS123(R) Treatment	Same as nonqualified options	Same as restricted stock except recognize compensation cost over the period when targets will probably be attained and true-up for actual vesting	Fair value at grant date reflects market condition using lattice model; expense recognized over derived requisite service period and not reversed if targets are not attained	Measured on the grant date (fixed accounting)	Considered liability award with mark-to-market fair value (using an option-pricing model); total expense equals cash paid to employee
U.S. Taxation	Same as nonqualified stock option	Same as restricted stock	Same as restricted stock	Not taxed at the time the shares are purchased, only when they are sold. A portion of the gain may be taxed as long-term capital gains if the shares are held for the required holding period.	Same as nonqualified stock option
Pros	(1) Same as nonqualified stock option, and exercise does not require tendering of an exercise price; (2) reduces dilution compared to broker-assisted exercise; (3) exempt from section 409(A) under AJCA	No FAS123(R) expense unless performance target attained; employee motivated to reach targets; shareholders also benefit if targets reached	Employee directly motivated to increase stock price; fair value per share generally lower than stock price at grant	Encourage saving and investing	Same pros as stock-settled SARs except for accounting under FAS123(R)
Cons	Same as nonqualified stock options	(1) Hard to set up proper performance criteria; (2) stock price may decline even though performance criteria are met	(1) FAS123(R) expense not reversed if targets not attained; (2) lattice model required to measure fair value	The potential compensatory cost incurred if the plan has a discount rate is more than 5% or provides a look-back feature	Same as nonqualified stock options except (1) Mark-to-market variable accounting under FAS123R; (2) subject to 409(A) under AJCA
Trend Predicted	Increase	Increase	Increase	Slightly Decrease	Decrease

- Optimize value for total compensation cost.
- Explore the emerging long-term incentive plan alternatives including SARs (whether settled in stock or in cash), various forms of stock options (ISOs, NQSOs, discounted options and premium options), performance awards, restricted stock and RSUs, ESPPs with no look-back feature, phantom stock plans, etc.
- Develop a holistic retentive long-term incentive plan mix that links pay to performance.

Launching Communication and Education for Implementing New Equity Plans

The various challenges involved in program design and implementation are as follows:

- Employee communication and education.
- Stock award administration, including systems and international and technical considerations for tax, accounting and securities laws, Section 409A and Sarbanes-Oxley compliance
- The tangible steps to take to implement new plans.

Companies must determine and design transition and communication strategies and plans for rolling out new types of equity compensation plans within the organization.

Conclusion

Back to the bottom line, now is the time for employers to embrace the new rules and regulations (such as FAS123(R), the AJCA section 409(A) and Sarbanes-Oxley). Employers must take a fresh look at the impact of these rules and regulations on the existing equity-based compensation programs and explore new holistic mixes of long-term incentive plans. Ideally such newly revamped equity plans and long-term incentive plans would comply with the new rules and regulations and drive corporate performance and shareholder value at the same time. There is no simple formula for a so-called "perfect" long-term incentive plan model. Each employer needs to go through its own growing pains to create its own "unique" rather than "perfect" model.

First published in *WorldatWork Journal*, Second Quarter 2006

Chapter 12

The ESOP Question: A Better Way to Ensure Ownership Broadly?

Corey Rosen, National Center for Employee Ownership

Employee stock ownership plans (ESOPs) were very popular in public companies in the 1980s. Companies borrowed billions of dollars annually through these plans to buy back their own shares, which were distributed to employee participants. In what seems like a déjà vu, accounting rules for ESOPs were changed in 1992. Suddenly, these plans could look more costly on the income statement, even though the actual cost did not change by one penny. Public companies decided to look at other ways to share ownership broadly, many settling on the accounting-blessed idea of stock options. But now that the FASB is headed toward requiring all forms of equity sharing to show as a charge to compensation on the income statements, it may be time to take another look at ESOPs.

The Ins and Outs of ESOPs

An ESOP is a kind of employee benefit plan. Governed by the Employee Retirement Income Security Act of 1974 (ERISA), ESOPs were given a statutory framework in 1974. Like other ERISA-qualified plans, ESOPs must not discriminate in their operations in favor of highly compensated employees, officers or owners. So, unlike individual equity plans, such as options or restricted stock, they are not meant as a way to reward one employee but not another, nor provide outsized benefits to higher-paid people.

ESOPs are subject to many of the same rules as 401(k) and profit-sharing plans. For example, a trustee who acts as the plan fiduciary governs them. The trustee can be anyone, although larger companies tend to appoint an outside trust institution. The trustee is considered the shareholder of record and is responsible for ensuring that the plan is operated in the best interests of plan participants.

The company usually funds ESOPs much as it would other benefits plans. Companies simply can make tax-deductible contributions of cash to buy stock or contribute the stock directly. Employees can contribute directly to an ESOP as they would a 401(k), but this is uncommon. Employees also can voluntarily reinvest dividends in company stock in the plan.

ESOPs can borrow money (the only plan able to do so) and use the proceeds to buy existing or new shares of company stock. Company contributions to repay the loan are deductible, so companies can deduct both principal and interest. Borrowing money is the most sophisticated use of an ESOP, called a "leveraged ESOP." In this approach, the company sets up a trust that borrows money from a lender. The company repays the loan by making tax-deductible contributions to the trust, which the trust gives to the lender. The loan must be used by the trust to acquire stock in the company.

The company can use proceeds from the loan for any legitimate business purpose. The stock is put into a "suspense account," where it is released to employee accounts as the loan is repaid. However, for purposes of calculating the various contribution limits described later in this article, the employee is considered to have received only his or her share of the principal paid that year, not the value of the shares released. After employees leave the company or retire, the company distributes to them the stock purchased on their behalf or the stock's cash value.

In return for complying with the anti-discrimination requirements, companies receive impressive tax benefits that are unavailable in individual equity plans or benefits plans. Consider the following:

- In closely held C corporations, owners can defer tax by selling to an ESOP; in S corporations, ESOP ownership profits are not taxed at the federal (and usually state) levels.
- Contributions are deductible to the company at the time they are made, but not taxed to the employee until distribution.
- The company can deduct the entire loan contribution it makes to the ESOP, with certain payroll limits described later in this article. This means the company, in effect, can deduct principal as well as the interest on the loan.
- The company can deduct dividends on the shares acquired with the proceeds of the loan that are used to repay the loan itself, as well as dividends employees voluntarily reinvest in the company or that are passed directly through to employees.

On the income statement, contributions of cash to buy stock or stock itself are a compensation cost when they are contributed. In a leveraged ESOP, the compensation costs equal the value of the shares released from the suspense account each year. Dividends paid on shares that have been allocated are a capital cost;

on unallocated shares they are a compensation cost. In a leveraged ESOP, the debt counts as corporate debt, with a "contra equity account" set up to balance this amount. Both are reduced as the loan is repaid. Allocated shares count against earnings per share (EPS) calculations, but unallocated shares do not. All shares in the plan, however, are outstanding in terms of standard dilution calculations.

Aside from their tax benefits, when combined with the right corporate culture, ESOPs can produce impressive performance gains. In 1999, in the largest study of ESOPs in public companies, Hamid Mehran (then of Northwestern University) found that ESOPs in 382 publicly traded companies increased the return on assets (ROA) 2.7 percent over what otherwise would have been expected. More than 60 percent of companies experienced an increase in their stock price in the two-day period after public announcement of the ESOP, with the average increase for all companies at 1.6 percent. Other research has shown that these gains are most pronounced when companies have corporate cultures that share financial information widely and seek to actively involve employees in decision-making, often through employee teams, at all levels of the company.

But ESOPs are not a magic wand. Most infamously, ESOP-owned United Airlines ended up going bankrupt. Enron had an ESOP, along with its 401(k) plan, while other corporate blackguards had a concentration of employer stock in their 401(k) plans. At United, neither the company nor the unions were seriously committed to the idea of an ownership culture and sharing ownership long-term (the ESOP was time-limited). And concentrating retirement assets in a single investment without a diversified savings alternative is not a good idea. But these disasters are not typical. As noted, ESOP companies typically perform better. Moreover, both public and private ESOP companies are more likely to have additional diversified retirement plans than comparable non-ESOP companies. For every failure, there are many successes.

Procter & Gamble, for example, has had an employee ownership plan since the turn of the 20th century, and it still is one of the richest ESOPs ever created. The stock price of RLI, a publicly traded insurance company committed to an ownership culture, was $19 three years ago. Today it's at $40—a price movement typical of its time as an ESOP.

Prior to 1992, companies only recorded the amount they paid for the shares as a compensation cost. For example, in 1988 a company borrowed money to buy stock at $20 per share. It repaid the loan through the ESOP for 10 years, releasing 10 percent of the shares each year. Each year, it would show a compensation cost of $20 per share. But after 1992—when accounting rules were changed—it would record the actual value of the shares released that year. In year three, if the shares were $26, it would record a $26-per-share charge for 10 percent of the shares released.

Public companies were less than thrilled. They were recording a charge they never actually paid for (the stock only cost them $20). The theory was that using the current market value was required, because that represented a cost to shareholders when the shares were sold later. As such, many public companies abandoned their ESOPs to look for greener accounting pastures. Today, all forms of equity may be similarly disfavored.

While ESOPs commonly are used in closely held companies, especially as a business-transition strategy, this article will focus on using an ESOPs in public companies as a broad-based ownership plan.

ESOP Applications
The following uses typically involve borrowing money through a leveraged ESOP, but a company can simply contribute new shares of stock to an ESOP, or contribute cash to buy existing shares, as a means to create an employee benefits plan.

Buy New and Existing Shares
The ESOP can buy both new and existing shares for a variety of purposes. The most common application for an ESOP in a public company is to use the leveraging features of the plan to match to 401(k) plan deferrals. For example, a company can borrow money to buy its stock at $40. It anticipates that over the next 10 years, as the loan is repaid, stock will go up an average of 10 percent per year. In year three, it will be almost $53. Essentially, for a $40 cash cost, the company releases shares to the 401(k) accounts worth $53. If this is not enough to meet the target match, additional cash or shares can be contributed. If it is more than enough, employees receive a windfall courtesy of stock price appreciations. Dividends (that may be paid on shares anyway) also can be used to repay the loan and are tax deductible.

Designate a Portion of the Plan as an ESOP
Even if the company does not borrow money to match the 401(k) deferrals, it might still designate the company stock portion of the plan an ESOP, because dividends that are paid on the stock can be deducted if passed through to employees or reinvested by employees (on a pretax basis) in company stock.

Divest or Acquire Subsidiaries

ESOPs often are used to divest or acquire subsidiaries, or even to go private. For example, a company may want to spin off a division; selling to employees may help retain jobs, keep a valued supplier or customer relationship, or be a strong message to remaining employees that the company, even with the restructuring, will watch out for their interests.

However, ESOPs can only pay the value of the business as a stand-alone entity. An ESOP could not match a synergistic buyer's offer. (Synergistic buyers will pay a premium for company shares if they believe the company will generate more tax earnings as part of their business than it would as a stand-alone business.) The ESOP can only pay a price based on what the business would be worth on a stand-alone basis. In the post Sarbanes-Oxley era, many public companies are going private. An ESOP can be an attractive mechanism for buying all or (more commonly) part of the company. Giving employees a stake in the new company and financing the transaction in pretax money can provide a big leg up. In some cases, companies may give employees the choice to move some of their 401(k) assets into the ESOP to help fund the plan, but this can only be done under the strictest fiduciary guidelines.

Buy Newly Issued Shares

Creator Louis Kelso first envisioned ESOPs as a means to buy newly issued shares in the company, with the borrowed funds being used to buy new productive capital. The company can, in effect, finance growth or acquisitions in pretax dollars while these same dollars create an employee benefits plan.

Rules for ESOP Loans

Typically, a lender loans to the company and the company reloans the money to the ESOP. The ESOP then uses the loan proceeds to buy new or treasury shares of stock (when the ESOP is used to finance growth) or existing shares (when the ESOP is used to buy shares of current owners). Of course, the ESOP itself does not have any money to repay the loan, so the company makes tax-deductible contributions to the plan, which the plan uses to repay the lender. In effect, the company can deduct the principal and interest on the loan, provided the requirements described below are met.

By selling bonds, the ESOP can borrow money from anyone, including commercial lenders or the company itself. Any loan to an ESOP must meet several requirements: It must have reasonable rates and terms, and it must be repaid only from employer contributions, dividends on shares in the plan and earnings from other investments in the trust contributed by the employer. There is no limit on the term of an ESOP loan other than what lenders will accept (normally five to 10 years), and the proceeds from the sale of shares to the ESOP can be used for any business purpose.

Shares in the plan are held in a suspense account. As the loan is repaid, these shares are released to plan participants' accounts. The release must follow one of two formulas. The simplest is that the percentage of shares released equals the percentage of principal paid, either that year or during whatever shorter repayment period is used. In such cases, however, the release may not be slower than what normal amortization schedules would provide for a 10-year loan with level payments of principal and interest. The principal-only method usually has the effect of releasing fewer shares to participants in the early years. Alternatively, the company can base its release on the total amount of principal and interest it pays each year. This method can be used for any loan, but must be used for loans of more than 10 years.

When dividends are used to repay ESOP loans, typically the company uses the money to buy shares from the unallocated (unpaid for) pool in the suspense account, releasing shares equal in value to the dividends to employee accounts. It is possible to run out of unallocated shares when dividends are paid; in that case, the company must contribute additional shares. It is not clear whether employees can contribute to the ESOP to pay down debt (and get more shares). Given the uncertainty, this practice is not recommended.

Limitations on Contributions

Congress made significant changes to contribution limits in all employee retirement plans in 2001. Generally, companies can deduct up to 25 percent of the total eligible payroll of plan participants to cover the principal portion of the loan and can deduct all of the interest they pay. Eligible pay is essentially all the pay, including employee deferrals into benefits plans, of people actually in the plan, of $205,000 per participant or less (in this year's dollars). However, company contributions to other defined contribution plans, such as stock bonus, 401(k) or profit-sharing plans, do not count in this 25-percent-of-pay calculation if the contribution is to repay an ESOP loan. If it is not, then the total contributions to all defined contribution plans must not exceed 25 percent-pay. On the other hand, "reasonable" dividends paid on shares acquired by the ESOP can be used to repay the loan, and these are not included in the 25-percent-of-pay calculations. If employees leave the company before they have a fully vested right to their shares, their forfeitures, which are allocated to everyone else, are not counted in the percentage limitations.

There are a number of limitations to these provisions. First, no single ESOP participant can get a contribution of more than 100 percent of pay in any year from the principal payments on the loan that year that are attributable to that employee, or more than $41,000 (in today's dollars), whichever is less. In figuring payroll, pay in excess of $205,000 per year (in today's dollars) does not count toward total contribution limits.

Second, if there are other qualified benefits plans, these must be taken into account when assessing this limit. This means that employee deferrals into 401(k) plans, as well as other employee contributions to 401(k) plans, stock bonus or profit-sharing plans, are added to the ESOP contribution and cannot exceed 100 percent of pay in any year.

Third, the interest is only excludable from the limits if not more than one-third of the benefits are allocated to highly compensated employees, as defined by the Internal Revenue Code (Section 414[q]). If the one-third rule is not met, forfeitures also are counted in determining how much an employee is getting each year.

How Shares Get to Employees

The rules for ESOPs are similar to the rules for other tax-qualified plans in terms of participation, allocation, vesting and distribution, but several special considerations apply. All employees older than age 21 who work for more than 1,000 hours in a plan year must be included in the plan, unless they are covered by a collective bargaining unit, are in separate lines of business with at least 50 employees not covered by the ESOP or fall into one of several anti-discrimination exemptions not commonly used by leveraged ESOPs. If there is a union, the company must bargain in good faith with it over inclusion in the plan.

Shares are allocated to individual employee accounts based on relative compensation (usually all W-2 compensation is counted), on a more level formula (such as per capita or seniority) or some combination. The allocated shares are subject to vesting. Employees must be 100-percent vested after five years of service, or the company can use a graduated vesting schedule not slower than 20 percent after three years and 20 percent per year more until 100 percent is reached after seven years. A faster vesting schedule applies when the ESOP contribution is used as a match to employee 401(k) deferrals. "Cliff" vesting must be complete in three years, and graduated vesting must start after two years and be completed no later than after six years.

When employees reach age 55 and have 10 years of participation in the plan, the company must either give them the option of diversifying 25 percent of their account balances among at least three other investment alternatives, or simply pay the amount out to the employees. At age 60, employees can have 50 percent diversified or distributed to them.

When employees retire, die or are disabled, the company must distribute their vested shares to them not later than the last day of the plan year after the year of their departure. For employees who leave before reaching retirement age, distribution must begin not later than the last day of the sixth plan year after their year of separation from service. Payments from the trust can be made in substantially equal installments over five years or in a lump sum. In the installment method, a company typically pays out a portion of the stock from the trust each year. The value of that stock may go up or down over that time, of course. In a lump-sum distribution, the company buys the shares at their current value, but can make the purchase in installments over five years, as long as it provides adequate security and reasonable interest. ESOP shares must be valued at least annually by an independent, outside appraiser unless the shares are publicly traded.

Voting Rules

The ESOP trustee actually votes the ESOP shares. The question is, "Who directs the trustee?" In public corporations, employees must be able to direct the trustee as to the voting of shares allocated to their accounts—regardless of vesting—on all voting matters. For unallocated and undirected shares, the trustee can either vote the shares, either at his or her own discretion or at the direction of the board, or the plan can be written to require mirror voting for those shares that have been voted.

Voting is not the same as tendering shares. So, while employees may be required to vote on all issues, they may have no say about whether shares are tendered. In public companies, this is a major issue. Almost all public companies now write their plans to give employees the right to direct the tendering, as well as voting, of their shares for several reasons.

Despite these rules, there is a gray area on how trustees should make decisions on issues involving the sale or merger of the company, whether that is accomplished through a tender offer or a vote. Looking to defend themselves against hostile acquisitions, most public companies write their ESOPs to provide employees with maximum control of plan assets, even naming them as fiduciaries for their shares and for a pro-rata share of unallocated stock. The U.S. Department of Labor (DOL) and the courts have found that, on allocated shares, trustees normally should follow participant wishes. On unallocated and undirected shares, trustees can be guided by these instructions, but ultimately must make an independent decision based on the best interests of plan participants as participants, not employees. So, if an offer is at a 50-percent premium, but everyone will lose his or her job, it could be hard to say no. Because of this uncertainty, ESOPs are a mixed bag as a takeover defense.

Reinvesting Dividends

The 2001 tax law made life easier for companies that wanted to allow employees to voluntarily reinvest their dividends in company stock. In the past, a convoluted arrangement called a "dividend switch-back" was followed. It required prior approval from the Internal Revenue Service (IRS) through a letter of determination. Essentially, employees had the dividends held by the payroll department and contributed to their accounts in the form of stock. It was deductible to the company and pretax to the employee (just as reinvestments are under the new law), but some employees with large account balances could find that their reinvestments were so large that they bumped up against annual contribution limits to defined contribution plans. This could result in a loss of contributions from the company that they otherwise would have received. Under this new law, this isn't a problem. Reinvested dividends do not count against the contribution limits, and no prior IRS approval is needed. For many public companies, this becomes one of the most attractive aspects of an ESOP, as it saves on taxes and encourages employee investment.

Financial Issues for Employees

When an employee receives a distribution from the plan, it is taxable unless it is rolled over into an IRA or other qualified plan. Otherwise, the amounts contributed by the employer are taxable as ordinary income, while any appreciation on the shares is taxable as capital gains. If the employee holds the shares after distribution, the portion that is taxable as ordinary income is immediately taxed, with a 10-percent penalty if the distribution is before retirement age. However, the appreciation is treated as "net unrealized appreciation" and is not taxed until sale, when it is taxed at capital-gains rates. Also, if the employee receives the distribution before normal retirement age and does not roll the funds over, a 10-percent excise tax is added.

While the stock is in the plan, however, it is not taxable to employees. It is rare, moreover, for employees to give up wages to participate in an ESOP or to purchase stock directly through a plan (this raises difficult securities law issues for closely held firms). Most ESOPs are either in addition to existing benefits plans or replace other defined contribution plans, usually at a higher pay level.

Diversification Issues and Concerns

Enron, WorldCom and other companies that encouraged excessive employee investment in company stock are powerful reminders that employees need diversification for retirement. ESOPs always should exist alongside more diversified plans. For example, if an ESOP is the match to a 401(k) plan, the company should discourage any significant investment in company stock with employee deferrals. Companies also may want to offer earlier diversification than legally allowed for the ESOP shares if the company match is a significant portion of total benefits for a more tenured employee.

Bills before Congress to require diversification of employer stock do not affect stand-alone ESOPs unless employees can buy stock in the plan. Those integrated with 401(k) plans would be required to offer diversification after three years of either stock being in the plan or employee tenure. However, the future of this legislation is very cloudy.

Administration and Compliance Issues

As part of ERISA, ESOPs face most of the same compliance and administration issues as 401(k) plans, profit sharing plans and, to a lesser degree, defined benefit plans. Most companies outsource their plan administration to firms with an expertise in the ESOP area. Given the complexity of these plans, this is generally advisable unless a company has a staff that can devote itself full time to administering the ESOP. Like other ERISA plans, companies must annually file a Form 5500 annual report on the plan (except for companies with fewer than 100 participants, which can file every three years) and must have the plan audited. Periodic changes in the law require plans to be updated. For public companies, these changes have almost always been the same as required for other defined benefit plans.

There are several ESOP-specific issues in plan administration that bear attention. While this article is not intended to provide a detailed description of these various issues, there are four that seem to cause the most problems:
- In most ESOPs, allocations are based on corporate contributions equal to a uniform percentage of pay, up to the aforementioned eligible limits. In some plans, however, ESOP allocations are used to match employee 401(k) deferrals. In those cases, companies must follow the 401(k) testing rules

and the ESOP rules to see if the plans meet anti-discrimination tests. ESOP anti-discrimination testing rules can be met if all employees who are eligible for the 401(k) are offered the same deal on the ESOP matching shares (i.e., 50 percent of the first 6 percent deferred is matched in ESOP shares). Combined plans can become cumbersome when the plan years do not match, potentially causing excess allocations. As such, it is always advisable to ensure that the plan years match.

- The use of dividends in ESOPs is very common in public companies. If they are used to repay a loan, then when a dividend is paid on shares held by the plan, the dividends attached to the shares that already have been allocated (i.e., been paid for) have to release unallocated shares equal in value to employee accounts. So, if a 3-percent dividend is paid on allocated shares with $10 million in value, then $300,000 in unallocated shares must be released. If share values have gone up since the loan, this is not a problem. But, if they have gone down, there may not be enough shares left to release. In that case, the company has to issue more shares.

- When an ESOP is used to match a 401(k) plan, it often borrows money to buy shares up front, and then releases them over time as the loan is repaid to match employee deferrals. If 10 percent of the loan is paid, 10 percent of the shares are released. If the share value goes up sharply over the loan period, then the company could end up making very large matches. Some companies have dealt with this by seeking to refinance the loan for a longer term so that fewer shares are released. The DOL does not approve of this approach in most cases as it violates the very intent of an ESOP, namely, for employees to share in future gains, not just be promised some standard matching percentage.

- As with 401(k) plans, if employees get company stock in their accounts, when they get a distribution they can keep the shares and pay no tax on the appreciation in value they achieved while the shares were in the plan (the so-called net unrealized appreciation rule). With low capital-gains rates in effect, many employees may want to take this course rather than sell the shares now or even roll them into an IRA and pay ordinary income tax when they withdraw amounts later. They would, however, pay ordinary income tax on the amount that was not due to appreciation, and possibly a 10-percent penalty tax (depending on their age) on top of that. Therefore, plan administrators need to track how much of the value was from appreciation and how much was from the basis of the stock (the amount the company paid to acquire the stock or the value of the shares when contributed) for each account.

ESOPs will not be right for every public company, but if the goal of an equity plan is to provide broad ownership to employees, and allocating this ownership based on relative pay or a more level formula is acceptable, then ESOPs deserve another look.

First published in *WorldatWork Journal*, Third Quarter 2004

Chapter 13
In the Hands of Employees
Dow Scott, Ph.D., Loyola University Chicago
Mark Reilly, 3C Compensation
John Andrzejewski, Anson Industries Inc.

Effective compensation programs must meet many requirements. They must align with the company's business strategy, be consistent with the pay philosophy of senior management, be perceived as fair by employees and be able to enhance company competitiveness—all while containing labor-cost increases.

Building compensation systems that can meet these expectations often results in an amalgamation of pay programs so complex they could befuddle even the most attentive employee or the manager who is trying to explain the plan. Furthermore, complex plans seem to have short shelf lives or require constant fine-tuning.

Consequently, when a compensation plan was discovered that was neither complex nor short-lived—and obviously was highly effective for one company— it was enough to catch even compensation veterans off guard.

About Anson Industries
Anson Industries was formed when United States Gypsum (USG) sold the division to two senior employees in 1941. Anson provides a range of construction services through four operating companies that concentrate on the installation of interior wall and ceiling systems and related exterior specialties, including commercial drywall, acoustical ceilings, and lath and plaster systems.

Anson Industries has 167 employees in eight offices in eight major cities. Each site operates independently and maintains its own profit-and-loss statement. There are 15 to 25 employees at each office who develop project bids and manage the work of about 1,250 craft workers hired from local unions. Although union workers are hired for specific jobs and have opportunities to work for a variety of employers in their local area, many choose to work exclusively for Anson. Conversely, Anson tries to maintain employment stability for its workers.

Anson has built a team of professional project managers who, along with highly skilled union construction crews, are able to handle very large jobs, including the Seattle Seahawks Stadium, Constellation Place in Century City, Calif., and Parkview Office building in Atlanta. The company has a strong reputation based on its ability to provide quality work at competitive prices and with flexible scheduling.

During the commercial construction boom in 2001, Anson Industries had revenue of $200 million, and its three-year compounded annual growth rate was more than 20 percent. In 2002, the economy and the war on Iraq caused revenue to decline. Though spending on commercial construction projects in 2002 was down 20 percent, Anson remained a strong performer and maintained profitability. (See Figure 1.)

Over the years, diversification across U.S. cities has proven to be a natural hedge against boom-and-bust economic cycles that plague many construction companies. When building in one city slows, it seems to be offset with greater-than-average building opportunities in another city.

Employee Ownership

There is a long tradition of employee company ownership in the United States—it is even encouraged by government through laws that provide a variety of tax advantages. In fact, 21,000 company plans facilitate company ownership, including employee stock ownership plans (ESOPs), stock bonus plans, profit-sharing plans, stock purchase plans, 401(k)s and broad-based stock option plans, according to data from the National Center for Employee Ownership (NCEO). And these

Figure 1
Anson Revenue

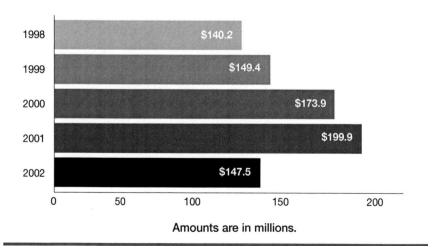

Amounts are in millions.

statistics do not include the various partnerships in which key employees have a major stake in company performance.

Not surprisingly, employee ownership has been linked to increased company performance. Giving employees a stake in the business is the reason most often attributed to enhanced company performance, and companies with ESOPs grow in sales, employment and productivity 2-percent to 3-percent faster each year than predicted without an ESOP, according to authors D. Kruse and Joseph Blasi in "Employee Ownership, Employee Attitudes and Firm Performance: A Review of the Evidence," in *The Human Resources Management Handbook*. Recently released results of the Employee Ownership Foundation's Economic Performance Survey said that more than 80 percent of the respondents' companies outperformed the Dow Jones Industrial Average, the Nasdaq Composite and the S&P 500.

However, employee-owned companies are not immune from serious problems. Consider United Airlines: Chapter 11 bankruptcy has wiped out the stock that employees once had invested in the company. Why is this airline giant having these problems? Was it the ESOP? Excessive union involvement? Something academic to the airline industry? Or was it a combination of all of these?

"While the ESOP did not cause United to fail, the ESOP has abjectly failed to help the company the way most ESOPs do," said Corey Rosen, NCEO executive director, in the Kruse/Blasi article. Rosen also said that actual ownership must be combined with a culture of ownership.

Anson Industries has succeeded in making this connection where United failed.

In 1954, the two owners who purchased the company from USG decided to retire, so they offered employees an opportunity to buy them out, thereby creating an employee-owned company. A rule was established that only employees could own stock, and they must surrender their stock upon retirement.

Every two years there is a stock offering to employees. A local bank provides loans of up to 50 percent of the stock price for employees to purchase Anson stock. Currently, senior management owns 60 percent of stock, and the rest of the employees own the remaining 40 percent. Though employees are not required to buy stock, 95 percent of the employee population owns stock. (See Figure 2.)

Anson also has a profit-sharing plan that covers all full-time salaried employees who have completed one year of service. The company's contribution is made at the discretion of the board of directors. Anson contributed $1.65 million in 2001 and $541,000 in 2002. Typically, all of the company's after-tax earnings are distributed to employees through either stockholder appreciation or profit sharing.

When employees want to sell their stock, the value is calculated as the current

Figure 2

Book Value Per Share

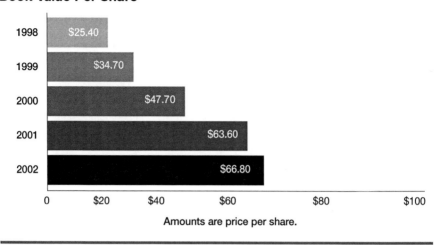

Amounts are price per share.

book value. The company has first right to buy the stock back and can spread the purchase of employee stock over a five-year period.

Stock also may simply be sold directly to other employees. A letter is sent to existing shareholders asking if they want to buy the stock at the current book value. If the offer is oversubscribed, the shares each person can buy are prorated among the buyers based on the amount they would like to purchase. The company repurchases any shares not sold this way.

Anson restricts the sale, transfer and assignment of stock. Shares owned by a terminated employee are offered to other employees for purchase or are purchased by the company at book value. The company repurchases all stock owned by an employee at his or her death. Stockholders who reach the age of 60 have the option to sell 10 percent of their shares back to the company once a year until their retirement, resignation or discharge.

Leadership

Anson Industries' leadership is unique in several ways.

Commitment to Employee Ownership

First, senior management has a long-term commitment to employee ownership. Although it is recognized that employee owners could sell or take the company public and receive a great deal more for the stock than the current book value, the company leadership is committed to keeping the company in employee hands.

Management also recognizes the danger of having any one employee own too large a share of company stock. Therefore, the president, who is the largest stockholder, is reluctant to purchase more stock. Clearly, the leadership is committed to the welfare of the company and all employees—it is not simply trying to maximize its own short-term earnings. Senior management recognizes that the employee ownership philosophy of Anson would change if someone owned too much stock.

Promoting from Within

The second unique feature about the company's leadership is that senior management has "grown up" in the company. It is the company's policy to hire newly "minted" college graduates and retain them throughout their careers. As a result, company leadership is not only committed to sharing ownership, it also is committed to a "promote from within" policy. Senior management is convinced that this policy ensures that everyone has a thorough understanding of business from the ground up.

Management has direct knowledge of customer needs and has established long-term relationships with labor unions that supply the contract labor. Anson is able to attract employees who want long-term careers with a company where they can own a piece of the business. Employees who appreciate their career opportunities and ownership potential are reluctant to leave Anson—as is apparent by the company's 1-percent turnover rate.

Company Culture

There is an advantage to having a relatively small company that is divided into even smaller local offices: Managers work closely with employees and customers, generating feelings of a small family business. Also, the company performance can be measured by office or by district. The profitability of jobs that are bid and managed at local levels provides very direct feedback regarding the success of the local business. District office managers' and project managers' bonuses are based on gross profit margin for the areas they manage and the business they sell.

Employee Involvement

Because most employees are owners, they participate in stockholder meetings and elect the members of the board. The annual stockholder meeting is a featured event each year and is well attended. At this meeting, employee owners have the opportunity to express feelings about leadership and how the company is managed.

Open-Door Policy

Finally, because of the organizational structure and leadership philosophy, employee participation can function at an informal level. Employees are encouraged to speak up, even to their bosses. As shareholders, they feel more empowered to submit suggestions to senior management. Given the nature of the business and the size of the company and its offices, this method of engaging employees seems to work well.

Lessons Learned

The first fundamental lesson that can be taken from Anson is that even very simple incentive tools can be used with great effectiveness. Sometimes it is easy to forget that it is not the tool that creates outstanding results, but how the tool is used. Obviously, Anson employees feel a strong sense of ownership. Do these feelings stem simply from the opportunity to own stock or earn profit-sharing bonuses? No. A feeling of ownership comes from an organizational culture that encourages employees to literally buy into the business, and then behave like owners.

Secondly, the compensation practices are consistent with the business strategy. The company uses a highly leveraged compensation strategy. For example, key positions receive a below-market salary and significant bonuses based on the total gross margin of their completed projects.

Finally, when employees purchase stock with their own money, it has a more powerful effect on behavior than stock option grants or shares in an ESOP. "Real" stock ownership provides both an upside opportunity and downside risk.

Is It Just a Small-Company Mentality?

Does Anson offer lessons just for small companies? Not necessarily. The underlying lesson is to develop feelings of ownership, which encourage employees to become business literate and engage management in the operations of the business. A related lesson is the respect management gives to its owner-employees by listening to their ideas and suggestions—after all, everyone at Anson is in it together.

First published in *workspan*, October 2003

Section V
Implementation
and Administration

Chapter 14

Implementing Pay Programs at McDonald's[1]: The Art and Science of Making Good Ideas Work

Lisa Emerson, McDonald's Corp.
Dennis Morajda, Performance Development International Inc.
Dow Scott, Ph.D., Loyola University Chicago

> *"It must be considered that there is nothing more difficult*
> *to carry out, nor more doubtful of success, nor more dangerous*
> *to handle, than to initiate a new order of things."*
>
> —Niccolo Machiavelli, *The Prince*, 1532

Those who propose to change or introduce new pay programs navigate a minefield of internal politics, turf battles and natural resistance motivated by fear and uncertainty. Pay affects not only employees' lifestyles but also their status within their organizations. For an employer, some of the largest financial decisions made each year are pay-related, and ultimately affect the organization's competitiveness and long-term survival. Within this context, human resources and compensation professionals are expected to deliver well-designed pay programs that improve performance in targeted areas of their organization (e.g., customer service, sales and production). However, absent proper implementation strategies, compensation experts often find it quite difficult to meet program objectives. Unfortunately, implementation planning is commonly treated as an afterthought by compensation professionals. Planning for implementation is pushed aside until the pay program has been designed and approved. Implementation is then hastily carried out with what little time and budget remain. This chapter provides a framework for effectively implementing pay programs and summarizes the successful strategy McDonald's followed to implement and communicate significant changes in its compensation programs.

Implementation ≠ Communication

Implementation and communication are often perceived as synonymous. While intertwined, these actions are distinctive. The implementation process integrates key staff and departments to carry a pay program strategy to fruition. Building understanding, acceptance and commitment for the pay program requires a coordinated effort from several departmental staffs, which may include finance, human resources, internal communications, information technology and line managers. Senior management often initiates the process by setting pay-program strategy and objectives. Line managers provide fundamental information about how the pay program needs to drive employee performance. Finance supplies the budgetary parameters within which the program should operate. Compensation experts with human resources support design the program, and the training function may be given the responsibility to educate managers and eligible employees about how the program works. Information technology facilitates the collection of employee and company performance data so payroll can make the promised payouts to employees. Successful pay program implementation requires program coordination and commitment from all key stakeholders to fully deliver a pay program that will drive the intended business results and reward employees for their contributions.

Communication is a critical component of a successful implementation. Communication experts help clarify and articulate key messages and effectively direct communications through available channels. Effective communication crafts the pay program's messages to gain the attention of eligible employees and their managers, and communication provides the information employees need to properly respond to the pay program's structure and obtain the desired rewards.

McDonald's Pay Implementation Strategy

In 2002, McDonald's faced disappointing global same-store sales and declining market share. Upon becoming CEO, Jim Cantalupo in early 2003 laid out a growth strategy that focused on getting more customers to dine more often in the approximately 30,000 existing restaurants rather than generating revenue growth from adding new restaurants. This change in business strategy gave McDonald's an opportunity to redesign its total compensation to better align pay with business needs and employee preferences. Prior to this shift toward existing restaurant revenue growth, McDonald's compensation strategy retained a heavy reliance on stock-driven rewards delivered deep into the organization. Now, compensation was shifted into areas where employees could actually see an impact on their jobs based on their level of responsibility. For some levels, this migration came out of stock-based awards and into shorter-term cash-based awards. In addition, McDonald's realigned its compensation strategy to be a customer-centric "Plan-to-Win." It accomplished this realignment through rewards that support initiatives around key drivers of its business (people, products, place, price and promotion) and that promote the financial discipline necessary to deliver solid shareholder returns. The annual incentive plan was redesigned to drive greater accountability for results, and a new three-year cash-incentive plan was introduced to deliver a better balance between stock-based awards and other performance metrics that were important to supporting long-term business objectives. The new total compensation strategy had six key objectives:

- Most effective use of available compensation dollars
- Better alignment of rewards with performance and service metrics that employees could impact through their day-to-day jobs
- Greater reward differentiation based on individual performance
- Value-added benefits and compensation programs that attract and retain talented people
- Addressing the needs of a diverse workforce
- Greater emphasis on employee understanding of the pay programs.

Based on these objectives, compensation professionals working with other stake-holders spent the better part of 2003 and 2004 reviewing and modifying virtually every U.S. compensation and benefits program for corporate employees and employees of corporately owned restaurants. It was recognized early on that a strong and systematic implementation process would be required because of the magnitude of these changes and their effect on how McDonald's employees would be rewarded. While implementation planning and communication began in the fall of 2004, the changes were effective in early 2005. A major concern was the potential for information overload and the difficulty human resources would encounter in helping employees and their managers understand the intent and mechanics of these changes. Another challenge was the geographically dispersed workforce, both at the staff and restaurant level. Therefore, the goal was to ensure that a consistent message was being delivered to all impacted employees.

The McDonald's brand is widely recognized by both employees and customers; connecting the brand to the revised total compensation program thus became the cornerstone of the communication strategy. McDonald's "addin' it up: my total compensation" program brand, which came to life in the third quarter of 2004, became the focus of the large change management, communication and education campaign.

This total compensation tagline was designed to be consistent with the previously rolled out ('i'm lovin' it) external marketing campaign. Prior to this campaign, less coordinated changes to McDonald's total compensation programs were the norm. Employees did not understand how total compensation programs were aligned with McDonald's business strategy and how those programs could drive performance.

Budgeted Implementation Concurrent with Sound Design and Realistic Objectives

Planning for implementation should commence early in the design process. Even in modestly sized firms, compensation plans are multimillion-dollar investments in talent acquisition, retention and motivation. Although a challenge for most companies, budgeting just .5 percent to 1 percent of this yearly expense (e.g., total annual wage/salary, performance bonus) for the implementation process can have a tremendous impact on the plan's overall success. Companies need to avoid the tendency to be "penny wise and pound foolish" by skimping on the implementation budget and then declaring the pay program a failure one to two years later when employees do not respond as expected. A structured plan and an adequately funded implementation process will improve the quality of the pay program's design, thereby focusing employee behaviors on desired results and building commitment for the program's success.

Elements of a Successful Pay Program Implementation

Successful program implementation is as much an art as it is a science because of the many factors that can affect it. These factors include culture, senior leadership style, turf politics and midlevel manager resistance. The science of an implementation is defined by a proven process for successfully implementing a program or change effort. The art springs from the creativity and imagination of the people involved in the implementation process who possess an intuitive understanding of the organization's culture and how best to present the program to create genuine interest, understanding, acceptance and enthusiasm. At McDonald's, compensation and benefits professionals demonstrated their cultural understanding by building on their well-known customer brand to communicate their new total compensation strategy and associated programs.

The Critical Role of Senior Management

As with any organizational change initiative, senior management sponsorship and support is vital for launching or updating a pay program. Without it, the project can easily fail. This leadership should come from outside human resources. An officer or business-unit head in a senior leadership role signifies that the change is not just an HR project but a directive that is intended to support the business. This senior leadership role cannot be emblematic or in name only; it must be a fully engaged role that is involved in the change process, keeps the project focused and builds commitment among the organization's other senior leaders.

Utilize Internal and External Resources

Although they possess considerable technical expertise, compensation professionals may have limited experience in successfully implementing major change initiatives. Fortunately, there are both internal and external sources available to offer assistance. Human resource development professionals have the expertise for assessing the learning needs of eligible employees and their managers, setting learning objectives and creating appropriate learning tools (e.g., live or video presentation, e-learning and scripted one-on-one interactions between employees and their supervisors). They also have considerable expertise evaluating employee and manager program perceptions, understanding, resulting behavior change and the program's impact on performance.

Communications and marketing professionals can contribute by creating key messages that focus employee attention on how new pay programs will affect them and by communicating to employees what they must do to obtain desired rewards. These professionals understand how to assess employee preferences for various types of media and how messages should be framed to achieve maximum impact. Marketing professionals have methods for evaluating the effectiveness of their marketing campaigns, and these evaluations will be helpful in determining who received what messages in support of the pay program.

Consulting firms are frequently engaged to help design pay programs, and if budgets permit, they can also play an important role in the implementation process. For McDonald's, Towers Perrin, a global human resources and management consulting firm, was instrumental in facilitating the implementation and communication around the "addin' it up" campaign. It acted as a true partner throughout the entire process. Working together, McDonald's internal staff and Towers Perrin were able to adapt a proven change-management approach to McDonald's culture. Towers Perrin began by gaining a complete understanding of the planned changes as well as the anticipated employee reactions to those changes. With this understanding, it worked with the McDonald's total compensation steering team to develop an implementation and communication strategy that reflected McDonald's unique needs. Each party was mutually respectful of the other's subject-matter expertise and the environmental considerations impacting these changes. Proven implementation strategies such as "addin' it up" require adjustment to fit the specific organization's culture, and working together to achieve that gentle balance is a critical aspect of the work of an external consultant and an organization. Both need to know when to rely on the other's experience and expertise.

Pay Program Design and Implementation Teams

Pay program design teams are widely employed but often function prior to and autonomously from the implementation process. Program design and implementation planning should occur concurrently, which requires coordination between the two functions—whether operating as two separate teams or as subgroups within a larger body. Pay program design traditionally relies upon the expertise of compensation professionals, finance, information technology and senior leadership from the functions eligible for the pay program (e.g., manufacturing, sales or customer service). Implementation experience comes from organization development, human resources development, marketing and communications. Successful coordination of such diverse expertise, and decentralized reporting relationships among the two teams, is challenging but essential for creating and implementing an effective pay program. At McDonald's, the implementation team was made up of many of the same members as the design team. This arrangement worked well because the change-management and communication expertise provided by Towers Perrin provided a needed external perspective.

McDonald's went a step further by chartering an employee advisory team. The team of 18 randomly selected employees representing a cross-section of corporate, field and restaurant-management staff was responsible for advising on communication and educational approaches as well as materials developed or commissioned by the design team. The advisory team operated as a standing "internal focus group" from whom the implementation team gained insight into the employee population and what communication strategies and informational materials would be most effective. Advisory team members' first-hand knowledge of the employee population and culture proved invaluable in identifying points of confusion and areas of potential employee resistance throughout the implementation process. The advisory team provided feedback on how employees might react to "addin' it up." Members reviewed key messages, design concepts and draft-communication pieces. It was particularly helpful to have respected vocal employees available to critique the implementation and communication process. By hearing the concerns of these critics, McDonald's was able to decide if and how it should adjust its approach or revise communication materials. On several occasions, the advisory team's perspective on communication materials led to adjustments to the messaging and the communication approach.

The advisory team met for an initial half-day kick-off meeting. The remainder of the group interaction was via conference calls and e-mails. Because of the heavy workloads most employees already face, one must be realistic about the amount and type of work such teams can undertake. McDonald's found that it needed to be very organized and well prepared for each touch point with the advisory team.

Collect Input/Feedback

In developing the implementation plan, McDonald's received important employee and management input, including recommendations to do the following:

Create a business conversation—Employees said, "We're businesspeople— talk to us like businesspeople." When it comes to communication, employees wanted honesty and wanted to understand the business reasons behind decisions—without any corporate spin.

Provide a complete picture—In the past, employees were confused by multiple "pieces" of information that were not always connected. Employees said, "I wish you'd just give it to us all at once." There was a real desire to understand how all the pieces fit together.

Communicate through a "familiar" credible executive—Employees wanted to hear from leadership prior to any announcement about total compensation changes. Many employees, especially those in the field, said it was more meaningful to get messages from their own business-unit heads than from top management.

Provide a "heads up" on key messages—Employees, especially those in the field, preferred to receive a voice-mail announcement prior to receiving an e-mail communication.

Mail communications to homes—Employees said they pay more attention to company communications when mailed to their homes.

Based on employee input, McDonald's, with the help of Towers Perrin, developed nine communication principles that were applied throughout the implementation process, as shown in the sidebar on page 192.

Communicate and Educate Systematically

Communication is an educational undertaking that enables employees to understand the "why" behind a pay program, "how" this will affect them and "what" behaviors are expected to earn the rewards. Once tactical communication principles are established, a communication campaign can be drafted and should model a sophisticated consumer-brand marketing campaign. If the goal is to inform, educate and ulti-mately sell a new or revised pay

> **McDonald's "addin' it up" 9 Key Communication Principles**
> 1. Keep it simple.
> 2. Eliminate spin.
> 3. Answer the "why."
> 4. Build connections (how rewards add up).
> 5. Use credible leaders to set the tone.
> 6. Get the message out and stay ahead of the grapevine.
> 7. Use multiple channels to capture attention.
> 8. Align messages.
> 9. Ask for feedback and make sure to listen.

plan to employees, then why not use the marketing tools and techniques that exist to break through the information overload and clutter prevalent in our work and personal lives? Give the pay plan its own identity—a look of its own (i.e., a brand). Choose a style, format and colors that employees will quickly recognize. Create a disruption; the format should cause people to take notice and want to read. You are competing with every other communication that comes across employees' desks, and you want to make sure that your communication catches their attention and is the one they read and look for. McDonald's "addin' it up" newsletter is an excellent example of an eye-catching piece that employees learned to rely on for information about their total compensa-tion, including pay programs. (See Figure 14-1 on page 193.)

Prepare a calendar summarizing content to communicate, when, to whom and how (mediums). Commence communications sooner rather than later, even if you don't yet know all the details. People need time to prepare for change. It is a good idea to plant the seed that something big is coming, which will build interest quickly without giving away too much detail. Communications will also need to continue well after the pay plan is implemented. Avoid delivering too much infor-mation at once, which can overwhelm employees. Pay programs are not the center of an employee's work life. Employees have job responsibilities with more imme-diate challenges than a pay-program change that may not affect them for several months. Build interest through short, bold, attention-getting communications. Start with an overview of the changes to set the stage and then communicate the details about a single aspect of the plan at just-in-time moments. Repeat key messages through different media in case employees do not understand or respond the first time. It is difficult to overcommunicate, but it is possible to overload with information if you do not appropriately time the communications.

Figure 14-1
Front Page of McDonald's "addin' it up" Newsletter

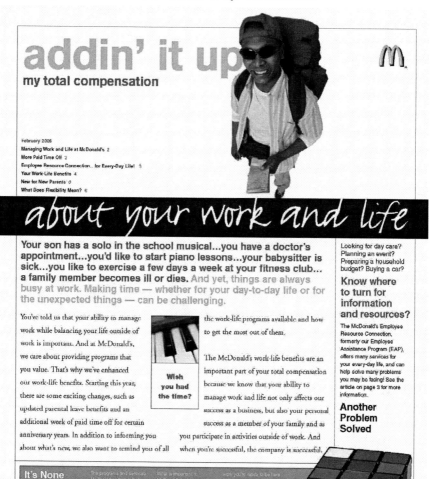

When organizations communicate messages en masse, the impulse is to carry them via e-mail—an efficient but not always the most effective means of communication. Do not discount the power of print material. People still love to read newspapers and magazines. Professional printed documentation such as newsletters have additional development costs and require time to distribute, but they are well worth the money and time if breaking through information overload is important to you. Mail the printed materials to your employees' residences in addition to workplace posting and circulation. Work-related mailed correspondence is often relevant for the entire family (e.g., insurance and benefits forms, retirement statements). Pay-plan communications may take on the same importance if mailed.

This is not to suggest that electronic communications such as e-mail, webcasts or podcasts should be ignored. A careful blend of multiple mediums, however, is ideal. People learn differently through different media. Employees in their twenties who are accustomed to technology may prefer electronic messages more than those in their forties who may find printed material a welcome relief. The message's intent can also dictate which media to use. For example, to get employees' attention directed to the fact that change was coming, McDonald's released an Adobe® Flash presentation to all managers that informed them, at a high level, that change was coming and that they needed to be ready to answer their employees' questions. It was different than anything that had been done at McDonald's in the past and caught employees' attention. McDonald's also implemented Adobe® Flash technology to deliver a 10-minute tutorial about the changes to the long-term incentive program, and explained the reasons behind the change and the differences between the different stock vehicles.

Training is the other key component of communication. Much of what employees learn about pay programs comes from their immediate supervisors. Therefore, supervisors need to understand the pay programs if they are to use them to motivate and retain employees. The human resources development department serves as an ally for developing educational materials. It is well versed in learning media (e.g., e-learning and webcasts) and can assist in curriculum and design. Because managers need to fully understand the specifics of the pay plan, they need to go through training modules prior to the training of their direct reports so that they can anticipate and be ready for questions. Use these early sessions to improve the module for the general employee population. For example, McDonald's capitalized on its "train-the-trainer" sessions. The "addin' it up" presentation for employees was presented to the HR staff responsible for orientating the entire domestic operation. As part of these HR trainer sessions, a panel of subject-matter experts fielded all questions from the trainees on the design and implementation. In some cases, these Q&A sessions lasted as long as three hours. All questions from these HR sessions were recorded, and appropriate answers were documented and bound in an answer book (30 pages in length) that was sent to HR trainers to use as a resource. New questions and answers were added as the general employee-training sessions took place.

Monitor Employee Reaction and Performance During the Implementation Process

Moving ahead on a planned implementation without monitoring employee perceptions and understanding is equivalent to flying a plane in a snowstorm without instruments. Employees and their managers who do not understand or are wary of a new compensation program can easily undermine the implementation and the program's ultimate success. Human resources development professionals also have considerable expertise in evaluating training programs. They have proven methodologies for determining if employees like the program, understand the materials and behave differently or perform more effectively because of the program. This expertise is also available from consulting firms that design and implement pay programs.

Employee opinion surveys and tests via the Internet have allowed implementation teams and compensation departments to amass pay-program feedback quickly and economically. A customized survey can be prepared in advance as part of the implementation plan and administered after employees have been introduced to the plan basics. Computer-based testing can help determine how well employees understand the pay program. For example, if a pay program contains multiple incentive options based on division, position or circumstance, employees should be able to review potential pay scenarios and calculate their total reward potential based on the program. If employees have difficulty with this task, the issues that caused difficulty should be quickly addressed. Fundamentally, a pay program must change employee behaviors to drive results. If the incentive plan is designed to encourage safety, then one must ask whether employees are following safety rules more conscientiously after the implementation of the incentive program.

Behavior change can be measured through observational methodologies, structured discussion groups (e.g., focus or nominal groups) and employee diaries. A variety of performance measures exist that can assess the impact of the pay program on company results. Pay program evaluation is examined in substantial detail in a later chapter, "Evaluating and Improving Incentive Pay Programs."

Build Flexibility into the Implementation Plan

This chapter is subtitled "The Art and Science of Making Good Ideas Work." Ensuring your implementation plan contains enough flexibility for a timely response to unexpected events demonstrates what is the "art" of this process. No pay program is perfectly designed, and its implementation cannot occur in a vacuum. Those individuals who are leading the implementation need to have the resources and must possess the proper frame of mind to accommodate sudden changes in the organization (e.g., layoffs, leadership change). They must be able to respond to up-to-the-minute information, such as survey or training feedback, so that they can modify the pay program as needed. For example, during the McDonald's "addin' it up" implementation, the compensation department noticed low participation for planned leadership webcasts on the new program. Realizing the importance of manager acceptance and understanding of "addin' it up," it quickly changed tactics and engaged leaders in a series of face-to-face group meetings. This action required far more time and resources than expected, but McDonald's leadership as a whole took notice of the seriousness given to the new program and responded in kind.

The implementation plan should recognize different operating cultures among business units and known geographical differences. Attempting a one-size-fits-all implementation plan usually creates more problems than the potential time-saving benefits of approaching implementation with a single plan of attack. The cross-functional and cross-level makeup of your design and implementation teams can pay large dividends when these differences are recognized at the outset.

Communication is a continuous process, not a single event. Build a process into the administration of the pay program; communicate to keep employees apprised of changes and to keep them from forgetting the value and specifics of the program. McDonald's still maintains an Employee Advisory Team that is now populated with new members representing a cross section of employees. Their input keeps communications fresh and provides an early warning when communication efforts are not producing their intended effects.

Conclusion

McDonald's Efforts Paid Off

Just how effective was the McDonald's "addin' it up" implementation plan? In the first year, more than 80 percent of employees indicated a better understanding of the value of their total compensation package due to the implementation and communication effort. In addition, 401(k) participation had increased, and a greater number of employees were taking advantage of wellness and prevention opportunities. The power of the newsletter communication was evident after the mailing of the *About Your Health* newsletter. Prior to the June 2005 issue, only about 1,500 employees had taken advantage of their new wellness benefits by having their annual physical. By the end of the year, more than 7,000 employees and dependents had undergone an annual physical. McDonald's goal of promoting health and wellness throughout the organization was achieved.

This chapter has presented the case for the relevance of proper pay-program implementation. When implementation is structured as a process of manageable steps that utilizes talent and resources both within and outside the organization, companies can achieve their stated objectives as they introduce a new or revised pay program. There is no circumventing the importance of systematic effort, careful planning and creativity to ensure the successful implementation of pay programs. Implementation is most effective when it is integrated with the design efforts and evaluation of the pay program.

To summarize, organizations are advised to do the following:

- Budget for implementation according to the plan's objectives. We suggest .5 percent to one percent of the plan's yearly payout or expense.
- Involve and coordinate individuals from finance, human resources, information technology, training and key line managers on a design or implementation team.
- Field pay-plan design and implementation functions as separate teams or as subgroups of one large team.
- Begin to craft the implementation strategy during the program-design phase. Don't postpone until late in the plan's design or approval process.
- Utilize available internal resources such as human resources development, communications and marketing along with expertise from outside consulting firms.
- Field an employee advisory team consisting of rank-and-file employees from across the organization to preview communication approaches and program features and respond to questions the employee population raises about the implementation process.

- Collect feedback from major stakeholders, senior managers, eligible employees and their managers on pay-program design, implementation and communication.
- Communicate! Communicate! Communicate!
  - Give the pay program its own identity—a style that grabs employee attention and maintains high future recognition.
  - Use a blend of electronic (e-mail, Adobe® Flash animation, webcasts) and printed communication to get the message out.
  - Create a calendar summarizing content to communicate, including when, to whom and how (mediums).
  - Avoid delivering too much content at one time or too soon.
  - Create an extensive training program about the pay plan for employees and their managers.
- Monitor employee reaction and performance during the implementation process.
- Build flexibility into the implementation plan.
- Keep communication processes going after the plan is in operation.
- Don't underestimate the value of using multiple communication channels—face to face, print, technology—to deliver and reinforce your messages.

Footnotes

1 "McDonald's" and "i'm lovin' it" are trademarks of McDonald's Corp. and its affiliates, used with permission.

Chapter 15

The Experience of Changing to an Integrated Compensation Software Program

George Kaspar, Exelon Corp.

This chapter provides a review of Exelon's experience in designing, implementing and administering an integrated compensation software program to collect employee ratings, merit adjustments, equity recommendations and annual/quarterly incentive bonus discretionary from managers. The core function of the program calculates complex annual incentive bonuses for the entire 17,000-employee workforce. This function is one of the main reasons Exelon, one of the nation's largest electric utilities with more than $15 billion in annual revenues, chose the software. If your company has decided to eliminate those awful spreadsheets used to gather employee performance scores and to calculate pay increases, incentive payouts and equity awards, the knowledge Exelon gained from its transition may be useful to you.

Reasons for Switching to Compensation Administration Software

The reasons for making an investment in compensation administration software become quite clear as the complexity and number of pay programs increases. The advantages of using integrated compensation software include the following:

- **More accurate data collection**—Have you ever received performance appraisal spreadsheets from managers and realized that one of them forgot to include a column when he or she re-sorted the spreadsheet, which caused all the records to be wrong? Or have you ever had a manager decide to add new or ineligible participants to the spreadsheet? A centralized compensation software tool has highly sophisticated data-entry controls (e.g., security rules) that can restrict users from adding or deleting employees as well as giving raises outside programmed parameters or rearranging system data.

- **More accurate and timely award payouts**—Compensation software systems are designed to calculate awards using your designated criteria. With spreadsheets, there is always the fear of formulas being wrong. Verifying the compensation software's computations by calculating your expected payout, independent of the system, will confirm your confidence in the software.
- **Better use of manager time!**—Compensation software is an efficient tool for collecting employee performance data, maintaining pay data and calculating incentive awards. Most compensation software systems let users input employee performance scores, salary increases, and incentive and equity awards all at one time. Centralized reporting makes it easy for senior management to review decisions of more junior supervisors or managers. Compensation software also provides bookmarking, which allows managers to go right to where they last worked in the system.
- **Other advantages:**
  - Improved security of confidential information
  - Improved compensation group review for outliers, adherence to guidelines, philosophy and strategy, etc.
  - Restriction of managers from viewing the performance of employees that do not report to them.
  - Increased control of spending and reporting for Sarbanes-Oxley and audit purposes.

By avoiding the designing, rolling out, collecting and verifying of spreadsheets, a tremendous amount of time is saved, and the process is greatly simplified.

Implementing a Compensation Software Package

A detailed plan is essential to successfully implementing a compensation software package. This section presents the plan followed at Exelon along with the lessons learned about saving substantial cost, time and effort.

Identify Business Needs and Software Requirements

The first step in selecting a new compensation software package and vendor is getting a clear understanding of your software requirements. Software requirements documentation—the **Software Requirement Specifications (SRS)**—needs to provide specific details for what you want the software to accomplish. The clearer your requirements, the easier it will be to select the right vendor, obtain accurate cost estimates and implement the program successfully. Exelon prioritized its needs in the following four categories:

- Necessary – Cannot pay or administer plans without the software meeting these requirements. If the compensation software cannot satisfy these requirements, it cannot be used, and the review committee will drop the software from consideration.
- Important – These requirements add considerable efficiency or capability but can be sacrificed if necessary to obtain other software features or cost advantages. The vendor should indicate how the system might be customized and how much the customization will cost.
- Nice to Have – These are a bonus, if included, but are not necessary to the system. For example, the software may not have the capability to lay out reports in the ideal format.
- Potential Future Needs – Although it is difficult to anticipate how compensation program designs might change in the future, software that can adapt to changes is desirable. However, if anticipated changes require software customization, proceed with caution, because cost and risk will increase.

Exelon categorized about 70 percent of its requirements as necessary, 20 percent as important, 9 percent as nice to have and 1 percent as potential future needs. Some of the requirements that Exelon identified as necessary included the following:

- Ability for managers to input all employee performance data for incentives, salary and equity award planning on one Web page
- System ability to calculate extremely complex bonus payouts by business units
- System ability to prorate calculations for new hires, rehires, temporary employees, employees on leave and part-time employees
- Capability to produce a total-compensation statement, stock option grant and incentive award calculation statement.

Obtain Management and Staff Commitment

Exelon's key players for identifying software requirements, supporting software development and administrating the compensation system consist of plan administrators, information technology (IT) and senior management sponsors.

- Compensation plan administrators are the best source of pay program knowledge. Administrators understand data and reporting requirements for calculating payouts and how to monitor and communicate the pay programs. At Exelon, compensation plan administrators design pay programs and provide program support for three main divisions: energy delivery, generation and business services. Working closely with human resources professionals, line managers and finance, they are critical for administering and signing off on the division compensation plan payouts for which they are responsible.

- Information technology (IT) support is a must. Exelon's IT group is very knowledgeable about its information systems; it actually developed and supported the old in-house incentive Visual Basic award system. IT supported the compensation software customizations, created interfaces between internal HR systems and the compensation software, and helped manage the relationship with the software vendor.

- Senior management sponsors at senior executive or director levels have a clear vision of what the software will be designed to accomplish. Sponsor commitment is critical when there is a need to approve emergency funding or to obtain support to overcome roadblocks or address critical design and implementation issues. Critical issues can escalate quickly when the vendor is not focused on a software fix that is needed immediately to avoid substantial delays in the development of the compensation software.

Select a Vendor and Compensation Administration Software

After completing the first two steps, you need to summarize the software requirements in a Request for Proposal (RFP). Vendors use the RFP to provide a cost and time quote for software customization.

Exelon evaluated each RFP response on three sets of criteria:

- **Meeting requirements**—How well did the vendor meet Exelon's software requirements? Vendors should specify what is standard to their package and what is considered customization. Preference should be given to the vendor whose core system functionality best matches your requirements. Customizations should be avoided, because they are time-consuming and costly.

- **Cost**—Compensation software can range from $100,000 to $400,000 depending on the size of the organization, required customization and support provided from the vendor. Furthermore, vendor costs can vary substantially. Comparing the costs of vendor software can be difficult because of inconsistent pricing methodology. Some vendors may charge more for the initial software but less for customization and upgrades. The cost to upgrade to a future software release can be substantial.

- **Professional references** – These should be reviewed carefully. Questions asked by Exelon included the following:
  - Did the vendor meet your timelines?

- How well does the system meet your needs?
- How many customizations do you have, and how did the vendor handle those?
- Did the vendor stay on budget? Are the costs for upgrades and customization what you expected?
- How well did the vendor develop and document the required customizations of the software?
- How does the vendor handle software training and support?
- Are you satisfied with the results?
- What problems or challenges have you faced related to the design, implementation and use of this software?

Exelon had three vendors that made the final cut: Authoria (AIM), Workscape and Peoplesoft Custom Consultant Programmers. Peoplesoft proposed to customize the needed functionality and interface their software with the Peoplesoft software used to manage Excelon's payroll and HR systems. Exelon liked this option, but the cost to program all customizations in Peoplesoft was more than double the cost of using other vendors. From Exelon's perspective, Workscape was very similar to Authoria, but it did not have a robust annual-incentive calculation tool to handle complex annual-incentive bonus plans. Although Workscape had better functionality for use with international employees, Exelon had few of these employees. Authoria was chosen because (1) its software had the ability to provide the calculations for Exelon's extremely complex incentive plans, (2) it had a lower overall cost, (3) it promised that it could deliver most of Exelon's software requirements, (4) it had references from an external Towers Perrin consultant who identified Authoria compensation software as "best in breed" and (5) it had positive feedback from other clients that use Authoria's compensation software.

Software Development and Customizations

After selecting the vendor, you need to finalize the SRS (see step 1). Depending on the number of software requirements and how well the specifications were outlined in your request for proposals, this step can be relatively easy or require substantial work. Finalizing the SRS should be done with the participation of compensation and equity plan administrators and IT support personnel at a meeting. The purpose of the meeting is for the vendor to meet your team and clarify any questions you have about the compensation software. Developing a clear understanding of the requirements and responsibilities may involve considerable discussion prior to reaching final SRS agreement. When both parties sign off on the SRS, it becomes the blueprint for customizing the compensation software for your organization. Any misunderstanding or change to the SRS will usually cost more money and delay the project. Exelon made 10 change orders in the SRS that added an additional $75,000 to the total project cost.

Customizing the vendor's compensation software is very costly and can result in software failures. Customization requires the following:

- Writing new computer code, which can become very complex, especially as the code writer tries to integrate the new capabilities of the software with existing capabilities of the standardized software package.
- Extensive testing, because changes in computer code that drive complex software can easily be broken or produce unintended results. Retesting is also required every time the vendor upgrades the software. Testing is a shared task between the vendor and the client; it can be very time-consuming and may transfer responsibility for errors to the client if those errors are not caught during testing.

Because writing and testing code requires substantial amounts of work, vendors typically bill clients by the hour for software customization. Unfortunately, Exelon learned this lesson the hard way. Roughly 25 percent to 35 percent of the total system costs were customizations. This is a significant amount of money. If Exelon had slightly changed the plan design or developed some workarounds, it could have saved $100,000 to $200,000. Workarounds are calculations that are done outside the system, with only the result entered into the system. Although workarounds could be a cost-efficient alternative to customization, they also can cause extra work and possible errors, so you have to weigh the cost against the administrative cost and the inherent risk of performing workarounds. The software customization at Exelon is so extensive because it tried to accommodate an extremely complex bonus-plan design. Thus, there is always a worry about what's going to break when updates or new code are/is applied. The lesson learned is that one should consider redesigning complex pay programs or reengineering pay processes so that they meet the vendor's standard system specifications—and so that customization isn't even needed. Exelon's plan is to upgrade to a new platform of the Authoria software in 2008 and, consequently, it will look very closely at where it can eliminate customizations.

Implementing and Testing Your Customized Compensation Software

After the system is developed and delivered, the real work begins. Usually the vendor provides a period of time for you to test the compensation software with your customizations installed. The vendor project manager for your account, however, will want to close the project and transition you to some form of customer care as soon as possible. Do not let this happen prematurely. Take your time to thoroughly go over the system and fully test your customizations. Authoria wanted to transition Exelon to customer care two months after delivery. It finally transitioned Exelon six months later. Having consistent support with one or two analysts who helped design the software is much better than working through an automated answering system (customer care) and waiting for someone who may not know your system to call you back in a day or two.

Software problems inevitably arise. A good relationship with the vendor helps in getting them solved quickly. Exelon had more than 200 software fixes within the first year of running the system. Because a vendor's support staff generally does not have the accountability that internal employees have, those support staff typically only do what they are told to do, and no more. Double-checking their work is an absolute requirement, and in many cases you have to monitor them closely until the job is done right. Some suggestions when dealing with vendors include the following:

- Request updates and proof that work is completed on schedule. If they cannot provide proof, request read-only access to their development site to view progress. Demand periodic sign-off verifying work is performed as scheduled. This last point is critical and should be clarified as part of the initial contract and statement of work.
- Know the vendor's organizational hierarchy so that you can obtain quick responses to serious issues or report unresponsive vendor staff. For example, Exelon had its vice president call the vendor's senior vice president directly about a problem, and then received immediate focus on its issue and a speedy resolution. Such an action is best taken as a last resort. Remember that you will have to deal with these people often and that demanding instant attention for noncritical issues will create relationship problems.
- Plan for vendor discontinuity. Vendor continuity is an issue in the software industry. The vendor can go out of business or be acquired by another company. If the company goes out of business, can you maintain the system until another software package is in place? As a backup plan, Exelon has its legacy system available in case this situation occurs. In the worst-case scenario, it could revert to collecting managerial input and calculating awards with spreadsheets.

Considerable administration time and skill are required to take advantage of the compensation software capability. We recommend a strong internal person for this role—someone who not only understands the technical aspects of compensation plans and their administration but who also has strong computer knowledge and experience. This compensation professional will be required to establish system rules or guidelines, which can include the following:

- **Performance**—If an employee receives an outstanding performance rating, what does that mean? You might establish a 7-percent maximum increase for employees rated as "outstanding," a 5-percent maximum increase for "average" employees and no increase for employees rated "poor." The software will disallow or alert managers when increases over the prescribed amounts are entered. Exelon adjusts these rules and guidelines annually, requiring salary, incentive and equity award program maintenance.

- **Budgets**—The compensation software calculates and manages budget dollars or stock shares for different business units or employee levels in your organization. For example, do your vice presidents have a higher budget pool than managers, or does one business unit get a higher budget than another? These guidelines must be established and entered into the software. At Exelon, the establishment of budgets is entered at the corporate level. Your company may decide to have the managers establish and maintain their own budgets within the compensation software.

- **Proration events**—Does your company prorate situations such as partial time in a job or business unit, new hires, terminations, part-timers, leaves of absence or temporary employees?

Implementing Exelon's new compensation software involved four major activities: training, communicating with stakeholders, testing the software with actual data and creating reports. Whenever complex software is implemented, one must expect a steep, if not bumpy, learning curve. Depending on the complexity of your incentive, salary and equity award plans, translating the designs into the compensation software can be confusing. Most vendors supply a training document and provide on-site training support for the compensation professionals responsible for administering the software. Compensation administration software is so complex that, while the support helps, you really need a dedicated person on the vendor's site to call when you run into problems. Even a small company should demand this type of service.

Training your managers and HR staff to use the software correctly is a challenge. Exelon was lucky to have an internal training and communications specialist who was a major contributor to the successful implementation of the compensation software package. At Exelon, training material was customized for the different groups that needed training (e.g., HR support, line managers and compensation specialists). Training at Exelon included the following:

- Classroom training was used for line managers where the software was demonstrated.
- Web-based training was used for managers and HR support. This training worked well because the workforce is spread out across the United States. Exelon still uses the Web-based training and considers it very effective.
- Recorded training sessions are used as a refresher for managers and HR support. This training was also useful for new managers and administrators.

Effective communication is a key element in overcoming resistance to the changes required by the new compensation software package. Exelon started the communication with software "demos" at the sponsor level of the organization. Once it had buy-in from the sponsors, the company communicated down the chain of command. Frequent communications will increase familiarity and reduce resistance when the software is rolled out. Items added to the communication plan included:

- E-learning programs to give managers a feel for the software and to show them, before implementation, some of the advantages they would soon enjoy
- Weekly or monthly manager updates about the implementation progress and the roles and responsibilities of managers who would be using the system
- Frequently asked questions (FAQs)–Included items like: How does this affect me? How do I access the system? and Who do I call if there are problems?

When developing and testing the software, it is important to verify the accuracy of the provided calculations. At Exelon, staff entered the data and the eligibility and performance parameters for each pay program (e.g., salary, merit or lump-sum bonuses, individual or team bonuses, equity award programs). An Exelon example of performance measures and how they are weighted appears in Figure 15-1 on page 208. In this example, we have one annual bonus-plan payout. For this bonus plan, we have five performance measures that are used to calculate the payout. The weighted performance measures are used to determine the amount of plan payout.

Many plans have modifiers such as shareholder protection hurdles or caps applied to awards. Modifiers can increase or decrease awards depending on performance. One must be sure to sequence pay-data modifiers properly. (Sequencing is the order in which modifications are made to awards.) For instance, your plan may have an "earnings per share" modifier calculated prior to the "individual performance" modifier, which could have a different payout than if you reversed the sequence of the two modifiers. In Figure 15-2 on page 208, an Exelon example of

Figure 15-1
Performance Measures

Performance Measure	Type	Weight
EPS - Incentive Earnings Per Share	Standard	25.00%
GenCo Operabng Net Income	Organizational	25.00%
Power Commercial Availabilty - Fossil	Organizational	15.00%
Power Hydro Equiv Availabilty	Organizational	10.00%
Power Net Operating Expenses	Organizational	25.00%

Total: 100.00%

plan modification sequencing, the sequence in the far left column orders the modification to the bonus plan.

In this bonus plan, "EPS award curtailment" will modify the award before the "peaking" modifiers we have listed as number two in the sequence is performed. If performance measures and modifiers are not placed in the correct sequence, the final calculations will be incorrect. The pay-program design and award calculations vary widely among pay programs, so care must be taken to ensure the sequence is absolutely correct.

- **Establish Key Identifier to Assign Employees to Plans**—There is usually some form of query tool in the compensation software used to assign employees to specific pay programs. Those queries establish the rules needed to assign a person to a plan. For example, a query could be set up with a filter to say that if I am in department 1000, I will be assigned to the energy department incentive plan, and if I am in department 2,000, then I will be assigned to the generation department incentive plan. At Exelon, it was necessary to customize the system to use a plan identifier (e.g., a code Exelon established) because the source HR/payroll system does not have 100-percent clean data, such as department numbers, and that could cause inaccurate plan assignments for individuals.
- **Test Plans with Spreadsheets to Mirror the Plan Payouts**—Exelon still

Figure 15-2
Plan Modification Sequencing

Seq.	Modifier	Mod Type	Component Tgt	Calc Meth
1	EPS Award Curtailment	Measure Group	Organizational	Cap
2	Peaking Environmental Indicator	Measure Group	Organizational	Multiply
2	Peaking Net Operating Expense	Measure Group	Organizational	Multiply
2	Peaking Station Clock Resets	Measure Group	Organizational	Multiply
2	Power Fleetwide OSHA Recordable Rate	Measure Group	Organizational	Multiply
3	ACSI Proxy Corporate	Total Plan	NA	Multiply
4	Individual Performance Modifier	Total Plan	NA	Multiply

uses spreadsheets to independently check the calculation of each of the pay programs in the compensation system. This is done by mirroring the incentive plan performance measures and modifiers in an Excel spreadsheet, entering the same performance and calculating the awards to see if the compensation software arrives at the same payouts. Exelon tests the incentive plan payouts twice: when the plans are developed and when the final awards are sent to payroll. It keeps records of test results for audit purposes.

- **Test Sample Payouts for Individual Employees**—The accuracy of the compensation software is tested again by taking a sample population of employees, manually calculating individual payouts and comparing them with the software payout results. Exelon creates a diverse sample that includes full-time, part-time, regular, temporary, prorated, standard and any other odd situation that may occur within that pay program. Exelon does this test of plan payouts twice: when the plans are developed and when the final awards are sent to payroll. Again, it keeps records of test results for audit purposes.

- **Test Managers' Input in Web-Based Worksheets**—Worksheets are the entry tool for managers to input employee performance for salary, incentive and equity award plans. Exelon has budget pools that limit the amount of money and equity managers can award to employees within the managerial input worksheets. When managers enter employee performance appraisal scores, they must manage their budget allocation to control spending. The budget pools should be reviewed closely to verify they are accurate. These pools can be calculated outside the compensation software system in Excel and cross-checked for accuracy. Doing this is important, because managers will be planning their employee awards based on their budgets. Exelon learned the hard way what can happen when this information is not checked closely enough. The wrong code in the compensation software system erroneously multiplied certain managers' budget pools by three.

Figure 15-3 on page 210 is a sample of one of the worksheets that Exelon managers use to develop performance plans for their employees. The worksheet provides data about the employee, including historical award payouts. Budgets at the bottom of the form automatically update as performance scores are entered. In the Authoria online worksheet shown in Figure 15-3, managers can input ratings, merit increases and lump -sum increases, as well as individual bonus-performance modifiers. They can also enter stock discretion awards, including stock options, restricted stock and performance shares for Exelon. While managers are entering the performance, they are receiving constant feedback from the system that tells them if they are over budget or if they

Figure 15-3
Performance Plan Worksheet

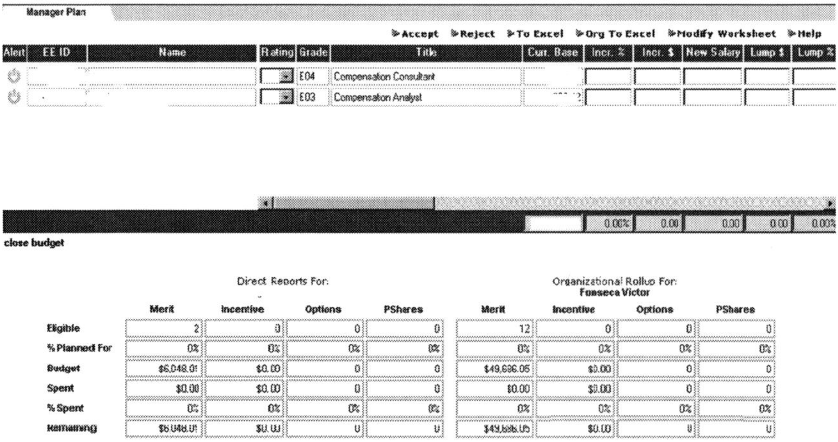

are entering performance scores that are higher or lower than specified by the guidelines. In some instances, the system will not allow performance scores entered outside the specified performance rules.

Security is always an auditable issue. As a result, you will find yourself taking responsibility for security administration when the compensation software becomes operational. Only a limited number of people with security clearance should have the ability to access the security administration of the system. At Exelon, the final access list is signed off by the vice president of human resources. Separation of control will please your auditors.

The single greatest benefit of a compensation software program is the ability to create reports. Previously, Exelon manually created compensation statement reports by using mail-merge functionality in Microsoft Word and linking all the data with a Microsoft Excel file. It did a triple check of all the data and physically produced statements before distributing the statements to managers for delivery to their employees. This task was time-consuming and prone to errors.

When you selected your software vendor and customized the software, considerable thought should have been invested in determining the reports required. Exelon had four main customized reports for employees and managers:

- **Total Compensation Statement**—Provides employees with a one-page statement showing all the compensation programs for which they are eligible and performance information for the year. Also included are next year's target opportunities for salary, incentive and equity award programs. This statement was produced by adding custom fields and tables to show next year's opportunity on the total compensation statements. Although giving employees their opportunity data was very labor-intensive, it was worth the effort.

An example of Exelon's Total Compensation Statement appears in Figure 15-4.

- **Annual Incentive Award Calculation Statement**—Details annual incentive payouts, including performance measures, modifiers and any individual factors incorporated into the bonus award calculation. This statement provides a breakdown of the employee's incentive award. Employees can go through each step of the calculation process to see what performance measures and modifiers added or subtracted dollars from their payouts.

- **Stock Option Grant Instrument**—Shows details and legal information about stock option grants given.

- **Organization To Excel Report**—Provides functionality allowing managers to export all their employees' data from worksheet forms into an Excel file. They can use this extract for planning offline or as a reference of what they planned for their employees.

Exelon learned that there was a need to have a lot of ad hoc reporting out of the

Figure 15-4
Total Compensation Statement

Total Compensation Summary Information

Personal and Confidential

Name:	Test	**Job Title:**	Test22
Employee ID:	111111	**Grade:**	E00

2005 **Performance Rating:** 3

Incentive Compensation Summary for 2005

2005 **AIP Award:**	Company Multiplier =	128.62%	$74,308
	Individual Multiplier =	110%	

2005 **Stock Option Grants:**	8,450 **Shares**	$108,825

Shares granted as of 1/24/05 are valued at an exercise price of $42.85 and 30% Black-Scholes. Options vest 25% over a 4-year period.

Total Direct Compensation Opportunity for 2006

2006 **Annualized Base Salary:**

Current Annual Base Salary	Merit Adjustment	(Effective 03/01/2006)	$182,067
$175,064 +	$7,002 (4.00%)		

2006 **Annual Incentive Target Opportunity: ( )**

system. It developed these reports by linking the compensation software with a reporting tool such as Microsoft Access. Doing this is especially helpful for running reports for financial accruing, data checking, data-entry monitoring, Sarbanes-Oxley reporting and so on. You may want to specify reporting functionality as a critical capability during the software-requirements process to be sure that you get the best possible reporting solutions and the ability to control your own reports without vendor intervention and costs.

Conclusion

Next year Exelon will upgrade its software to the latest version of Authoria's Compensation Advisor and switch its software from being managed on the intranet IT network to having Authoria manage and host the software on its network. Thus, Exelon will not have to maintain the network and Compensation Advisor software with internal IT hardware and staff. Most compensation software vendors prefer to host their own software so that they do not have to maintain many different versions of their software across many different customers' sites. Hosting also allows the vendor to more efficiently make fixes or upgrades for all clients. To end users like Exelon, the transition should be seamless.

Exelon has found that integrated compensation software is an administrative tool that is more accurate and cost-effective than the spreadsheets and Microsoft Word statements that Exelon once used. These compensation tools are starting to evolve into even more complex software suites that now offer tools for recruiting, performance management, employee advising and communications. However, you should be aware that the skill sets needed for effectively using these compensation software tools are scarce. If the internal expert leaves the company, it could be very difficult to quickly fill that role.

Author's note: I would like to thank John B. Nolan, CPA (executive compensation consultant at Exelon Corp.), for his critical review of this chapter and his helpful suggestions.

Chapter 16

Evaluating Pay-Program Effectiveness: A National Survey of Compensation Professionals

Dow Scott, Ph.D., Loyola University Chicago
Dennis Morajda, Performance Development International Inc.
Thomas D. McMullen, Hay Group

Editor's note: The authors are grateful for the help provided by Richard Sperling, Hay Group, in the development of this paper.

Given that compensation is often the largest controllable expense for an organization, it would seem that HR management and senior executives would calculate return on investment (ROI) for annual merit budgets, incentive pay plans, health and welfare benefits programs and equity programs. This is not the case.

According to a recent study conducted by Hay Group, Loyola University Chicago and WorldatWork, 62 percent of compensation professionals report that their organizations do not attempt to measure the ROI of their compensation programs (Scott, McMullen, Sperling 2005). Moreover, organizations that measure ROI are split between doing this informally and using quantitative data to evaluate their pay programs. What is even more astounding is that the majority of compensation professionals feel that their programs are either effective or highly effective. How can compensation professionals believe their programs are effective without knowing if these pay programs provide a reasonable ROI?

So why don't most organizations measure the ROI for their compensation programs?

There are a number of possible answers. For some organizations, the compensation department may not be involved in this activity-measuring; ROI may be in the purview of finance or operations. For others, measuring ROI may not be feasible because measurement and monitoring systems are not in place—it may just be too difficult and time-consuming. The functional silo orientation in many HR functions may be a contributing factor; the compensation staff focuses on direct compensation, the benefits group focuses on benefits costs and incentive pay programs may be the purview of specific operational areas. For example, sales departments often design and administer sales incentive programs. Finally, it may not occur to compensation professionals that traditional methods of assessing the value of pay programs have significant limitations. Benchmarking pay programs with other companies, an often-used compensation practice, may indicate if pay program costs are aligned with competitors, but it does not indicate the economic or perceived value of the pay program, which is by far the more important consideration.

However, even if an organization calculates ROI for its pay programs, ROI evaluation by itself is not enough since this information provides little insight into why ROI exceeded, met or did not meet management expectations. Furthermore, since ROI, like many financial tools, is a lagging indicator of effectiveness, by the time these results are calculated, damage may already have been inflicted by misaligned or poorly designed pay programs.

In this first installment of a two-part series, the authors advocate a systematic and comprehensive pay-program evaluation process that provides an accurate assessment of the compensation program's contribution to the business and offers insight into how to improve both program quality and effectiveness.

For many organizations, it appears that compensation is considered to be just a cost of doing business. However, *Fortune* magazine's "Most Admired Companies" were much more likely to assess ROI (64 percent as compared to 38 percent of all companies), and 21 percent (as compared to 9 percent) report using financial or operational data in assessing ROI for their compensation programs (Scott, McMullen, Sperling 2005). Although senior executives may not hold compensation professionals to the same ROI analysis standard as their colleagues in other organizational areas, a variety of end-result measures to evaluate their pay programs are used by the organizations that measure ROI. They include revenues, profits, employee retention, controlled or lowered labor costs, productivity, ability to recruit and employee-satisfaction measures. Unfortunately, because the use of these measures and evaluation processes across organizations is inconsistent and absent a systematic process for data collection, the value of these evaluation methods is limited insofar as determining trends within the profession.

Approaches for Evaluating Human Resources Programs

One does not need to look far to find successful approaches for evaluating human resources programs; human resources development (HRD) and performance management (Kaplan and Norton's Balanced Scorecards) are relevant comparators. HRD has taken a lead on the introduction of more rigorous evaluation processes within the HR function because training and development programs are often perceived as valuable but unessential by senior management. As a result, these programs are often cancelled or delayed and HRD staffs decimated when their organizations face financial challenges. In response, HRD professionals have been forced to develop systematic processes of evaluating training programs that better demonstrate their business value. The authors believe that these evaluation techniques developed by HRD professionals have direct applicability to the compensation profession and can substantially improve the ability to design and implement effective pay programs. As in HRD and Balanced Scorecard evaluation processes, comprehensive pay program evaluation can do the following:

- Demonstrate the contribution pay programs make to the "bottom line."
- Provide necessary feedback for improving pay-program effectiveness, given the constant changes in the work and business environment.
- Identify problems early in the program's rollout.
- Build employee and management commitment to the pay program by engaging them in the evaluation and improvement process.
- Hold management responsible for using the program as designed.
- Better communicate pay values, policies and programs to employees and managers. Evaluation is not just an opportunity to collect information, it represents an opportunity to clarify and communicate management priorities, values and willingness to listen to employee concerns.

Recommended Pay-Program Evaluation Framework

Pay-program evaluation can be thought of in terms of two dimensions as shown in the matrix in Figure 1 on page 216. Building on what has been learned by HRD (for example, Kirkpatrick 1998 and Phillips 1997) and performance management professionals (Kaplan and Norton 1996), the first dimension focuses on the different evaluation perspectives that should be considered in the evaluation process, that is, employee reaction, understanding, behavior change and impact on end results.

The balanced scorecard emphasizes that it is not enough to judge outcomes, but one must also examine how those outcomes were obtained to provide a fair evaluation and to provide the information the employee needs to improve.

The second dimension of the proposed framework is the evaluation process, which has been developed by researchers and evaluation experts over many years. We have divided the process into six steps:

1) Setting goals or objectives
2) Identifying evaluation criteria
3) Selecting an evaluation methodology
4) Collecting and analyzing data
5) Interpreting findings

Figure 1

Pay-Program Evaluation Matrix. Customer Service Representative— Monthly Incentive Pay Program

	Reaction (Level 1)	Understanding (Level 2)	Behavior (Level 3)	End Results (Level 4)
1. Program Goals	CSRs and their managers feel the bonus program: • Is administered equitably • Rewards performance fairly • Measures performance accurately • Pays out if CSRs perform	CSRs and their managers understand: • The goals of the bonus program • How performance is measured • How and when performance will be rewarded	• CSRs resolve the customer problem/request on the first call. • CSRs follow up with the customer problem or request if not resolved on the initial call. • CSRs handle 15% above the minimum number of calls during peak hours.	• Improved customer satisfaction • Increased sales revenues from new and existing customers • Improved CSR productivity • Increased CSR retention
2. Evaluation Criteria and Measures	Employee opinion survey measures to assess employee perceptions about bonus program; e.g. equitable administration, fair performance measures, accuracy of performance measures and likelihood of receiving rewards for performance	E-learning program that has multiple-choice questions to test CSRs and their manager's working knowledge of the program	• Track calls that are handled on the initial customer call. • Track unresolved first calls to determine if CSR has followed up with customer. • Track number of calls handled during peak hours.	• Customer satisfaction survey scores (sampled monthly) • Sales revenues by new and existing customers • Number of calls processed monthly • CSR retention rates (monthly)
3. Design Evaluation	Employee perceptions of bonus program benchmarked with perception of other pay programs and changes in perceptions measured over time	CSRs and their managers must, on average, score 85%; employees receiving less than a 70% will receive additional training.	Behavioral data measured over time to determine if improvements are associated with the bonus program	Measures outcomes over time to determine if improvements are associated with the bonus program
4. Data Analyze and Collection	Conduct survey and analyze data, for example, t-tests, regression and ANOVA	Averages and total scores	Collect data and use time-series analysis	Collect data and use time-series analysis CSR retention rates

The evaluation levels are adapted from Kirkpatrick's evaluation model (for example, 1998). Behaviors and outcomes are defined by management in terms of what is valued (outcomes) and what management believes drives those outcomes (behaviors), so in some cases what one organization defines as a behavior may be defined as an outcome by another organization. Since both behavioral and end results unfold or happen over time, similar evaluation designs and statistical methods may be applied as noted in this example.

6) Developing and implementing program improvement strategies.

To collect accurate information that exposes both the value of the pay program and suggests methods for improvement, the evaluation process steps must be followed and the pay program examined from as many of the four perspectives as possible.

Figure 1 illustrates the evaluation framework by applying it to a monthly bonus program for 110 customer service representatives (CSR). The monthly incentive pay program is not fully developed because organizational-specific characteristics such as culture, job duties and technology will have a substantial impact on the overall design of the evaluation process.

Dimension I: Evaluation Perspective

This paper adapts Kirkpatrick's model to articulate the different perspectives that should be considered in the evaluation process. Kirkpatrick's (1998) framework has four evaluation levels: (1) reaction, (2) learning, (3) behavior and (4) results. Ideally, evaluation should take place sequentially on all four levels because each provides a unique perspective for assessing their value and effectiveness. The adaptation of these four perspectives can be described as follows.

Reaction to the Pay Program (Level 1)

The most fundamental evaluation of a pay program is how it is perceived; not just by program participants (that is, eligible employees) but also by their managers. Pay programs often require employees to change their behavior or accept changes in the way they are compensated. A common reaction, especially if employees do not understand the new pay program, is the belief that the organization may be trying to cheat them by demanding more work for less pay. If employees feel the pay program is unfair either internally (that is, in comparison to other employees) or externally (that is, in comparison to pay programs they might be eligible for in other organizations), regardless of the program's merit or the sophistication of its design, it will meet resistance. Furthermore, employees may be dissatisfied with rewards offered or how the program is administered. By the same token, managers who have a negative view of the pay program will be unenthusiastic supporters and will likely not use the pay program as intended. Arguably, negative perceptions of virtually any pay program are going to undermine its effectiveness.

Some managers are reluctant to ask employees how they feel about pay programs because it may open the door for complaints. Although this may be true, employee expectations can be managed, therefore minimizing these complaints.

Employee and manager perceptions of a pay program or policies can be assessed several different ways. The most common methods include employee opinion surveys, focus groups and interviews.

Employee Opinion Surveys

Confidential employee opinion surveys focused on pay-program goals, design and administration can provide an accurate and cost-effective assessment of perceptions for large employee groups. However, employee opinion surveys require professional assistance to obtain information that accurately reflects employee perceptions. A recently published *WorldatWork Journal* paper by Scott, Morajda and Bishop (2005) provides more information on the design and administration of employee opinion surveys.

Focus Groups

Small employee groups are often used to determine how employees will react to an HR program. Focus groups must be carefully structured and use competent and unbiased facilitators to obtain accurate assessments of employee views about pay programs. Because participants may have questions, the facilitator should understand the company's pay package and how it is administered. It is also recommended that employees with different types of pay packages be placed in different focus groups.

Interviews

Although requiring a substantial investment of time, one-to-one interview feedback may provide the most in-depth understanding of how employees feel about their pay. Interviews must be highly structured and in sufficient numbers to provide comparative information across different employee groups, for example, income levels, gender, age and race. Interviewers, like focus-group facilitators, should understand the pay system and be perceived by employees as unbiased and able to keep individual information confidential.

Managers often assert that they can informally determine employee reaction to HR programs or policies by simply keeping their "ear to the ground." Unfortunately, information collected informally can be biased, resulting in inaccurate assessments. First, just because some employees are willing to speak up does not mean they are representative of major employees' opinions on the subject. Second, employees often "pull their punches" when dealing with superiors who can affect their jobs, pay and employment. Third, even the best managers may hear only what they want to hear (especially if they were involved in the pay program's design). As a result, more formal (as opposed to informal) methods to assess employee reactions to pay are encouraged.

Pay Program Understanding (Level 2)

The second evaluation level focuses on how well employees and their managers understand the pay program. If the pay program is not understood, one cannot expect employees to perform or to behave in the desired way, and the confusion associated with limited program knowledge will create frustration and resentment. Knowledge of the pay program includes understanding the program's goals, how it benefits the organization and employee and what employees must do to receive the rewards.

A straightforward way for assessing understanding is to administer tests over program policies and descriptive materials. New e-learning technology utilized by human resources development professionals makes this relatively easy and cost-effective. In addition to being an evaluative tool, testing also enhances learning by holding employees and managers responsible for understanding the required material. A variety of testing methods can be initiated to evaluate employee understanding based on the level of knowledge required.

In the CSR illustration, if the bonus program is straightforward, a multiple-choice test should suffice. Integrating an e-learning module where employees and managers can learn about the pay program and have their level of understanding tested at the same time is likely the most practical route. Thus, employees are able to learn the materials when they are ready (or by a deadline established by management) and absorb this information at their own pace. Testing is not about grading an individual; it is a tool to encourage learning and to ensure everyone understands the program. The appropriate e-learning materials can be repeated until a passing score is achieved. E-learning also enables management to monitor who has successfully completed the training and identify questions employees are having difficulty answering. Finally, the e-learning module is available on-demand when new employees are hired or when employees require a refresher course.

Work Behaviors (Level 3)

For a pay program to impact organizational outcomes or increase ROI, employees must behave differently by putting in more effort, working more efficiently or focusing their actions to be more effective. When pay programs are developed, management frequently pays little attention to what employees will do differently to increase productivity, sales or profits. However, unless the linkage between behavior and end results is established, employees will have little influence on pay-program outcomes. With no "line of sight," employees will become frustrated and will not be motivated by the pay program.

For a pay program to be effective or have the desired end results, three things must happen. First, employees must perceive a pay program as fair and worthy of their efforts (Level 1). Second, employees must understand how the pay program works and how to obtain the rewards (Level 2). Third, employees must exhibit the behavior that will generate the desired outcomes (Level 3). Of course, if the behavior change is unrelated to the end result, then the program will not generate value.

Job behaviors can be identified and quantified through a variety of analytical methods including observation, behavioral event interviews or expert panels. These methods provide insight into how critical job behaviors influence desired organizational results. Although compensation professionals are usually familiar with these job-analysis techniques as they are used to determine the internal and market value of work, HRD and performance management professionals can help identify critical behaviors linked to positive end results.

As most managers know, desired changes in behavior may not occur due to work climate, peer pressure, work requirements, technology limitations and negative reinforcement by supervisors. As such, behavioral measures can provide important insight into why a pay program may not have a positive impact on desired results. The challenge is in finding behavioral measures that are reliable and valid.

In our CSR example, the three behavioral measures chosen to affect performance are: (a) CSRs resolve the customer problem or request on the initial call; (b) CSRs follow up with the customer problem or request if not resolved on the initial call; (c) CSRs handle at least 15 percent above the minimum number of calls during peak hours. The major assumption at this level is that these are the behaviors that will drive the desired end results specified in Level 4 (End Results). In fact, there may be a strong rationale for rewarding a CSR for exhibiting these Level 3 behaviors rather than simply expecting these behaviors and rewarding desired results. First, it may be difficult, costly or impossible to reliably measure outcome. Second, the desired results may be impacted by numerous other factors in addition to employee behavior. For example, increased sales may be driven more by the economic health of the United States and company marketing efforts than by the efforts of the CSR.

End Results (Level 4)

Obviously, it is the end results that management expects to gain from the pay-program investment. End results measures include revenues, net profits or cost savings in the production process. End results also can be quantified in terms of reduced employee absenteeism, increased sales of specific products or reduction in waste which can be attributed to the pay program. However, given senior-management responsibility to owners and the desire to invest scarce company resources where they will have the most impact, examining the results from a cost/benefits perspective or ROI perspective is intuitive.

Sales revenue and the savings associated with improvements in selected outcome measures are usually available. Unfortunately, it is often difficult to isolate the effects of a pay program on desired results. For the example in Figure 1, sales revenue and productivity improvements are easily measured, and from this information the payouts for the monthly bonus program can easily be calculated. The estimated costs of designing and administering the bonus program can be made. However, improvement in customer satisfaction survey scores is not easily translated into financial value for the company. Furthermore, it may be difficult to attribute the value of increases in sales revenues, productivity and customer satisfaction to the monthly bonus program. Sales increases could be attributed to other factors such as improvements in the economy (that is, customers simply have more money to spend) or the company's new marketing effort.

Given the fact that other factors besides the behaviors of the employee may substantially influence outcomes in some situations, behavioral measures may provide the most accurate measures for assessing the value of a pay program.

Despite these inherent weaknesses, attempting to evaluate pay programs in terms of their effect on end results and their ROI is a worthy goal. This information allows management to make comparisons with other investment needs and to determine the true value of the pay program to the company. The evaluation processes described in dimension II can help clarify the value added by the pay program.

Dimension II: Evaluation Process

This paper's model, as shown in Figure 1, focuses on four evaluation perspectives and, to a lesser extent, how to measure or assess the achievement of these different perspectives. In addition, utilizing a systematic evaluation process obtains accurate information for each of these perspectives. The six steps in this evaluation process are briefly summarized in the following. A more detailed treatment of the evaluation process and statistical methods can be obtained from numerous research studies and HRD textbooks (for example, Werner and DeSimone 2006).

Setting Goals or Objectives (Step 1) and Identifying Evaluation Criteria (Step 2)

Effective evaluation requires setting specific program goals with measurable evaluation criteria to determine if these objectives are met. For example, CSR bonus program goals could include the following:

1. Increase CSR productivity.

2. Improve customer satisfaction.

The measures associated with Goal 1, increase productivity, require number of calls handled by CSRs for designated periods of time (for example, shift, hour or week) to be counted. Management must decide if certain types of customer problems are more difficult and deserve more weight in the calculation. If two CSRs are involved in handling a customer problem, how is the call credited? Even with inherent issues surrounding results measures, quantifiable data is often available and utilized to evaluate CSRs.

Even if CSR productivity represents a sound measure and translates into cost savings, increased productivity may not capture how the customer feels about this experience or whether this experience will influence future purchasing decisions. If management believes customer satisfaction drives future sales, then this measure gains importance. As managers of call centers know, productivity can increase at the same time customer satisfaction plummets. However, in both cases, if productivity or customer satisfaction decreases, no one may know why.

Although seldom explicitly considered when establishing pay-program goals, one should consider employee reactions to the program and employees' program knowledge. First, if CSRs do not think the program is fair or motivational, their reactions will seriously impact their response to the program. Second, if CSRs do not understand the workings of the program, how can they focus their efforts on what management believes will drive their success? As a result, clearly articulated pay-program goals and evaluation criteria and measures are essential for each of the three evaluation perspectives described in Dimension I.

Selecting an Evaluation Methodology (Step 3) and Collecting and Analyzing Data (Step 4)

The evaluation methodology is important in determining the impact that a pay program has on the outcomes (Level 4) desired by management. For example, customer satisfaction may be heavily influenced by the promises of the salesforce or quality of phone-answering technology, neither of which the CSR controls. Evaluation methodology can determine what influenced increased customer satisfaction, the pay program or the new technology.

A fairly common approach is to compare the performance of employees who are participating in the pay program with those who are not. In this case, the use of new technology would be available to both groups. Statistical tests can then determine if participating employees reacted more positively, were more likely to behave as desired or were more likely to obtain the expected program results.

Collecting before and after measures for each of the comparison groups enhances the accuracy of these comparisons. The most sophisticated of the comparison designs is called a Solomon Four, which is described in evaluation and HRD textbooks (for example, Werner and DeSimone, 2006). T-test, ANOVA and regression are statistical tests often used to determine if significant differences in attitudes, knowledge, behavior or results occur across these groups.

In the CSR example, a comparison would be made between a group of CSRs who are eligible for the monthly bonus and a control group of CSRs who have similar demographics and terms of how they are managed but do not receive the monthly bonus. Again, measuring the criteria from each perspective before and after the implementation of the bonus program is ideal to control factors that may bias the results. However, this evaluation method can be problematic given potential management reluctance to implement a two-tier pay system for employees doing similar work.

Time-series analysis is a second common method for evaluating pay programs and offers an alternative to making comparison among employee groups. This evaluation method collects a series of before and after measures of employee attitudes, knowledge, behaviors or results over time. If a significant change was made at the time the pay program was implemented, the change is attributed to the pay program (that is, assuming another event did not supersede the effect of the program). For example, customer satisfaction is measured each week by asking a random sample of customers who have called in to complete a short satisfaction survey. Once this data has been collected for 10, 20 or more weeks, the bonus program is implemented. The data continues to be collected for the next 10 or more weeks. If the level of customer satisfaction increases significantly after the bonus program was implemented and absent external events affecting customer satisfaction, then we can likely attribute the bonus program. Time-series analysis can determine if a significant change in sales occurred post program implementation. Of course, the same evaluation method can be used to determine if the new technology also affected customer satisfaction.

There are numerous statistical techniques to analyze pay-program evaluation data. This paper is not intended to offer a detailed treatment of methodological or statistical issues associated with program evaluation because specific situations will determine the appropriate analytic methods. Statisticians, books and articles can provide detailed information on research and statistical methods. Although computer-application software has made running these statistics easy, it is important that correct evaluation design and statistical tests are chosen.

Interpreting Findings (Step 5) and Developing and Implementing Program-Improvement Strategies (Step 6)

The key to interpreting findings generated from Step 4 is to clearly articulate the evaluation goals to be answered at the beginning of the process for each level of evaluation and then develop appropriate measures, collect data from employee groups specified by the evaluation design and use appropriate statistical techniques. If these steps have been carefully followed, interpreting findings involves packaging the information in readable form for the stakeholders to consider. We have found that graphic displays of data focused on specific issues are most effective.

In the CSR example, presenting the findings to CSRs and their supervisors and managers participating in the program is important. First, because this data were collected from them, often with their knowledge, employees will want to know what was found. Second, discussing the findings with employees and their supervisor can provide important insights as to why employees perceived the pay program as they did or how the pay program influenced their behavior. For example, employees may know why customer satisfaction decreases toward month's end.

Finally, if we are to improve the effectiveness of pay programs, program-participant and manager involvement in the evaluation process will foster considerable commitment to improving the pay program. Previous research initiatives found that approximately four of five organizations do not involve employees in the design of compensation programs, and compensation professionals report that building better line of sight and effective program communications are viewed as two of the top challenges in pay-program design (Scott, McMullen, Wallace 2004).

Pay programs must change because of the constantly changing competitive environment. Effectively changing programs involves numerous people, and it is essential to have a strategy for implementing change. Building commitment for change is absolutely essential. It is important to build into the design of a new pay program the elements required for effective evaluation and a plan for implementing changes as they are suggested. Implementation of important program changes is most often the "weak link" in the evaluation process.

Conclusion

Pay-program evaluation requires careful thought and a commitment to using the feedback to improve these programs. Given the substantial investment made in pay programs and the impact they have on organizational effectiveness, comprehensive pay-program evaluation makes good business sense. Unlike other HR programs, management cannot just cancel pay programs when the economy "softens." Even so, systematic evaluation can add significant value to pay programs when one goes beyond measuring a financial-oriented ROI. The authors' recommended approach, similar to the Balanced Score Card, reduces the dangers of overdependence on "lagging" financial indicators and considers employee perceptions, knowledge and behaviors associated with pay programs, which form the basis for getting desired results. When management wants to know why the pay program did not meet expectations, compensation professionals will be better prepared with answers and, more importantly, suggestions as to how these pay programs can be improved.

First published in *WorldatWork Journal*, Second Quarter 2006

Selected References

Burkholder, Beth. 2002. "Orchestrating a Finely Tuned Incentive Plan." *workspan*, August, 16 – 23.

Burchman, Seymour; Jones, Blair. 2006. "Executive Compensation as a Support for Growth Strategy." *WorldatWork Journal*, Third Quarter, 39 – 46.

Burchman, Seymour; Jones, Blair. 2005. "Should Do, Can Do, Will Do: Setting Incentive Goals That Yield Results." *WorldatWork Journal*, Second Quarter, 24 – 33.

Burchman, Seymour; Jones, Blair. 2004. "The Future of Stock Options from Starring Role to Ensemble Player." *WorldatWork Journal*, First Quarter, 29 – 38.

Chen, Yvonne. 2003. "Paying for Performance in a Down Market." *workspan*, December, 40 – 43.

Conlin, Robert S. 2003. "Driving Corporate Change with Technology and Pay for Performance." *workspan*, August, 42 – 45.

Ellis, Christian M.; Laymon, R. Glenn; LeBlanc, Peter V. 2004. "Improving Pay Productivity with Strategic Work Valuation: Applying a Business-Centered Approach at Five Companies." *WorldatWork Journal*, Second Quarter, 56 – 68.

Ericson, Richard N. 2004. "Pay for The Right Stuff: Do's and Don'ts of Performance Measurement at the Senior-Management Level." *WorldatWork Journal*, Second Quarter, 80 – 87.

Ericson, Richard N. 2003. "The Microsoft Ripple Effect: Is It Your Time for an Equity Overhaul?" *workspan*, September, 16 – 19.

Ericson, Richard N. 2002. "Addressing Structural Issues in Executive Incentive Plan Design." *WorldatWork Journal*, First Quarter, 59 – 70.

Ferracone, Robin A. 2004. "Break from the Herd: Meeting the Long-term Performance Challenge." *WorldatWork Journal*, Second Quarter, 45 – 55.

Frocham, Martin Ibanez. 2005. "Executive Pay the Latin Way." *WorldatWork Journal*, Fourth Quarter, 72 – 79.

Gilles, Paul. 2002. "Relative Performance: Long-term Incentive Design Considerations." *WorldatWork Journal*, First Quarter, 30 – 34.

Jones, Blair; Hatfield, Clare. 2005. "Strategic Work Valuation: Compensating the Right Executives the Right Way." *WorldatWork Journal*, October, 23 – 28.

Jones, Blair; Leach, David; Purewal, Jesse. 2003. "What's Next for the Compensation Committee? Exceeding Expectations in a Difficult Time." *WorldatWork Journal*, Fourth Quarter, 6 – 14.

Kao, Tina; Kantor, Richard. 2004. "Total Rewards: From Clarity to Action." *WorldatWork Journal*, Fourth Quarter, 32 – 40.

Klein, Andrew; McMillan, Alisa; Keating, Kimberly M. 2002. "Long-term Incentives in Not-for-Profits—An Emerging Trend." *WorldatWork Journal*, Third Quarter, 63 – 71.

Karolyi, Darrell. 2003. "Is Overhang Overstated?" *WorldatWork Journal*, Third Quarter, 47 – 54.

Kurlander, Peter; Barton, Scott. 2004. "Improving Your Odds: Successful Incentive Compensation Automation." *workspan*, January, 30 – 33.

Lawler, Edward E. III. 2003. "Pay Practices in *Fortune* 1000 Corporations." *WorldatWork Journal*, Fourth Quarter, 45 – 54.

Merriman, Kimberly. 2005. "Avoiding the Performance Pay Employee Entitlement Trap." *workspan*, May, 64 – 68.

Pentolino, John. 2002. "Making the Case for Sales Incentive Administration Software." January, *workspan*, 8 – 10.

Reda, James F. 2002. "Till Wealth Do Us Part: The Truth Behind Executive Employment Arrangements." *WorldatWork Journal*, Second Quarter, 34 – 43.

Reilly, Mark. 2005. "Pay for Performance or Pay for the Masses?" *WorldatWork Journal*, Fourth Quarter, 16 – 21.

Reiman, Paul J. 2004. "Are Your Sales Compensation Plans Working as Designed?" *WorldatWork Journal*, Fourth Quarter, 16 – 24.

Rogers, Phil. 2006. "Incentives Can Drive Success in Workplace Wellness Programs." *workspan*, February, 55 – 56.

Romweber, Jane; Fox, Robbi. 2006. "Employment Contracts: What Directors Need to Know." *WorldatWork Journal*, Second Quarter, 16 – 23.

Scott, K. Dow; McMullen, Thomas D.; Wallace, Marc; Morajda, Dennis. 2004. "Annual Cash Incentives for Managerial and Professional Employees." *WorldatWork Journal*, Fourth Quarter, 6 – 15.

Shives, Gregory K.; Scott, K. Dow. 2003. "Gainsharing and EVA: The U.S. Postal Service Experience." *WorldatWork Journal*, First Quarter, 21 – 30.

Somelofske, Martin, J.; Bhayani, Rahim; Levin, Sarah. 2003. "Stock Options: 'The Reports of My Demise Are Greatly Exaggerated' " *WorldatWork Journal*, First Quarter, 48 – 56.

Stoskopf, Gregory A. 2004. "Using Total Rewards to Attract and Retain Health Care Employees." *WorldatWork Journal*, Third Quarter, 16 – 25.

Wagner, Frank H.; Kazmlerowski, Mark J. 2006. "High-Technology Equity Programs: Powerful Forces for Change." *WorldatWork Journal*, First Quarter, 42 – 51.

Weinberger, Theodore, E. 2002. "Flinching Bias Blues: The Down Side of Kinked Payout Plans." *WorldatWork Journal*, Second Quarter, 71 – 77.

Zingheim, Patricia K.; Schuster, Jay R. 2006. "Best-Practice Incentives for Contact Centers and Distribution Centers: Driving Customer Satisfaction." *WorldatWork Journal*, Third Quarter, 32 – 38.

Zingheim, Patricia K.; Schuster, Jay R. 2005. "Revisiting Effective Incentive Design: Still The Major ROI Reward Opportunity." *WorldatWork Journal*, First Quarter, 50 – 58.

WorldatWork Surveys (www.worldatwork.org/library/research/ surveys)

2005 – 2006 Strategic Reward and Pay Practices: The Need for Execution Survey Report

2005 - The State of Electronic Communications in Compensation and Human Resources

2005 – Bonus Program Practices

2005 - Key Sales Incentive Plan Practices

2004 - Strategic Performance Measurement and Rewards Systems Survey

WorldatWork Bookstore (www.worldatwork.org/bookstore)

Colletti, Jerome A. and Cichelli, David J. 2005. *Designing Sales Compensation Plans*. Scottsdale: *WorldatWork*.

Davis, Michael L., and. Edge, Jerry T. 2004. *Executive Compensation: The Professional's Guide to Current Issues and Practices*. Ashland: Windsor Professional Information.

Delves, Donald P. 2006. *Stock Options and the New Rules of Accountability*. Scottsdale: *WorldatWork*.

Ellig, Bruce R. 2002. *The Complete Guide to Executive Compensation*. New York: McGraw Hill.

Ericson, Richard. 2004. *Pay to Prosper: Using Value Rules to Reinvent Executive Incentives*. Scottsdale: *WorldatWork*.

Lawler, Edward E. 2000. *Rewarding Excellence: Pay Strategies for the New Economy*. Hoboken: Jossey-Bass.

Overton, Bruce B.; Steele, Mary T. 2004. *Designing Management Incentive Plans.* Scottsdale: *WorldatWork.*

Sotherland, Jude. 2003. *When Pay Plans Go Wrong: Managing Compliance Issues Before the Audit.* Scottsdale: *WorldatWork.*

Wilson, Thomas B., and Malanowski, Susan. 2004. Rewarding Group Performance. Scottsdale: *WorldatWork.*

WorldatWork. 2002. *The Best of Sales Compensation: A Collection of Articles from WorldatWork.* Scottsdale: *WorldatWork.*

WorldatWork. 2001. *The Best of Variable Pay: Incentives, Recognition and Rewards.* Scottsdale: *WorldatWork.*

WorldatWork Courses (www.worldatwork.org/education)

GR6 – Variable Pay

C12 – Variable Pay, Incentives, Recognition & Bonuses

C5 – Elements of Sales Compensation

C6A – Advanced Concepts in Executive Compensation

T11 – Fundamentals of Equity-based Rewards

C17 – Market Pricing – Conducting a Competitive Pay Analysis

Sales Compensation for Complex Selling Models

Equity 101 – Online Learning

About the Editor

Dow Scott, Ph.D., is a professor of human resources and industrial relations at Loyola University Chicago. His teaching, research and consulting focus on helping business leaders create high-performance organizations and build employee commitment.

Scott has led numerous consulting projects and developed diagnostic tools for assessing company and leadership performance and capability. He has consulted with diverse organizations including AT&T, Groendyke Transport, Landstar Systems, Sara Lee Corp., Marsh Inc., Central Federal Saving, Hebrew Home of Maryland, Abbott Laboratories, Hay Group and USG.

He has received national recognition for contributions in areas of team and company productivity improvement, employee selection, employee commitment and leadership development from the Academy of Management, Southern Management Association, and the Society of Human Resource Management, and has been awarded over $1.2 million by government and business to further his applied research.

Scott has published papers in more than 100 journals, books and conference proceedings, including the *Academy of Management Journal, Compensation and Benefits Review, Training and Development Journal, WorldatWork Journal, Journal of Applied Psychology, Journal of Management,* and *Personnel Psychology.*

About the Authors

John Andrzejewski is CEO at Anson Industries Inc., one of the country's largest specialty contractors, with annual revenues near $200 million and offices throughout the United States.

G. Michael Barton, SPHR, is the human resources administrator at Trover Foundation in Western Kentucky. Trover is a major medical complex that includes a 401-bed hospital and nine physician clinics. Since 1972, Barton has taught a variety of college-level courses in business and health-care administration.

Currently, he is a lecturer in Healthcare Administration at the University of Southern Indiana (USI). At USI, Barton teaches graduate and undergraduate courses on human resources management, organizational behavior, organizational communications, health-care administration, benefits administration, leadership and strategic planning.

He has published four books, including *Culture at Work* (WorldatWork Press, 2006) and *Recognition at Work* (WorldatWork Press, 2006), now in a second edition, and has more than 20 articles in professional and academic journals. He has conducted more than 200 seminars on diverse topics such as managing change, negotiation skills, recognition management, cultural assessment, performance management, continuous quality improvement, leadership and communications. He has served on the faculty of WorldatWork since 1997. Barton holds a master's in business administration and a bachelor's from the University of Evansville.

Gibson J. Bradley is a director in the global compensation unit at Procter & Gamble's world headquarters. His responsibilities include compensation governance and executive compensation design on a global basis. He has been working in the field of human resources for more than 25 years, with extensive experience in the design of leading-edge compensation plans. His experience includes that of a senior HR generalist and as the top compensation and benefits professional in several leading companies. Bradley graduated summa cum laude from Cornell College, where he was elected to Phi Beta Kappa.

Chuck Cockburn has been president/CEO of Watermark Credit Union since September 2001. He has more than 25 years' experience in the credit-union industry. He worked 12 years for the National Credit Union Administration and served as president/CEO of four other large credit unions, including the largest in New York State and Massachusetts. He earned a master's in business administration from the George Washington University.

Jerome A. Colletti is managing partner of Colletti-Fiss LLC, a management-consulting firm headquartered in Scottsdale, Ariz. His firm is a leading source of expertise and insight on strategic compensation issues affecting the productivity of sales and customer-contact employees.

A management consultant since 1977, Colletti provides advice to top managers on the design and implementation of compensation plans, particularly variable pay arrangements, and how they reward employees for sales success, customer retention and customer loyalty. He is the author of more than 70 publications and has been a Cert 5 (Elements of Sales Compensation) course instructor for WorldatWork since 1979. He is the co-author of *Sales Compensation Essentials* (WorldatWork Press, 2006), as well as the WorldatWork course, Sales Compensation for Complex Selling Models.

Paul Davis is the president of Scanlon Leadership Network. In this role, Davis helps member organizations implement and maintain Scanlon Plans, develops Scanlon-related training programs, organizes Scanlon-related conferences and workshops, speaks on Scanlon philosophy and writes on Scanlon. He also serves as a staff liaison to the Scanlon Foundation and Scanlon consultancy.

Lisa Emerson is vice president of global total compensation at McDonald's Corp. In this role, she leads McDonald's global total compensation function, which includes global compensation and benefits. She has responsibility for developing global total compensation strategy, programs and frameworks. In addition, she serves on the McDonald's human resources leadership team, which is responsible for developing human resources strategy for McDonald's throughout the world.

Emerson began her McDonald's career in 1997 as director of compensation planning. Before joining McDonald's, she spent five years at Kraft Foods, N.A. as director of compensation and eight years at Ameritech as director of compensation, benefits and HRIS.

Mary S. Fiss is a partner in the management consulting firm Colletti-Fiss LLC. She has extensive experience in the development and implementation of team and individual compensation, reward and recognition, professional development and performance management programs. Fiss works with clients on issues and challenges related to increasing salesforce productivity through the effective use of compensation and management-education programs.

Fiss is frequently quoted in popular business publications and is the author of more than a dozen articles, book chapters and books. She and Jerome A. Colletti co-authored the book, *Compensating New Sales Roles: How to Design Rewards That Work in Today's Selling Environment,* published by AMACOM.

Robert J. Greene, Ph.D., CCP, CBP, GRP, SPHR, GPHR, is CEO of Reward $ystems Inc., Glenview, Ill. He has more than 30 years of consulting experience following work in major corporations. He has published more than 80 articles and book chapters and was the first recipient of the Keystone Award from the American Compensation Association (now WorldatWork) for achieving the highest level of excellence in the field. He consults on HR strategies and program design and is a member of the faculty for the DePaul University MSHR and MBA programs.

Clare Hatfield is a consultant at Sibson Consulting. Hatfield's consulting experience has been in both the performance and reward and change sides of client organizations, focusing mainly on executive compensation and top-team development initiatives. Her specific experience includes the development and implementation of reward programs for senior executives and key employees and the design of executive-change workshops. Based in the United Kingdom, Hatfield has served clients in various industries, including professional and financial services, real-estate management, and leisure and hospitality services.

Robert L. Heneman, Ph.D., is a professor of management and human resources in the Fisher College of Business at The Ohio State University. His primary areas of research, teaching and consulting are in performance management, compensation, staffing and work design. He has been published in more than 60 publications and has received more than $1 million in funds for his research. He is a recipient of the WorldatWork Distinguished Total Rewards Educator Award. Heneman has consulted with organizations throughout the world. His most recent books are *Business-Driven Compensation Policies: Integrating Compensation Systems with Corporate Strategies* (AMACOM) and *Strategic Reward Management: Design, Implementation, and Evaluation* (Information Age).

Blair Jones is a managing principal at the Semler Brossy Consulting Group. She helps clients motivate and retain their talent in ways that contribute to sustained shareholder-value creation. Jones has expertise in performance management and executive rewards design and has worked with leadership teams across a number of industries, including automotive, health care, retail, telecommunications, professional services and consumer products. She works extensively with companies in transition. Before joining Sibson Consulting in 1991, Jones worked for Bain & Co., helping clients develop pricing and marketing strategies.

George M. Kaspar, MIS, CCP, is executive compensation consultant for Exelon Corp. Kaspar is also the business project manager for implementing and maintaining AIM/Authoria Compensation Advisor software for Exelon Corporation.

Stéphane Lebeau is the director, strategic rewards and talent management, for Akamai Technologies Inc. in Cambridge, Mass. He is responsible for the design, implementation, communication and administration of the company's base pay programs, incentive compensation and equity-based compensation. He also oversees Akamai's talent-management strategy, which develops talent and leadership to further enhance the company's strengths. LeBeau is the adviser to the management committee and the board of directors on organizational design and total remuneration issues.

He is an associate of the Society of Actuaries (ASA). He holds a bachelor's degree in mathematics specializing in actuarial sciences from the University of Montreal, and certificates in business and management from Harvard University and MIT Sloan School of Management.

Thomas D. McMullen is the U.S. reward practice leader for Hay Group based in Chicago. He has more than 20 years of combined HR practitioner and compensation consulting experience. His work focuses primarily on total rewards and performance program design, including rewards-strategy development and incentive-plan design.

Robert L. Moore, Ph.D., is currently Elbridge Amos Smith Professor of Economics at Occidental College, where he has taught since 1978. He received his doctorate in economics from Harvard University, specializing in labor economics and public finance. In addition to authoring three textbooks, his articles have appeared in journals such as the *American Economic Review*, the *Quarterly Journal of Economics*, the *Review of Economics and Statistics,* and *Economic Inquiry*, among others. His research relating to the economics of human resources management (personnel economics), co-authored with Edward P. Lazear, has focused on seniority-based incentive plans as well as the incentive effects of pensions for retirement and turnover behavior.

Dennis Morajda, MSIR, is vice president of Performance Development International Inc. (PDII). His practice areas focus on developing high-performance organizations, building dynamic work cultures, designing and administering customized attitude surveys and evaluating human resources programs. He has assisted clients in reducing employee turnover and evaluating employee selection/training programs. He also has experience in team building, continuous improvement and performance evaluation.

His recent published research focuses on evaluating compensation programs—going beyond return-on-investment (ROI), base and variable pay practices and effective application of employee attitude surveys.

Mark Reilly is a founding partner of 3C Compensation Consulting Consortium, a boutique firm located in Chicago and Pittsburgh. 3C's sole focus is on compensation consulting. Reilly is based in Chicago and focuses on executive compensation and incentive-plan design. He has 18 years of consulting experience. Before he formed 3C, he worked for large consulting firms based in New York, Philadelphia and Princeton. He also worked for Continental Bank and Ameritech.

Reilly has consulted to companies on total compensation, strategy, long- and short-term incentive-plan design and executive severance. He has authored and co-authored papers in both *WorldatWork Journal* and *workspan*. He is a frequent speaker and is regularly quoted in *The Wall Street Journal*. Reilly holds a master's degree in finance and marketing from Northwestern's Kellogg School of Management and a bachelor's degree in finance and economics from Boston College.

Corey Rosen is executive director and co-founder of the National Center for Employee Ownership (NCEO), a private, nonprofit membership, information and research organization in Oakland, Calif. He co-founded the NCEO in 1981 after working for five years as a professional staff member in the U.S. Senate, where he helped draft legislation on employee ownership plans. Prior to that, Rosen taught political science at Ripon College.

He is the author and co-author of numerous books and more than 100 articles on employee ownership. He also is co-author (with John Case) of the forthcoming book, *Equity*, to be published by Harvard Business School Press. Rosen was the subject of an extensive interview in *Inc.* magazine in August 2000, has appeared frequently on CNN, PBS, NPR and other network programs, and is regularly quoted in *The Wall Street Journal*, *The New York Times* and other leading publications. Rosen has a doctorate in political science from Cornell University.

Donna Stettler is a senior manager in the executive compensation practice of Deloitte in Chicago. For more than 11 years, her work has focused on executive compensation for public and private companies in a variety of industries. Stettler assists her clients in the development of multifaceted compensation programs that include annual and long-term incentive programs and all types of equity-based compensation arrangements. She has directed engagements to assess market-compensation levels and the competitive posture of pay programs, including the facilitation of customized compensation surveys and studies. Stettler is recognized as an expert on the accounting and tax consequences of executive compensation and is a frequent speaker on these topics.

Robert Todd is the manager, compensation and stock plan administration, for Akamai Technologies Inc. in Cambridge, Mass. He provides in-depth critical analysis to Akamai's management on current and proposed equity compensation strategies and initiatives. Todd also serves as an adviser to the Corporate Executive Services Board of Charles Schwab & Co., and provides guidance on current regulatory and accounting developments as they relate to equity compensation practices.

Todd holds a master's in business administration with a concentration in finance from Boston University, Boston, Mass.

Jon Werner is a professor in the department of management at the University of Wisconsin-Whitewater. He received his master's in business administration and doctorate from Michigan State University. The focus of his teaching and research is various aspects of human resources management, including training, compensation and strategic human resources issues. His research has appeared in numerous leading management and psychology journals. He is co-author of books on human resources development and merit pay, and he has consulted with numerous organizations.

Linda Zong, CCP, CBP, GRP, is a consultant for the human capital/total rewards practice at Deloitte Consulting LLP in Los Angeles. She provides consulting and thought leadership in compensation, benefits and total rewards management. She has published numerous articles in journals including *Compensation and Benefits Review, Journal of Compensation and Benefits*, the *Corporate Board, Sarbanes-Oxley Compliance Journal, Journal of Deferred Compensation, Journal of Pension Planning & Compliance* and *Journal of Private Equity*. She earned a master's in business administration from the University of Maryland, an master of arts from Shanghai International Studies University and a bachelor of science from the University of Shanghai for Science and Technology.